Lust for Glory

Lust for Glory

An Epic Story of Early Texas and the
Sacrifice That Defined a Nation

Stephen L. Hardin

State ✦ House
Press
Abilene, Texas

State❤House Press

State House Press
1 McMurry University, #637
Abilene, Texas 79697-0001
325-793-4682
www.mcwhiney.org

Cataloging-in-Publication Data

Names: Hardin, Stephen L., author.
Title: Lust for glory: an epic story of early texas and the sacrifice that defined a nation / Stephen L. Hardin
Description: First edition. |Abilene, TX: State House Press, 2018. | Includes bibliographical references and index.
Identifiers: ISBN 9781933337753 (softcover)
Subjects: LCSH: Texas History Revolution, 1835-1836. | Texas History To 1846.
Classification: LLC F390.H2892018 (print) | DDC976.403

This paper meets the requirements of ANSI/NISO, Z39.48-1992 (Permanence of Paper).
Binding materials have been chosen for durability.

First edition 2018

Cover illustration: *Fight for the Inner Courtyard* by Gary S. Zaboly
Cover Design by Rosenbohm Graphic Design

Printed in the United States of America
Distributed by Texas A&M University Press Consortium
800-826-8911
www.tamupress.com

I gratefully dedicate this book to the
memory
&
legacy
of

James W. Pohl, Ph.D.

Teacher—Mentor—Exemplar

I know how much I owe him;
I hope he knew how much he meant to me,
which was,
in both cases,
everything.

Contents

Supplemental Vignettes

Preface

ost Texans agree that the twenty-five years between 1821 and 1846 are the most exciting, tragic, and momentous in their state's history. They begin with the arrival of the first of Stephen F. Austin's U.S. colonists and Mexico's independence from Spain; they close with Texas annexation and its transformation from an independent nation into one of twenty-eight united North American states. The intervening years witnessed the climactic showdown between two military giants—Antonio López de Santa Anna and Sam Houston—who faced off for the first and only time across the sodden prairie of San Jacinto. The victory there guaranteed the future of the Texas Republic and was a crucial link in the chain of events that converted northern Mexico into the American Southwest. Still, it is not that glorious triumph at San Jacinto that stamped the Texas soul, shaped the Texan identity, and led to the development of what some label "Texas Exceptionalism." No, the event that wrought all that was instead a calamitous defeat that had occurred some seven weeks before on the outskirts of San Antonio de Béxar. It is admittedly a bit incongruous, but it is not the redemption of San Jacinto that Texans exalt but, rather, the sacrifice at the Alamo.

As a professor of Texas history, I often complain that my students "Remember the Alamo," but forget everything else. They are not alone in that. Our fascination with the anguish, heroism, and drama of that epic last stand has produced a form of historical nearsightedness. To comprehend—to truly appreciate—that encounter with all its heartbreak and grandeur, we must know something of what came before and what followed.

This book investigates the most extraordinary and captivating of all periods of Texas, and dare I say, American history. It is an account of early Texas, covering the years of colonization, revolution, republic, and the precious legacy that they left all Texans. It does not pretend to be a general survey history of the state. Rather, I have focused on the events and personalities of this remarkable quarter-century, one that many note with pride but recall with difficulty. For those of a certain age, it has been a long time since their seventh-grade Texas history class—this book is for them.

But it is also for those students currently enrolled in a Texas history course. And their teachers. And, I hope, their parents. Although I make my living as an academic, I have made every effort not to write like one. I have tried to make this book accessible to the widest possible audience. The average young adult, grades 7 through 12, should be able to read this book, with only the occasional help of a dictionary. More than thirty years of scholarship inform the narrative, but one will search in vain for any trace of a footnote. You'll just have to take my word for it. I have, however, included an extensive bibliography and encourage readers to avail themselves of its contents. The wisdom of the award-winning author David McCullough continues to inspire: "No harm's done to history by making it something one would wish to read." Some of my associates may look askance at my approach and style, so be it. I did not write this book for my colleagues down the hall, but for my neighbors down the street.

Some of those neighbors are lifelong natives of the state. Others, "got here as fast as they could." I hope that the information will prove helpful and amusing to both types. Together in the pages that follow, we will examine the arcs and episodes of this amazing epoch. Readers will encounter historic personalities. Some like Sam Houston and David Crockett remain fixed in our collective memory. Others like Jean Louis Berlandier and Richard Bullock are commonly forgotten, but are no less fascinating for that.

So come and explore the Texas Heroic Age. You'll find heroes alright but also plenty of villains. But mostly, we'll get to know folks who are much like us—flesh-and-blood human beings who scrape by, rear their children, and each day strive to attain their own notions of honor. We will learn of their virtues and their vices. Both made them the people they became. And if you close the book with a better appreciation of those people, their period, and the unique culture they left us, your scribbling friend will be content.

Acknowledgments

This book began as an online "Texas Revolution and Republic" course for Schreiner University. Being an obsessive fellow, I felt the need to write down each lecture. Although I admire those who are, I've never been an off-the-cuff speaker. While we were filming the lectures, Donald S. Frazier, my friend and colleague at McMurry University, observed: "Steve, you may not know it but you've produced enough material for a book—and we just happen to operate a publishing company."

He was correct; I didn't know it. I never viewed these pages as anything more than notes for the class, scraps I'd toss once the lectures were "in the can." Don argued that if we published a book, it would serve as a handy companion volume for students taking the course. He also suggested that the book's format would lend itself to general readers, Texas History teachers, and their students. At any rate, those are the folks I had in mind as I wrote it.

At length, I allowed Don to persuade me to process the episodes into a book. If you don't like it . . . blame him. It was his bright idea.

Which I now gratefully acknowledge.

This is my second book with State House Press. Once again I am reminded how blessed I am to work with friends who are both personable and professional. I've already mentioned Dr. Donald S. Frazier President and CEO of the McWhiney History Education Group, an organization that does much more than publish books.

Scott Clowdus has moved on to greener pastures but during his time as Chief Operations Officer he contributed considerable talent and energy in sailing this project into port. Chief Financial Officer Susan Frazier, performed yeoman service in pinning down wayward images and keeping me (and everyone else) on task. From the start, I wanted to make this book accessible to the widest possible audience. To achieve that, I invited Project Manager Claudia Gravier Frigo to rein in the abstract jargon. I am, after all, a college professor and an indecorous grandiloquence frequently blights my discourse. (See what I did there? The manuscript was full of that crap.) While grappling with my prose, Claudia and I enjoyed some epic disagreements. I say *enjoyed* because we both appreciate the delightful variability of the English language and agree that affable argument fosters the editorial process. I know that her dogged advocacy of the forthright over the highfalutin made this a better book—certainly a more readable one. Thanks, Claudia; I'll miss our collegial clashes.

During their holiday visits to Abilene, I pressed my son and daughter-in-law into service. Walker and Gretchen are both fine writers and editors. Together we workshopped the title and hashed out the general tone of the book. Like Claudia, they talked me out of the worst of my academic extravagances. My daughter, Savannah, also supported the project. She inherited her mother's razor wit and frequently employs it to cut her old man's ego down to size—which he requires and appreciates. I pledge that this year's Christmas will be book-free, with nothing but family time, fine dining, and loads of game playing. As for next year? Well, I make no promises. I love them more than I can express. While I pine for the children that they were, I admire the adults they have become. What a lucky guy I am to have these astonishing people in my life.

My wife, Deborah, is an award-wining seventh-grade Texas history teacher at Mann Middle School in Abilene, Texas. Throughout this process, she has served as a sounding board, cheerleader, and editor. On countless occasions I have asked her, "Would teachers find this helpful?" And she always had an answer. On a daily basis, she shares her knowledge, passion, and dedication with her colleagues and students. But she is not alone. Thousands of fourth- and seventh-grade teachers toil in the trenches to introduce the state's rich legacy to the next generation. They all have my respect and admiration.

But only one of them has my love.

Stephen L. Hardin
Abilene, Texas
2018

Aftermath: March 6, 1836

The soldiers had struggled and died in darkness. Yet, as dawn began to crack over San Antonio de Béxar, it faintly illuminated the shattered fort. The soft light exposed sights of death and destruction that horrified even those who had fought the battle. Those visions seared themselves into the memory of Mexican officer José Enrique de la Peña, who recalled the grisly spectacle: "The bodies, with their blackened and bloody faces disfigured by a desperate death, their hair and uniforms burning at once, presented a dreadful and truly hellish sight. What trophies—those of the battlefield!"

Mexican survivors of the carnage remained in a condition of uneasy tension and continued to shoot at shadows. When a terrified feline scurried among the ruins, a shaky and superstitious *soldado* shouted, "It is not a cat, but an American!" In a berserk frenzy, his comrades cornered the helpless mouser and tore it to pieces with their bayonets. The Mexican assault troops had witnessed their companions get mangled by artillery, riddled by rifles, and gutted by Bowie knives. Having survived the slaughter, they were unwilling to take more chances.

Generalissimo Antonio López de Santa Anna made a grand entrance into the compound. He had always been careless with the lives of his men, and he now surveyed the bloodbath with remarkable indifference. Before the attack, he had not bothered to set up a field hospital. Ramón Martínez

1

Caro, Santa Anna's personal secretary, recorded that "more than a hundred of the wounded died afterward as a result of the lack of proper medical attention and medical facilities in spite of the fact that their injuries were not serious." Caro bitterly recounted how, "those who lingered in pain and suffering without the proper comfort or relief" envied their comrades who had died instantly.

During the assault, the garrison's non-combatants had huddled in the sacristy of the church. As Mexican soldiers flooded into the room, they herded those non-combatants into a protective corner. For more than fifteen minutes, musket fire peppered the building and continued even after the last Texian rebel lay dead. Then came silence, which, for the wives and children of the fort's defenders, was even more ominous than the noise of battle. An impeccably uniformed, English-speaking Mexican officer entered the sacristy. It was Colonel Juan Almonte, who had received his education in the United States. "Is Mrs. Dickinson here?" he inquired.

And she was. Susanna Dickinson, the wife—now widow—of Artillery Captain Almaron Dickinson, crouched with the others, holding her infant daughter, Angelina. Traumatized by that morning's events and frightened out of her wits, Mrs. Dickinson hesitated to identify herself. "Is Mrs. Dickinson here?" Almonte snapped impatiently. "If you value your life, speak up. It's a matter of life and death." Only then, did she step forward.

As Colonel Almonte led mother and child out of the church and into a hazy fog of black powder smoke, the sun was rising over the hills behind the fort. The battle was over, but a few nervous soldados continued to shoot off their muskets haphazardly. As she walked across the courtyard in front of the church, one of those careless rounds caught Mrs. Dickinson in her right calf. Colonel Almonte determined that her wound, although painful, was not serious and hastened her along. The longer that they remained inside the fort, the more likely it was that the young widow and her baby would receive lethal injuries.

"As we passed through the enclosed ground in front of the church," Mrs. Dickinson later testified, "I saw heaps of dead and dying." Amid the

Santa Anna ordered his soldiers to burn the bodies of the Alamo defenders. This image shows them performing that doleful duty. *Courtesy of Gary Zaboly, illustrator, An Altar for Their Sons: The Alamo and the Texas Revolution in Contemporary Newspaper Accounts.*

turmoil, one of those bodies demanded her special attention. "I recognized Col. Crockett lying dead and mutilated between the church and the two story barrack building, and even remember seeing his peculiar cap lying by his side." Almonte escorted mother and child into Béxar and took them to the home of their close friends Ramón and Francisca Músquiz.

Santa Anna ordered his soldiers to inter their slain companions in Béxar's Campo Santo. And what of the rebel corpses? Santa Anna commanded them burned. Mexicans spent the rest of the day stripping the Texian bodies, tying ropes around their ankles, and dragging them to twin funeral pyres. Pablo Díaz, a local Tejano, related how "grease of different kinds, principally tallow was melted and poured over the two pyres." By five o'clock in the afternoon, the soldados had collected all the dead Texians, piled them in layers, and set them all alight. "The dense smoke from this fire went up into the clouds, and I watched it while the fire burned for two days and two nights." After two days, the flames had not entirely consumed the cadavers. Díaz reported seeing, "[c]harred skulls, fragments of arms, hands, feet, and other members of the bodies of the dead defenders." The stench, he avowed, was almost unbearable.

Captain Fernando Urizza had approached Santa Anna in the bloody compound; the callousness of the general astonished him. Referencing the corpses, His Excellency casually remarked: "These are the chickens. Much blood has been shed, but the battle is over. It was but a small affair."

In military terms, Santa Anna was correct. Compared to the Napoleonic and Mexican Revolutionary battles that preceded it, the assault on the tiny border outpost was little more than a skirmish. The Duke of Wellington suffered more casualties (5,365) at Talavera during the Peninsular Wars almost thirty years before than the total number of combatants in this engagement. So judging simply by the statistics, it was a "small affair."

Yet, numbers alone can never convey the real meaning of the Battle of the Alamo. It quickly transcended history and entered the realm of myth. The fall of the fort provided a potent rallying symbol, filling Texians with a righteous anger—an anger that would bear fruit on the boggy field of San Jacinto. Today, the Alamo is the most-celebrated military engagement in Texas history; each year more than a million tourists visit the battle site and pay homage to the valor and determination of the defenders. But what were the circumstances that led to the battle and what were the consequences of it?

The pages that follow will provide answers to those questions—and many more.

SETTLEMENT

January 1821 – September 1835

1821: A Tale of Two Republics

In 1821, U.S. President James Monroe enjoyed widespread popularity. Indeed, one contemporary journalist branded the years of his administration the "Era of Good Feelings." In the aftermath of the War of 1812, it reflected a sense of national purpose and unity. The period witnessed the Federalist Party fade from the political landscape, terminating the partisan wrangles between it and Thomas Jefferson's Democratic-Republicans. Yet, Jefferson would have found it difficult to recognize the coalition he had initiated. In the face of hard truths, party regulars had adopted many Hamiltonian doctrines. So much so, that old Federalists were now comfortable in what had been, but was no longer, an opposition party. By seeking domestic unity and (he hoped) eliminating factions, President Monroe endeavored to build a national consensus—and, from 1817 to 1824, he largely succeeded.

Citizens were even able to assess the calamitous War of 1812 through a veil of self-congratulation. A fellow would have been utterly optimistic, or wholly delusional, to claim a U.S. "victory" against the British. Truthfully, the exhausted belligerents judged that the struggle was not worth the candle and cut their losses—and declared a "*status quo ante-bellum*." Still, Americans preferred to accentuate Andrew Jackson's final triumph at New Orleans and disregard the shameful surrender of Detroit, the trouncing at Bladensburg, and the burning of their national capital in Washington. They dubbed the conflict the "Second War of Independence," and it

Independence Day Celebration in Centre Square (1819) by John Lewis Krimmel. Full of hope and optimism, Americans celebrate Independence Day. During the "Era of Good Feelings," they had much to celebrate. At the same time, citizens of the fledgling Mexican Republic did not share the same confidence. *Courtesy of the United States National Portrait Gallery.*

had yielded some positive results. In the Old Northwest, it shattered the power of hostile tribes and evicted British fur traders from U.S. soil. Of more psychological and symbolic import, the Americans had stood up to the British. And, by God, never again would the British choose to face the Americans.

The year before, Americans demonstrated that they were willing and able to cooperate for the common good. Preserving the balance of power between slave and free states, congressmen enacted the Missouri Compromise, which admitted Missouri as a slave state and Maine as a free state. The statute regulated slavery in the western territories by excluding the South's "peculiar institution" in the former Louisiana Territory north of the parallel 36°30', except within the boundaries of the proposed state of Missouri. For a time, Americans hailed the 1820 agreement as an essential conciliation, almost equaling the Constitution in its substance. Ultimately, it could not avert the slide toward civil war. Nonetheless, many historians assert that it postponed the hostilities for decades.

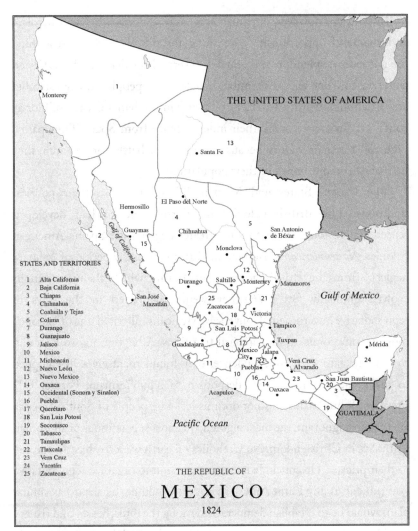

STATES AND TERRITORIES

1 Alta California
2 Baja California
3 Chiapas
4 Chihuahua
5 Coahuila y Tejas
6 Colima
7 Durango
8 Guanajuato
9 Jalisco
10 Mexico
11 Michoacán
12 Nuevo León
13 Nuevo Mexico
14 Oaxaca
15 Occidental (Sonora y Sinaloa)
16 Puebla
17 Querétaro
18 San Luis Potosí
19 Soconusco
20 Tabasco
21 Tamaulipas
22 Tlaxcala
23 Vera Cruz
24 Yucatán
25 Zacatecas

THE UNITED STATES OF AMERICA

Gulf of Mexico

Pacific Ocean

THE REPUBLIC OF

MEXICO

1824

Map by Donald S. Frazier, Ph.D.

Notwithstanding the general mood of contentment, not all Americans harbored good feelings. The Panic of 1819 damaged them all, but had utterly devastated poor folks living on the frontier. The first peacetime financial crisis in the United States, it brought about a general collapse of the national economy that persisted through 1821. Many destitute citizens prayed for a way—and a place—to begin anew.

In Mexico, however, circumstances were different. Selfless heroism and shameful opportunism, a yearning for the old order and a thirst for autonomy, splendor, and squalor—were all evident in the afflicted country; conflict and contention had left the people craving stability and a national identity. In 1821, following more than a decade of bloody conflict, Mexicans secured their independence from Spain. They paid a high toll for their victory because during their battle for freedom, they had sacrificed one-tenth of their population.

The United States and Mexico differed most in their political traditions. The British colonies in North America had developed representative foundations to a far greater degree than Spain's American colonies. *Norteamericanos* had benefited from a lengthy period of "salutary neglect" from the British government, during which their institutions evolved gradually. By 1776, they were experienced in the ways of representative government. Conversely, Mexicans inherited one of Europe's most uncompromising monarchical traditions. After fighting so long and so hard to gain their independence, they found themselves ill-equipped to make the transition from despotism to republicanism. Former U.S. President John Adams was not optimistic: "The people of South America are the most ignorant, the most bigoted, the most superstitious of all Roman Catholics in Christendom. No Catholics on earth were so abjectly devoted to their priests." He concluded, that any attempt to organize representative government in any Latin American nation would be "as absurd as similar plans would be to establish democracies among the birds, beasts, and fishes."

Although such views were remarkably prejudiced, he was not entirely wrong. By 1821, public education was rapidly becoming available to most U.S. children. Indeed, the United States was among the world's most literate societies. The few Mexican intellectuals emphasized the need for communal schooling, but the prevailing chaos made progress impossible. Some estimates reported illiteracy rates as high as 99 percent. Small wonder then that the ruling 1 percent regarded the majority as ignorant savages, more to be restrained than educated.

Even when the revolution ended, Mexicans continued to die in droves. City dwellers, who were primarily *mestizo*, illiterate, and dismissed by the ruling elites as "rabble," lived mostly in ground-level lodgings that flooded each rainy season. Such conditions promoted a glut of diseases and an appallingly high mortality rate. Fully one-third of all urban deaths were those of children younger than age three. Those living in the country fared little better because famine was a cyclical occurrence. So, too, were outbreaks of smallpox and another local disease that resembled smallpox but affected only those of Indian lineage.

Like the United States, Mexico consisted of many regions; unlike the United States, however, wretched roads and rugged landscapes made many of them virtually inaccessible. Consequently, most who lived outside Mexico City identified more with their region than the nation. Of all the Mexican states, Tejas was the remotest from the capital in Mexico City. There, the native Mexicans—*Tejanos*—battled against a brutal terrain, an erratic climate, and belligerent Comanche, Apache, and Kiowa Indians. Although government officials could tempt few interior Mexicans to relocate to such a godforsaken place, a norteamericano named Moses Austin presented what seemed like a feasible plan.

Moses Austin and the Power of a Dream

Moses Austin shared many characteristics with his biblical namesake: Both blazed trails later followed by their people to new homelands; both crossed bodies of red water (in Austin's case a Red River instead of a Red Sea); and each perished before seeing the settlement of his promised land.

As a young man, Austin had a hard time staying put. A native of Durham, Connecticut, he was born October 4, 1761. At twenty-three years of age, he moved to Philadelphia to partner with his elder brother Stephen in the dry goods business. He later relocated to Richmond, Virginia, to open a second dry goods store. In 1785, he married Mary Brown, the daughter of an affluent iron mining family.

And it was in mining that Austin made his mark. Always ambitious, Austin started his own establishment in southwestern Virginia. In 1789, he traveled there to inspect a lead mine site that showed great promise. By 1791, his family had joined him in present-day Wythe County. Moses, his brother Stephen, and several other business partners developed the region. The tiny village around the mines became "Austinville." To enhance the productivity of his venture, Moses imported experienced British miners and smelterers. So important were Austin's innovations that he became one of the principal founders of the U.S. lead industry. Scholars of this commerce refer to its second phase as the "Moses Austin Period." Indeed, his advances continued to guide the industry until the introduction

13

The interior of San Antonio de Béxar's Spanish Governor's Palace (built 1749). It was here that Moses Austin and Felipe Enrique Neri, Baron de Bastrop, worked their will on Governor Antonio María Martínez. *Courtesy of the National Park Service.*

of heavy machinery in the mid-1860s. Austin's fame grew apace with his fortune, and even in locales far removed from Virginia, Americans began to call Austin the "Lead King."

By appearances, Austin's future looked bright, but the Lead King occupied a rickety throne. Moses and Stephen had incurred heavy debt, which triggered the collapse of their Virginia mines. Moses abandoned Austinville to evade debtor's prison; Stephen stayed behind to face creditors and attempted to recoup what remained of their Virginia business. Stephen resented that Moses had absconded, leaving him to manage the disagreeable consequences, and the brothers remained estranged for the rest of their lives. Virginia courts laid claim to most of Moses's property and broke up the brothers' various operations. To escape the heavy hand of the law, Moses left town, the county, the state, and even the country. The former Lead King cast about for a suitable place of exile—and he found one.

Austin heard about the wealthy lead deposits in Missouri, which was part of Spanish Louisiana at the time. In December 1797, he and a companion investigated the mines. The following year, Spanish authorities granted Austin one square league of land—some 4,428 acres—and he became a Spanish citizen. He further promised that he would lure U.S. families to colonize the sparsely settled region.

As a Spanish subject, Austin prospered beyond his wildest dreams. He operated a portion of Mine à Breton, near what is now Potosi, Missouri. It was there in 1798 that he founded the first Anglo American settlement west of the Mississippi River. Always the enthusiastic entrepreneur, Austin greatly increased his assets. From the British miners he had previously employed, he learned how to operate the more efficient reverberatory furnace. As a result, he came to dominate virtually all of Missouri's smelting operations. Success finally crowned his industry, and according to some reports, he amassed a fortune in excess of $190,000.

Austin was not a Spaniard for long. In 1800, the Treaty of San Ildefonso restored the Louisiana Territory to France, and so he briefly found himself a subject of Napoleon. Yet, with the Louisiana Purchase of 1803, Austin was again an American—an extremely well-to-do American.

Once more, Austin was the Lead King, and he began to live like one. With the proceeds from his mines, he built an imposing mansion that he called Durham Hall. Money flowed like water or, more accurately, like molten lead. Beginning in 1805, and continuing for the next four years, his mine produced some 800,000 pounds of the ore annually.

It was too good to last. Aaron Burr's conspiracy, the War of 1812, and the dropping price of lead eroded Austin's bottom line. He sought to remedy the situation by joining in a scheme to increase the money supply by founding the Bank of St. Louis. Yet, during the Panic of 1819, the bank failed, wiping out Austin's fortune and leaving him and his family destitute.

And once again, Austin sought to rebuild his fortune in a Spanish province. In 1820, he rode to San Antonio de Béxar with a design to bring U.S. colonists into Spanish Texas. Unimpressed, Governor Antonio María Martínez spurned the scheme and ordered Austin out of the country. Crestfallen, Austin was about to depart when he encountered an old friend, Felipe Enrique Neri, Baron de Bastrop, who interceded with the governor. The baron was persuasive. The following year, the governor awarded Austin a land grant and permission to settle three hundred families in Texas.

This statue of Moses Austin stands in San Antonio's Main Plaza. It faces the Spanish Governor's Palace where Austin, Baron de Bastrop, and Governor Martínez collaborated to initiate Anglo American settlement in Texas. Sculpture by Waldine Tauch. *Courtesy of the Library of Congress.*

Ever the optimist, Austin must have believed his fortunes were on the rise; however, it was not to be. On his return trip, he contracted pneumonia and died shortly after arriving in Missouri. His son, Stephen F. Austin, would ultimately realize the colonization plan.

Moses Austin was the first of his type—one common in Texas lore—the wildcatter, the schemer and dreamer who found it easier to amass a fortune than to hold it. It would vex him to learn that nowadays his countrymen chiefly remember him as the father of Stephen F. Austin. Veiled in the shadow of his illustrious offspring, the recognition for which he yearned still eludes him. Yet, both in temperament and aptitude, it was the son—not the father—that providence had marked for greatness. Moses cleared a path into the wilderness but had christened his heir with remarkable foresight.

His middle name was "*Fuller.*"

Stephen F. Austin and
the Old Three Hundred

N ever was there a more reluctant colonizer than Stephen Fuller Austin. Dismayed by his father's many failures, he traveled to New Orleans in November 1820 where he met attorney Joseph H. Hawkins and began to study law. But a letter from his mother informed him that his father Moses, then desperately ill, had bequeathed his Texas enterprise to him. On June 31, 1821, Austin was in Natchitoches, Louisiana, when he learned that Moses had died. Stephen noted: "He was one of the most feeling and affectionate Fathers that ever lived. His faults I now say, and always have, were not of the heart."

All Moses's hopes and aspirations now rested on Stephen's shoulders. Responding to duty's call, Stephen abandoned his own ambitions for a legal career and, with considerable ambivalence, took up his father's mantle at twenty-four years of age.

Austin's doubts were well warranted. Seeking confirmation of his father's grant, he rode to San Antonio de Béxar, arriving on August 12, 1821. Along the way, he learned Mexico had achieved its independence from Spain. Would victorious Mexicans honor an agreement made by the Spaniards they had just deposed? In Béxar, Austin met influential Tejano leader José Antonio Navarro and began a lifelong friendship. Navarro helped Austin navigate the confusing procedures of Spanish and Mexican law. Finally, Governor Antonio María Martínez—the same man

The Log Cabin by Henry McArdle. Upon receiving news of an Indian raid, Stephen F. Austin grabs his long rifle with his right hand, while he closes a book titled, *The Laws of Mexico*, with his left. Surrounded by his colonists—including an enslaved man peeking through the window—all eyes are on the *empresario. Courtesy of the Texas State Library and Archives.*

who had previously authorized Moses's grant—reapproved it, recognizing Stephen's leadership, under the same terms. Martínez further granted Stephen permission to explore between Béxar and the Brazos River for a suitable location for a colony. Having selected the tract he wanted, Austin began to advertise in New Orleans, proclaiming that inexpensive acreage along the Brazos and Colorado rivers was now open for U.S. settlers. By the end of the year, settlers had begun to arrive.

It looked like the Texas venture was about to bear fruit when news arrived from Mexico City that upset all Austin's plans. Notwithstanding Governor Martínez's approval, the *junta instituyente,* Emperor Agustín de Iturbide's new Congress, rejected the Spanish land grant. Undeterred, Austin made the lengthy and grueling journey to Mexico City, teaching himself to speak Spanish along the way. Once there, he convinced the junta instituyente to endorse Moses's grant, as well as Iturbide's law of January 3, 1823, which authorized the employment of *empresarios*, or land agents, to stimulate immigration. In March 1823, just when it seemed that Austin's Texas plans were about to gel, Iturbide abdicated and the Congress negated the immigration law once more.

Empresario Colonies in Texas, 1824–1835

Map by Donald S. Frazier, Ph.D.

Redoubling his efforts, Austin, now fluent in Spanish, worked his will on the new Congress. In April 1823, the Congress approved a contract allowing Austin to transport three hundred Anglo American settlers to Texas, but he remained in Mexico City to help officials hone their new constitution. In 1824, a new immigration law passed Congress. It authorized each Mexican state to oversee its public lands. In March 1825, the legislature of Coahuila y Tejas passed a law that revived Iturbide's empresario system.

Largely because of Austin's determination and perseverance, conditions in Texas began to improve. By the end of 1825, the first three hundred families had arrived in Austin's first colony. They are known as the "Old Three Hundred." Although other empresarios operated in Texas, Austin was by far the most effective. Between 1825 and 1829, Mexican authorities were so impressed with his exertions that they granted him contracts to settle an additional nine hundred families. As empresario, Austin

Map by Donald S. Frazier, Ph.D.

possessed considerable civil and military authority over his colonists. Even so, he exercised his power with a light hand, and settlers came to admire his prudence and fair play. The early immigrants struggled at first, but by 1829, Austin could boast to his brother-in-law: "This is the most liberal and munificent Govt on earth to emigrants—after being here one year you will oppose a change even to Uncle Sam."

Austin did not exaggerate. The Mexican government was so openhanded that U.S. newcomers could hardly believe their good fortune. A head of family, if a farmer, received one *labor* (177.1 acres), or if he was a stock raiser, a *sitio* (a square league or 4,428.4 acres). Consequently, few immigrants admitted to being farmers. These land-hungry *norteamericanos*

Austin's Other Colonies

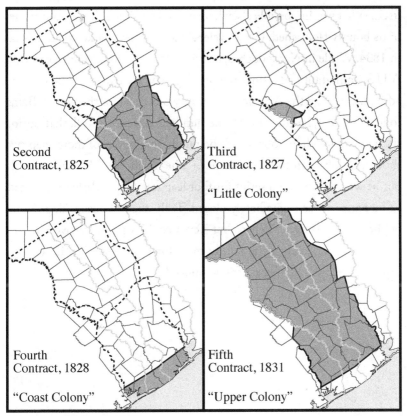

Map by Donald S. Frazier, Ph.D.

may have never owned a horse or punched a steer, but once in Texas, they became "ranchers." In return, the Mexican government required the U.S. settlers to convert to Roman Catholicism (at least on paper), provide evidence of their good character (again on paper), and improve their grants within two years (in theory). That was it. Yet, some ingrates whined about the twelve and a half cents an acre Austin charged as a surveying fee. Even so, most colonists understood how good they had it. After paying all administrative fees, a league and a labor together ran about thirty-eight cents an acre. If the grantee did not have enough money in pocket, he could pay it over time.

21

Mexican Texas offered more opportunity than the "land of opportunity" itself. What was impossible elsewhere proved possible in Texas, and stories of its bounty flourished. U.S. traveler Amos Andrew Parker visited Texas in 1834. While in Nacogdoches, he witnessed an astonishing transaction. A U.S. immigrant had a fine-looking dog, which a native Tejano came to admire. He asked the American what he would take for the hound. Being fond of the pet, he priced it at one hundred dollars. (Recall, that during the 1830s a hundred dollars had the purchasing power of more than two thousand dollars in today's currency.) The Tejano said he had no cash, but he would sign over a script for four leagues of land. Parker recounted: "The bargain was immediately closed. Truly, the old adage, 'dog cheap,' ought to be reversed." Where but Texas could a person arrive virtually penniless and exchange the family mutt for more than 17,712 acres of prime real estate? Man's best friend, indeed.

The Mexican Constitution of 1824 and the Struggle for the National Soul

n 1824, Mexican liberals finally crafted the form of government they had been fighting to attain since the beginning of their revolution in 1810. With Agustín de Iturbide now out of the way, leaders began reorganizing the system along federalist-liberal lines. They envisioned an arrangement that allowed significant regional sovereignty, while keeping the central government comparatively feeble. During the autumn of 1823 through January 1824, delegates from the various Mexican states gathered to endorse a national charter. On October 4, 1824, that document became part of Mexico's first constitution, the Federal Constitution of the United States of Mexico. Among the signatories of that historic contract was *Tejano* delegate Juan José María Erasmo Seguín.

The Constitution of 1824 owed much to its predecessors. It mirrored the U.S. Constitution of 1787, but it also drew from the 1812 Spanish Constitution of Cadiz. A liberal document by Spanish standards, the Cadiz charter greatly influenced many state and federal officials. Undercutting Mexico City's traditional influence, the 1824 Constitution sanctioned state participation in national matters but allowed for greater regional self-rule. Hypothetically, it removed distinctions between all races and castes. Mexican politicians learned, however, that it was easier to eliminate such divisions on paper than in hearts and minds. Allegedly, eradicating class differences, the 1824 Constitution nevertheless retained special privileges—or *fueros*—for clergymen and soldiers. Although pledg-

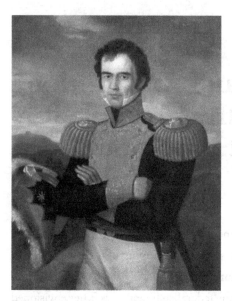

Following the adoption of the Constitution of 1824, general and political leader, Guadalupe Victoria—he was born José Miguel Ramón Adaucto Fernández y Félix—served as the first president of the United Mexican States. Victoria, Texas, is named in his honor. *Author's collection.*

ing freedom of speech, it incongruously recognized only one religion: Roman Catholicism. Despite those inconsistencies, most Mexicans believed their new constitution was a vast improvement over all previous legislation and signified a brighter future.

Yet, others had no faith in the new government. The conservative *centralistas* asserted that Mexico could never achieve true unity unless, and until, the central government consolidated authority. Their liberal rivals—the *federalistas*—countered that unless the individual states seized the lion's share of power, the wealthy, the church, and the military would strangle the infant republic in its crib. Federalists, moreover, supported U.S. colonization for the economic growth it fostered; the centralists opposed it.

Labels can create confusion. In U.S. history, federalists were men like James Madison, Alexander Hamilton, and John Jay who supported a powerful central government. Quite the opposite was true in Mexico; Mexican federalists advocated strong state governments but a weak central regime. The two factions never organized into formal political parties. Rather, they were communities of interest with profound philosophical differences. In 1824, Mexicans were still trying to find their footing and forge a national identity. The centralists and federalists nurtured vastly different visions of what Mexico should be, and each sought to define the national soul. Their altercations shaped Mexican politics for the next four decades and placed Texas on the path toward revolution.

Back in Texas, U.S. colonists read Mexican proclamations with mixed emotions. During the Spanish colonial period, the province of Tejas—which one disgusted official reviled as "more remote than Lapland"—had proven an administrative nightmare. It was, furthermore, a nightmare that the Mexican Congress had inherited. On May 7, 1824, Congress addressed the problem by simply fusing the troublesome region with Coahuila and established the hybrid state of Coahuila y Tejas. Yet, it neglected to stipulate a border, leaving the question of Texas's southwestern limits wholly unanswered. Erasmo Seguín resisted the legislation and attempted to maintain a separate identity for Tejas. Yet, the citizens of Coahuila, who greatly outnumbered those in Texas, easily brushed aside Seguín's opposition. On August 18, officials approved a federal colonization law. Respecting one of the major tenets of Mexican federalism, it allowed states considerable latitude in administering immigration within their own boundaries. The law did, however, impose *some* restrictions. Foreigners, for example, could not reside within thirty miles of the coast; neither could they settle within sixty miles of the international (read U.S.) border. Mexican federalists may have supported U.S. immigration, but they did not entirely trust the Americans.

For the most part, the Constitution of 1824 delighted U.S. settlers—and for good reason. The heirs of George Washington, Thomas Jefferson, and James Madison could not help but approve that Mexico had adopted a constitutional republic. At first glance, the differences between the U.S. Constitution of 1787 and the Mexican Constitution of 1824 seemed trivial. It was true that the Mexican Congress, not the people, elected the president. Nor did the new constitution recognize separation of church and state, a principle Americans greatly valued. But these disparities were mere irritants, not deal breakers.

Stephen F. Austin and his Anglo American colonists placed their hopes in the promises of Mexican federalism—as did native Mexicans. During the years of Spanish rule, communal loyalty to a distant sovereign and a sanctioned religion provided a sense of political and cultural continuity. Yet, independence had undermined or, in some cases, entirely shattered those ties. Worse yet, nothing had emerged to take their place. Mexicans who lived beyond the boundaries of Mexico City identified with their own region—*la patria chica* ("the little homeland") they called it. The illiterate 99 percent of the population found it difficult to even comprehend the concept of a nation-state. For them, federalism meant that each state would determine its own destiny without interference from a far-flung central government. As Anglo American settlers interpreted the ruling, they had official sanction to recreate U.S. culture and traditions in Texas.

The Fredonian Rebellion

aden Edwards and Stephen F. Austin were both Texas *empresarios*—which is about all they had in common. Truthfully, it is difficult to imagine two individuals who were more dissimilar. Edwards was a speculator; Austin was a colonizer. Edwards was shrill and abrasive; Austin was soft-spoken and diplomatic. Edwards was loyal only to his appetites and ambition; Austin was devoted to his colonists and the Mexican Republic. Edwards was slapdash and, ultimately, a failure; Austin was attentive and successful. Even so, the pair were to play key roles in a bewildering episode historians note as the Fredonian Rebellion.

After Moses Austin blazed the trail, Edwards was among the Americans flocking to Mexico City seeking Texas lands. There, he first met Stephen F. Austin while both were pursuing government contracts. Their relationship was cordial. Austin even aided Edwards maneuver the maze of Mexican bureaucracy. After lobbing for three years, Edwards finally secured an empresario grant from the state government in Saltillo. It authorized him to settle eight hundred families in eastern Texas. The contract demanded that Edwards acknowledge all previous Spanish and Mexican land titles, organize a militia, and finally, that he submit his deeds to a state land commissioner for certification. Edwards agreed to all those stipulations.

Map by Donald S. Frazier, Ph.D.

Situated north and east of Austin's Colony, the Edwards Colony occupied an expansive section that encompassed the community of Nacogdoches, which boasted a long and intricate past. Contrasting Austin's grant, the district had long embraced a polyglot mixture of Frenchmen, Spaniards, and more recently, Anglo Americans. Already a camping ground for the Caddo Indians, Spaniards had established Nacogdoches as early as 1716. In addition to the Caddo, a band of Cherokees had recently moved into the region. Notwithstanding their ethnicity or nationality, few occupants of the area were able to provide land titles, given the region's convoluted history. Those who could, likely concocted forgeries. Many of the original families had populated the Piney Woods for generations and considered Edwards a gatecrasher.

His demeanor did nothing to soothe the original inhabitants' concerns. Arriving in Nacogdoches in August 1825, Edwards asserted that only he had the power to establish the legitimacy of surviving land claims. He further required written proof of ownership, else claimants must forfeit their land and the empresario would auction it to the highest bidder. Bigotry provoked his actions. Edwards disparaged poor people or those of a different race. If he could force out the humbler settlers, he could disperse their holdings to affluent Southern planters.

Of course, few of the original settlers could produce any documentation. Most *Tejano* families worked land that Spanish authorities had granted more than seventy years before. Before Edwards's arrival, written deeds had never been an issue; few of the original Hispanic settlers could even read them. Expecting tension between Edwards and the locals, Luís Procela, the acting *alcalde*, and José Antonio Sepulveda, the town clerk, took it upon themselves to authenticate Spanish and Mexican land titles. Infuriated, Edwards charged them with forgery. His behavior alienated the old inhabitants who were already skeptical of their new empresario. By December 1825, Edwards had recruited fifty U.S. families to inhabit previously settled plots near Nacogdoches—a circumstance that provoked the initial occupants even further.

Reports of Edwards's oppressive tactics arrived on the desk of Governor José Antonio Saucedo in San Antonio. The governor and other Mexican officials began to view the irksome empresario with a disapproving eye. In 1826, during a period when Edwards was absent from Texas, he left his colony in the hands of his business partner and younger brother, Benjamin. Nine years younger than Haden, Benjamin inherited all of his big brother's grace and charm, a gift of debatable value. Haden's record of severity, along with the haughty and contemptuous tone of Benjamin's correspondence, persuaded Mexican officials that the Edwards brothers did not justify all the vexation, so in October 1826, they rescinded Haden's contract.

The Edwards brothers faced financial ruin; Haden had sunk more than fifty thousand dollars of his own money into the project and now stood to lose it all. On December 16, 1826, the brothers, with only thirty supporters, entered Nacogdoches. On December 21, they proclaimed the Republic of Fredonia, which just happened to share the same boundaries as Edwards's former colony. Almost immediately, the self-styled "Fredonians" endorsed a peace treaty with the neighboring Cherokees. The revolutionaries then hoisted their new flag. Denoting the allied ethnic groups, it sported one white stripe and another in red. Emblazoned on the standard were the words, "Independence, Liberty, and Justice." The rebels dispatched couriers to Louisiana seeking reinforcements from the U.S. Army, which wanted nothing to do with the harebrained conspiracy. Another messenger rode south to invite Austin and his colonists to join the insurgence. Austin, of course, declined the offer and responded with a stern warning: "You are deluding yourselves and this delusion will ruin you." Green DeWitt's colonists went so far as to adopt a resolution declaring their "contempt and disgust" for Edwards.

His subsequent actions only bolstered Austin's belief that Haden Edwards had lost his mind. On December 13, 1826, Colonel Mateo Ahumada and Governor Saucedo marched with a Mexican army against the Fredonians. Then, on December 21, Edwards declared that, henceforth, the Republic of Fredonia would incorporate all the land from the Sabine River to the Rio Grande. Edwards gambled that the other U.S. empresarios would back his play. He lost that bet. Instead, Austin summoned Texas militiamen to unite against those he called, "a small party of infatuated madmen." Austin attempted to negotiate with Edwards, but he rebuffed all overtures. On January 22, 1827, Colonel Ahumada's force was quickly approaching Nacogdoches. The house of cards that was the Fredonian Republic began to collapse from within. As his followers absconded, Edwards finally came to understand that he was facing disaster. On January 28, 1827, the former empresario fled toward Louisiana, abandoning Texas, his colony, and his fantasies of the Fredonian Republic. The rebellion was over, and Ahumada's soldiers had not fired a single shot.

Following this bizarre incident, Mexican federalists began to question their policy of U.S. immigration; Mexican centralists, of course, had always opposed it. Texas was simply too remote for officials in Mexico City to discern the intentions of the U.S. colonists. They needed a patriot of proven judgment to inspect the province and gauge conditions.

General Manuel de Mier y Terán was just such a man.

Mier y Terán and the Comisión de Límites

The many attainments of General José Manuel Rafael Simeón de Mier y Terán seemed to justify such a grandiose name. Born in 1789, he earned a degree from the College of Mines, distinguishing himself in engineering and mathematics. During the Mexican wars for independence, he sided with the republicans and served as an artillery officer. In 1821, he fought alongside General Agustín de Iturbide to drive out the Spaniards. During the early 1820s, the new government enlisted him in an array of positions. In 1822, he was a member of the committee on colonization of unoccupied lands in the first constituent congress. In 1824, he rose to the rank of brigadier general and later served briefly as minister of war. In a nation where the majority was illiterate, Terán appeared an intellectual giant.

In 1827, President Guadalupe Victoria selected him to lead a scientific and boundary expedition into Texas to observe and document the natural resources, the American Indians, and to finally verify the Mexican–U.S. boundary between the Sabine and the Red rivers. That was the official rationale for the expedition. Unofficially, the president tasked Terán to secretly ascertain the number and motives of the U.S. immigrants. He was an unlikely choice; the president was a federalist, and Terán was a centralist. Nevertheless, the general's loyalty and acumen were beyond reproach. Notwithstanding Terán's politics, his was a reliable opinion.

In 1828, General Manuel de Mier y Terán led a boundary commission into Texas. Although the general admired Stephen F. Austin, he did not entirely trust his motives. Mier y Terán's recommendations resulted in the Law of April 6, 1830. *Courtesy of the Texas State Library and Archives.*

The expedition was an elaborate enterprise. Leaving Mexico City on November 10, 1827, Terán traveled in a "prodigious" coach, ornately carved, inlaid with silver, and escorted by mounted dragoons. A number of authorities accompanied him: Rafael Chovell, a mineralogist; Lieutenant José María Sánchez y Tapía, a cartographer and illustrator; and Jean Louis Berlandier, a Swiss botanist and zoologist. All kept careful records and sketched the flora and fauna on their journey.

On March 1, 1828, the Boundary Commission reached San Antonio de Béxar. The bounty of the countryside moved Berlandier to eloquence: "Peach trees were in bloom at the end of February, nut trees burgeoned, the willow and the poplar were covered with catkins—in a word, all Nature was already animated although winter was not yet past." Even so, Béxar's citizens made a less favorable impression: "Poor farmers live there in wretchedness, insulted at every turn by the Indians." The Bexariños also failed to impress Sánchez, who observed:

> The character of the people is care-free, they are enthusiastic dancers, very fond of luxury, and the worst punishment that can be inflicted upon them is work. Doubtless, there are some individuals, out of the 1,425 that make up the total population, who are free from these, failings, but they are very few.

On April 27, the comisión arrived in San Felipe de Austin, the capital of Stephen F. Austin's colony. The *empresario* received the general with appropriate deference. Their relations were respectful and proper but never warm. Each sized up the other like boxers before a prize fight. Terán never recorded his impression of Austin, but Sánchez did. Austin's efforts to please repelled him. As he logged in his diary, "the diplomatic policy of this empresario, evident in all his actions, has, one may say, lulled the authorities into a sense of security, while he works diligently for his own ends." Stymied by the Brazos River floodwaters, the expedition remained in San Felipe for two weeks. Nacogdoches was the next destination, but inclement weather, muddy roads, and a plague of mosquitos prolonged their travel to three weeks.

Terán well knew that Nacogdoches had been the hotbed of the Fredonian Rebellion and he expected the worst. As he approached that troubled community, what he witnessed confirmed his fears: "As one travels from Béjar to this town, Mexican influence diminishes, so much that it becomes clear that in this town that influence is almost nonexistent." Lieutenant Sánchez also noted that the Nacogdoches *Tejanos* had embraced the speech, dress, and manners of their U.S. neighbors: "Accustomed to continuous commerce with the North Americans, they have imitated their customs, and so it may truthfully be said that they are Mexican only by birth, for even the Castilian language they speak with considerable ignorance."

Terán thought Nacogdoches Americans cut from an entirely different cloth than Austin's deferential colonists:

> The North Americans are haughty; they shun society by inclination and because they disdain it. They devote themselves both to industrial enterprises and to the hardest labors—as well as to the grossest vices—with exceptional ardor. They do not think they have relaxed from their grueling tasks until drunkenness dulls their senses, and in that state they are fierce and scandalous.

According to Terán, Austin's colony was the only one where the U.S. immigrants even tried to "understand and obey the laws of the country and where, as a result of the enlightenment and integrity of its empresario, they have a notion of our republic and its government."

As far as Terán could tell, the U.S. settlers were still devoted to their Madisonian institutions: "They all go about with their constitution in their pocket, demanding their rights and the authorities and functionaries that [it] provides." The *norteamericanos* may never have read the Mexican Constitution of 1824, but they knew all about the Philadelphia charter of 1787.

Like the Lewis and Clark Expedition before it, Terán's Boundary Commission made momentous contributions to scientific knowledge. Even now, its records provide historians with the best source material for the study of Texas during its colonial period. But Mexican officials were more interested in the general's secret report on foreign immigration. When they finally received it, the commentary set into motion a series of events that was to shake Texas to its foundations.

The Law of April 6, 1830 and the Disaffection of Texas

While Manuel de Mier y Terán toured Texas, political upheaval threatened to tear Mexico apart. In 1827, Vice President Nicolás Bravo Rueda instigated a centralist rebellion, which federalist Generals Vicente Guerrero and Antonio López de Santa Anna promptly slapped down. The 1828 elections pitted the federalist Guerrero against a centralist candidate, Manuel Gómez Pedraza. Returns from ten of the nineteen states pronounced Gómez Pedraza the victor. Nevertheless, federalists refused to transfer power, claiming that the opposition candidate had fraudulently pressured the army to confirm him. Pandemonium reigned as the two rival governments, each supported by its own soldiers, disputed the presidential succession. The federalists finally won the upper hand, forcing Gómez Pedraza to surrender the executive office. It was ironic that the federalists—Mexicans who ostensibly supported constitutional government and the rule of law—refused to acknowledge the results of the first national election sanctioned under the Constitution of 1824.

Under the watchful eye of military authorities, President Guerrero faced multiple challenges as he strove to manage a government of dubious legitimacy. In July 1829, a Spanish force, in a bid to reclaim the country, landed at Tampico. In August, President Guerrero dispatched Santa Anna to confront the invaders. The Mexican general besieged the Spaniards and, in October, forced them to surrender. Following the Spanish defeat, Mexicans of every stripe hailed Santa Anna as the national "savior."

Once Santa Anna sent the Spaniards packing, the federalist president enacted sweeping reforms, which, in September 1829, included the "Guerrero Decree" that abolished slavery throughout Mexico. Guerrero tenaciously retained the emergency powers granted him during the Spanish invasion. Although that threat had passed, this dictatorial authority enabled his restructuring of the government—and infuriated conservatives. Guerrero pushed too far too fast, alienating even many moderates. In early 1830, the centralist vice president, Anastasio Bustamante, led a successful coup against Guerrero and assumed the executive office.

Now that centralists had seized control, they could take up General Terán's recommendations concerning Texas. He urged the government to bolster current presidios and construct new ones. He further proposed expanded coastal trade between Texas and other Mexican states. This would, he explained, diminish the commercial influence of the United States, which he had recently observed in Nacogdoches. Finally, to offset the mushrooming Anglo American population, he advised transporting European and Mexican colonists into Texas. Terán did not mince words: "Either the government occupies Texas now, or it is lost forever."

Centralists had always taken a hard line against Anglo American immigration, and they intended not merely to draw that line but also to enforce it. Terán's recommendations both instigated and informed the Law of April 6, 1830, a provocative directive that actually exceeded his suggestions. More than simply relocating Europeans and interior Mexicans into Texas, the decree forbade any more migration from the United States and canceled all unfinished *empresario* contracts. Americans could relocate anywhere in Mexico, *except* in territory adjacent to the United States—in other words, *not* in Texas. Quite enough Anglo Americans already lived there. The law further banned Southerners from bringing their slaves into Texas, in line with the Guerrero Decree. Even so, the president, a mestizo of African descent, might have also wished it to reduce the pace of U.S. settlement. Paradoxically, abolishing slavery was one liberal reform that the conservatives supported. On this issue, at least, the interests of federalists and centralists coincided.

The Colonization Law of 1824 specified that Congress could pass such draconian legislation only under "imperative circumstances." Lucas Ignacio Alamán y Escalada, Bustamante's minister of foreign relations, personally drafted the Law of April 6. He suffered no doubts that conditions in Texas presented a clear and present danger and warranted swift and formidable countermeasures. Alamán believed that U.S. migrants were participants in a U.S. conspiracy to wrest Texas away from Mexico much like their countrymen had previously attained Louisiana and Florida from Spain. Alamán insisted, "Where others send invading armies, [the Americans] send their colonists."

The Law of April 6, 1830, placed U.S. settlers in Texas on notice that centralist administrators would not permit them to reconstruct their former U.S. lives on Mexican soil; as much as they might have disliked the prospect, they would finally have to assimilate. When news of the decree arrived in Texas, the U.S. colonists were outspoken in expressing their resentment and anxiety. Empresario Stephen F. Austin cautioned patience and attempted to tap down mounting tensions. Firmly, but tactfully, he wrote to both General Terán and President Bustamante arguing against the new law. In the fullness of time, Austin was able to obtain an exemption for his contract and that of fellow empresario Green DeWitt. They were able to prove they had acted in good faith and had brought in the requisite number of colonists. Austin and DeWitt managed to save their enterprises, but other empresarios were not so successful. Austin retained his loyalty to the Mexican Republic, but the torrent of punitive decrees emanating from the centralist Congress weakened his confidence in the Mexican government.

Additionally, the April 6 law distressed the *Tejano* elites. Their Anglo neighbors not only provided useful allies in the struggle against Indian marauders, but their industry was also beginning to turn Texas around economically. If a rising tide lifts all boats, it seemed that centralist demands were forcing U.S. boats out of port. Because they were more familiar with Spanish and Mexican legal traditions, because they believed that the centralists might be more receptive to native petitioners, and because it was in their own interests to do so, Tejano leaders took the helm in contesting the despised ruling.

Law of April 6, 1830: What It Required

The Mexican Minister of Foreign Relations, Lucas Alamán y Escalada, initiated this decree. He did so in an attempt to halt (or at least slow) the torrent of immigration from the United States into Texas. An upshot of General Manuel de Mier y Terán's warnings and recommendations, the legislation encouraged counter-colonization of Texas by Europeans and citizens from the Mexican interior, inspired military occupation, and increased coastal trade.

The edict stated the following:

- It authorized a loan to finance the cost of transporting colonists to Texas.
- It opened the coastal trade to foreigners for a period of four years.
- It authorized the position of federal commissioner of colonization to supervise *empresario* contracts in accordance with the general colonization law.
- It forbade the further introduction of slaves into Mexico.
- It intended to prohibit or limit immigration from the United States through Article 11. Alamán, not Mier y Terán, proposed this restriction. Texian settlers especially despised this article.

Notwithstanding his opposition to Article 11 and the law's restrictions on slavery, Mier y Terán became federal commissioner of colonization. News of the law unsettled Texian settlers. Ever the peacemaker, empresario Stephen F. Austin attempted to calm their fears. At the same time, however, he did lodge protests with Mier y Terán and President Anastasio Bustamante. His objections bore fruit. Austin managed to secure exemptions from certain clauses the law for his contract and for that of fellow empresario Green DeWitt. But Alamán's legislation shattered the bonds of trust between the Texian colonists and the Mexican government. Historians can now trace the chain of events that were to lead to revolt and bloodshed to a single date: April 6, 1830.

Los Tejanos

Tejanos were, and long had been, an isolated people. Spaniards—and after 1821, Mexicans—valued Tejas only as a defensive buffer against French, British, Indian, and finally, U.S. encroachments. Beginning in the early eighteenth century, tight-fisted officials dispatched clerics, soldiers, and settlers to the *frontera* but never in numbers sufficient to achieve dominion or provide for their safety. Removed by distance from the seat of viceregal power, Tejas colonists learned to fend for themselves. That de facto abandonment nourished a culture detached from the rest of the country. Tejanos developed their own customs, clothing, music, tactics, and food. On those rare occasions that government bureaucrats did venture into Tejas, they found the inhabitants unfamiliar, uninformed, and uncouth. During General Manuel de Mier y Terán's 1828 inspection, Lieutenant José María Sánchez noted: "The Mexicans that live here are very humble people, and perhaps their intentions are good, but because of their education and environment they are ignorant not only of the customs of our great cities, but even of the occurrences of our Revolution."

True. Beyond the mainstream of Mexican life and culture, Tejanos developed their own societal formations, their own economic concepts, and their own political principles—with scarcely a thought to events in Mexico City. They, probably more than any other Mexicans, were proud natives of *la patria chica*, but in their case, a not-so-*little* homeland. Tejanos

41

Even American colonists who disliked Mexicans in general admitted that *Tejanos* were unexcelled at working cattle. Indeed, the Anglos incorporated nearly all of their practices and gear. *Courtesy of the San Antonio Missions National Historical Park.*

scraped out an existence in a hostile borderland; their priorities were their families, their communities, and their region. What, after all, had Mexico City ever done for them?

Tejas had always been a military frontier. Sons and grandsons of hardy presidial troopers, boys grew up on horses brandishing arms. Instead of the smug condescension they normally received, Tejanos thought that interior Mexicans owed them their appreciation for securing the frontera. They expected government authorities might, at least, acknowledge their many contributions. In one petition, Tejanos entreated exclusive legislation "for their worthy status as inhabitants of the frontier, who have undergone sacrifices and risks unknown to the people of the interior, and for which the latter are indebted to the former." Yet, assistance, or even gratitude, was rarely forthcoming. The official response was always the same: The coffers are empty; do the best you can; you're on your own. But no one knew that better than the Tejanos themselves. If faraway lawmakers in Mexico City could not help them, they would turn to people who could.

Tejas traditionally suffered from a miniscule population, which was the reason that Tejano elites championed Anglo American emigration. Writing the same year that the centralists dictated the Law of April 6, Béxar resident Francisco Ruiz declared: "I cannot help seeing advantages which, to my way of thinking, would result if we admitted honest, hardworking people, regardless of what country they come from—even hell itself." U.S. frontiersmen were proven Indian fighters, which the beleaguered Tejanos welcomed. Anglos were also improving the regional economy, raising both cattle and cotton in abundance. Lacking the means to produce even basic commodities, Tejanos increasingly relied on U.S. trade. In a petition to federal officials, Béxar's city councilmen described their plight:

> Although it grieves us to say so, we should state that the miserable manufacture of blankets, hats, and even shoes was never established in Texas towns. Lack of these articles has obliged us to beg them from foreigners or from the interior of the republic, two or three hundred leagues distant.

For all those reasons, Tejanos opposed punitive legislation that might drive U.S. colonists away.

Wealthy Tejanos believed the financial development of the state (and, indeed, their own prospects) interconnected with the U.S. colonists, their cotton economy, and ultimately, their slaves. Cotton, after all, did not plant or pick itself. Consequently, Tejanos joined Stephen F. Austin and Green DeWitt in opposing both the 1829 Guerrero anti-slavery decree and the 1830 Law of April 6. Although Political Chief Ramón Musquiz admitted that slavery was "unfortunate," he nonetheless condemned freeing *Texas* slaves as hasty, especially as the primitive region was just starting to show a profit. Austin's friend and collaborator, José Antonio Navarro, introduced a cynical legal loophole whereby U.S. planters might still bring their slaves as "indentured servants." Neither the Guerrero Decree nor the Law of April 6 placed any restrictions on personal servants. Changing their title, of course, made no difference in how those wretched souls lived day to day. To restate Shakespeare: That which we call a slave, by any other name, would be as shackled.

Tejanos and U.S. colonists got along well enough when they came into contact, but such opportunities were infrequent. Again, the reason was distance. Each group settled in population clusters. Tejano communities developed in three widely separated areas: San Antonio de Béxar, the political hub of Texas; the Nacogdoches region, buried deep within the Piney Woods; and the Victoria–Goliad district, where open-range ranching flourished. For their part, most U.S. colonists lived in East Texas and on the rich bottom land drained by the Brazos River. Between the settlement clusters lay wide-open, vacant spaces. Vacant, that is, unless Indian raiders were on the warpath.

The arrival of Austin's colonists trapped Tejanos between two realms. They had no desire to have centralists in Mexico City, or even federalists in Saltillo, dominate Tejas and impede its progress. Then again, neither did they want to surrender hegemony to Americans still damp from the waters of the Sabine River.

Tejanos and the Anglo colonists needed each other, which is not to say they always trusted each other. And although both sides might have wished for better, they had to make do with the material at hand. Mexicans frequently described *norteamericanos* as drunken adventurers. In a remarkably frank exchange, one report to a state official read: "Let us be honest with ourselves, Sir, the foreign *empresarios* are nothing more than money-changing speculators caring only for their own well-being and hesitating not in their unbecoming methods." U.S. settler, Mary S. Helm, returned the compliment by describing Mexicans as the "debris of several inferior and degraded races, demoralized by a long course of indolence and political corruption." It was in this climate of distrust and derision that some U.S. colonists thought themselves obliged to depend on Tejanos less and grab their fortunes and futures with their own hands.

"Disturbances": Anahuac, Velasco, and Nacogdoches

Centralist officials began to transfer forces into Texas to enforce the Law of April 6, 1830. President Anastasio Bustamante designated General Manuel de Mier y Terán commandant general of the Eastern Interior Provinces. His new title carried with it the responsibility of supervising both civil and military affairs in the states of Tamaulipas, Nuevo León, and Coahuila y Tejas. Terán ordered the construction of six additional Texas presidios to prevent smuggling and impede U.S. immigration. These initiatives resulted in a series violent confrontations between U.S. colonists and centralists troops. Traditional Texas histories euphemistically classed these clashes as "troubles" or "disturbances." Actually, these flare-ups were in the U.S. tradition of civil disobedience, not unlike Shays's Rebellion or the Whiskey Rebellion, in which citizens challenged taxation they considered repressive and a government they deemed unresponsive.

General Terán established a presidio at Anahuac on Galveston Bay and placed Colonel Juan Davis Bradburn in command of the post. It was an ill-fated choice. Born in Virginia in 1787, his parents had christened him *John* Davis Bradburn. He came to Texas first as a filibuster but later joined the fight for Mexican Independence, changed his first name to "Juan," rose through the ranks of the Mexican army, and became a dutiful and dedicated centralist. At first, U.S. colonists in Anahuac received the news of Bradburn's appointment with "great pleasure," but his haughty demeanor soon dampened their enthusiasm. His duties under the April 6 law included enforcing Mexican customs regulations, dispensing licenses to Anglo attorneys, and reviewing land titles. The federalists had previously granted the U.S. immigrants tax exemptions, but the time allotted had expired. President Bustamante and his centralist cohorts anticipated that tariff revenues would cover the costs of the new presidios securing the approaches into Texas from the United States.

To locals, Bradburn seemed self-important beyond purpose. Moreover, the "depraved character" of his troops—many of whom were convicted criminals serving out a prison sentences with military service—became intolerable. Bradburn was an American by birth, and many speculated that to prevent charges of favoritism he was more severe than a native Mexican might have been. Of course, as a centralist officer it was his duty to dissuade U.S. immigration. Nevertheless, he appeared to take too much enjoyment in his work.

George Fisher was another former U.S. citizen that Anahuac settlers wished had stayed in the United States. Appointed customs collector in 1831, he insisted ships would have to pay their duties to him in Anahuac. But most U.S. captains were bound for Velasco at the mouth of the Brazos River. Thus, they had to sail some 140 miles out of their way simply to satisfy the dictates of this petty bureaucrat. That, and they further resented having to pay any Mexican tariffs at all.

In 1832, matters came to a head when Bradburn arrested two mouthy lawyers, Patrick Jack and William Barret Travis, who had been trying to incite the locals to rebellion. On June 10, 1832, Anglo citizens in Anahuac determined to rescue the troublemakers, and armed insurgents occupied a number of the town's buildings. In the skirmish that followed, five centralist soldiers and one Anglo colonist died. After the clash, the rebels regrouped along Turtle Bayou and waited for the arrival of artillery purportedly on the way from Brazoria.

It was fortunate for the dissidents that news had arrived that General Antonio López de Santa Anna, an avowed federalist and the erstwhile

In this Charles Shaw illustration, Mexican soldiers haul a defiant William Barret Travis and Patrick Jack into the brick kiln that serves as a makeshift jail. American citizens of Anahuac shout their outrage. *Courtesy of the San Jacinto Museum of History.*

"Savior of Mexico," had launched a coup against Bustamante's centralist regime. The Anglo insurgents, of course, favored the federalist faction because it supported U.S. immigration and state rights. Indeed, during the skirmish on June 10, the mob at Anahuac took as their battle cry, "*¡Viva Santa Anna!*"—ironic considering the role he would play in Texas just four years later.

On June 13, the Anahuac dissenters drafted what they called the "Turtle Bayou Resolutions." In the document, they declared themselves loyal Mexicans who supported Santa Anna and the Constitution of 1824. They insisted that they had taken up arms only to resist "the present dynasty" and its "*many* despotic and arbitrary acts."

On June 26, Brazoria residents, employing a schooner armed with a cannon and between 100 and 150 riflemen, besieged Fort Velasco, commanded by centralist commandant Domingo de Ugartechea. Once they had exhausted all their ammunition, Ugartechea and his garrison hoisted the white flag. But the fighting had been fierce. The Anglo insurgents lost seven killed and fourteen wounded; three of the fourteen later died of their wounds. The centralist garrison suffered five killed and sixteen wounded.

Meanwhile, back in Anahuac, Bradburn was feeling the pressure. He called on centralist garrisons in Nacogdoches and San Antonio for reinforcements. On June 19, Colonel José de las Piedras, commander of the Nacogdoches presidio, led one hundred troops southward to assist his beleaguered comrade. Fortunately for all concerned, Piedras was more diplomatic than Bradburn. When he arrived within thirty miles of Anahuac, he opened talks with the angry Anglo citizens, who supplied him with a list of grievances. Piedras offered a number of concessions. He agreed to reestablish a town council at Liberty, release Jack and Travis to civilian authorities, and demand Bradburn's resignation. On June 28, the insurgents gladly accepted his terms; on July 1, Piedras entered Anahuac without incident. Triumphant, the mob released Jack and Travis from their eight-week confinement.

With order restored in Anahuac, Piedras returned to Nacogdoches; the poor man had no idea that he was riding into a maelstrom. Inspired by the events at Velasco and Anahuac, Anglo colonists in and around that Piney Woods community marched on the centralist garrison there. Like Bradburn, Piedras had angered the Anglo community by attempting to enforce centralist dictates. On August 2, after a bitter street fight, Piedras and his centralist garrison evacuated Nacogdoches and retreated toward Béxar. Yet, members of the "National Militia," under James W. Bullock and James Bowie overtook them and forced their surrender. Piedras had suffered forty-seven killed and more than forty wounded. With that, all centralist forces found it prudent to flee eastern Texas. Shortly afterward, Travis boasted: "Mexicans have learned a lesson, Americans know their rights and will assert and protect them." The young firebrand seemed to have forgotten that, *legally*, he was himself a "Mexican." Presumably, he purposely *remembered* to forget it.

The bloody episodes of 1832 may well have provoked a wider upheaval had cooler heads not prevailed. Although a centralist, Terán interpreted the Law of April 6 with remarkable restraint, instructing his officers to conduct themselves with discretion. Ironically, U.S. settlers respected the native Mexican officers more than U.S.-born officials like the "martinet" Bradburn and the "busy-body" customs collector Fisher. As he always did, *empresario* Austin cautioned patience and temperance. But these clashes had not been mere "disturbances"—as many as sixty-five men lost their lives and dozens more suffered serious wounds. Most U.S. colonists craved peace and scorned those agitators who had incited mayhem. More reflective men planned to assemble in October—and they proposed to defend their rights, not with bullets, but a petition.

The Convention of 1832

I n 1832, the Anglo American settlers of Mexican Texas grappled with many thorny issues, not the least of these involved what to call them. Residents of Spanish and Mexican heritage were, and always had been, "*Tejanos.*" But what to call U.S. Mexicans? Several designations were in contention: Texicans, Texasians, Texionians, and even Texilingans. Still, the term most often employed by the people themselves was *Texian.* The non-Hispanic white residents of Mexican Republic Texas—and, later, the Texas Republic—continued to employ Texian as an expression of self-identification until annexation to the United States in 1846. Not until the early statehood period did *Texan* come to predominate. Accordingly, for the remainder of this book, I will use *Texian* because it is the more historically appropriate label.

Residents of Texas—both Tejano and Texian—kept a watchful eye on affairs in Mexico City. Centralist Anastasio Bustamante had previously deposed liberal president Vicente Guerrero. The federalist champion attempted to regain power, but he fell into Bustamante's hands and a reactionary group hauled him before a firing squad. A U.S. official, known for his disapproval of Mexicans, nonetheless described Guerrero as "one of the most distinguished chiefs of the revolution." The illegal execution of a national hero disgusted both Tejanos and Texians. But Guerrero was merely the latest in a long list of slain Mexican leaders. In 1824, Agustín de Iturbide, also a popular idol, had faced a federalist firing squad. During the U.S. election of 1828, challenger Andrew Jackson had despised the incumbent president, John Quincy Adams, but he did not shoot him when he won. Some Anglo colonists began to wonder if John Quincy's father, John, had been correct; were Latin Americans even capable of sustaining a constitutional republic? All the same, many Texian planters were delighted to learn that the author of the 1829 anti-slavery decree was now gone.

On July 3, 1832, the same day that an Anahuac mob freed Patrick Jack and William Barret Travis from confinement, Mexico lost one of its most devoted patriots. With civil war roiling the interior and Texas in revolt, General Manuel de Mier y Terán could read the handwriting on the wall. Overwhelmed by events and in declining health, he retired to a quiet church, and like a Roman patrician, fell on his sword. Shortly before his suicide, he had penned a note in which he observed: "Texas is lost." Just days before his death, he dispatched a final missive to Austin. In it he lamented: "The affairs of Texas are understood only by you and me, and the two of us are the only ones who can regulate them; but there is no time." The general was right. He had been the only Mexican official who had truly understood conditions in that embattled province—and now he was gone.

With calm temporarily restored in Texas and General Antonio López de Santa Anna challenging Bustamante in the interior, Texians believed the time was ripe to advance their interest in a more diplomatic manner. In August 1832, the San Felipe de Austin *ayuntamiento* (town council) announced a convention. It called for delegates representing Texas settlements to assemble there on the first day of October. Stephen F. Austin believed the meeting premature but was unable to deter its proponents and finally decided to play a part. Fifty-eight delegates eventually assembled in Austin's namesake town. They represented every Anglo municipality, but the Tejano enclaves of San Antonio and Victoria declined the invitation. The caucus proved to be a predominantly Anglo affair, addressing predominantly Anglo concerns.

During the six days that the convention remained in session, the delegates discussed several items. The delegates elected Austin as president of the convention—somewhat ironic considering his opposition to it—and then got down to the business of drafting a petition. It requested that the government lift the prohibition on U.S. immigration, exempt Texas from custom duties until 1835, and—with the recent trouble in Anahuac fresh in mind—create a mechanism whereby citizens could dismiss corrupt customs officers. The request further entreated the government to separate Texas from Coahuila. This motion contained an explanation that Texas and Coahuila were radically different in their climate and economy. It further pointed out that Coahuila boasted nine times the population of Texas, and its citizens routinely outvoted Texians on matters they deemed essential. The Anglo representatives were adamant, however, that their request for an independent statehood was in no way a pretext for complete separation from Mexico itself.

Rafael Manchola, the *alcalde* of Goliad, arrived in San Felipe just as the convention was adjourning. He was the only Tejano delegate at the convention, and given his tardiness, his participation was negligible. Even so, Manchola offered to play a crucial role. He agreed to accompany Anglo American representatives when they presented the petition to government officials; the appearance of a convention controlled by recent immigrants worried Manchola, Austin, and several other delegates. They hoped Mexican administrators would be more likely to accept their plea if they knew at least one Tejano had participated in its preparation.

Tejanos had valid reasons for not wishing to involve themselves in these proceedings. The vast majority of the ruling elites opposed separation from Coahuila. Native Mexicans realized that the moment Texas achieved an independent legislature, they would live at the whim of Anglo colonists, who already greatly outnumbered them.

Ramón Músquiz, the political chief in Béxar, was a federalist and a champion of Anglo colonization, but he was also an official of the Mexican Republic and subject to its laws and procedures. Accordingly, he ruled the San Felipe gathering out of order. In Spanish and Mexican practice, all complaints commenced in the ayuntamientos, not in extemporized citizen assemblies.

Although such conventions might be commonplace in the United States, he chided, the Anglo settlers no longer lived there. Músquiz assured the Texians that their petition would only serve to anger and estrange officials in Saltillo and Mexico City and do more harm than good. As a practical matter, there would be no point in forwarding the proposal as long as Bustamante and the centralists remained in power in Mexico City. For all those reasons, he opted to exercise his authority as political chief and did not forward the proposal on. And with that, all the labor of the Convention of 1832 came to naught.

Many Texians were, of course, disappointed that their efforts at playing nicely with Mexican officials had achieved nothing. They believed that Músquiz was being overly formal and that Mexican procedures were needlessly ambiguous. Whaddya mean, the people can't call a convention whenever they want? What kind of government is that? Well, a *Mexican* government, as it turned out. Santa Anna finally ousted Bustamante in December 1832, but the convention had met the first week of October. Austin and Músquiz had been correct; the timing of the convention had been premature. Nevertheless, many Texians denounced the Mexican government and its agents as indifferent. Now, more strident voices prepared to make themselves heard.

The Convention of 1832: A Response to the Law of April 6, 1830

The Convention of 1832 was the first political assembly of Anglo American colonists living in Mexican Texas. Representatives from the various Texian townships wanted changes from the Mexican government, but at the same time, they wanted to express loyalty to their adopted country. On October 1, 1832, fifty-five delegates gathered at San Felipe de Austin to draft a petition requesting reforms in the way the Mexican government ruled Texas. They elected Stephen F. Austin to serve as the convention's president. The conference was almost entirely an Anglo American affair; no delegates from San Antonio de Béxar, Goliad, or Victoria—areas of *Tejano* settlement—participated.

The commissioners produced a petition that made several specific requests:

- That Mexican officials delay collection of customs duties until 1835.

- That Mexican officials grant Texas citizens the means by which they might remove crooked customs officers.

- That Mexican officials issue land titles in a more timely manner.

- That Mexican officials agree to sell public lands to raise funds for bilingual schools.

- That Mexican officials work harder to prevent new settlers from infringing on lands promised by treaty to Indian tribes.

- That Mexican officials repeal Article 11 of the Law of April 6, 1830. Delegates took pains to explain that the degree did nothing to halt the flow of dishonest squatters, but only barred law-abiding immigrants.

- That Mexican officials grant Texians permission to muster militia companies as protection against Indian raids.

- That Mexican officials make Texas an independent state, completely separate from Coahuila.

- Delegates understood that the request to separate Texas from Coahuila would be controversial. They highlighted the differences in economy and weather between Coahuila and Texas. The petition also noted that Texas's inadequate representation in the state legislature made it impossible to pass laws that met Texian requirements.

- Finally, Texian delegates swore that their request for independent statehood was not merely a ruse to achieve secession from Mexico.

continued

As the convention was about to adjourn, Goliad's *alcalde* Rafael Manchola, rode into San Felipe. He was the sole Tejano at the convention. Texian delegates correctly believed that their petition might meet with more favor if at least one Tejano name appeared on the document. Austin subsequently wrote, "we have just had a convention of all Texas, native Mexicans and foreign settlers—all united as one man." Such a statement was more than a little insincere. In truth, most Tejanos wanted nothing to do with the San Felipe meeting.

The work of the Convention of 1832 came to naught. Ramón Músquiz, the political chief in Béxar, ruled the convention out of order and the petition made it no further than his trash bin. Subsequently, the Béxar *ayuntamiento* composed a petition that echoed much of the wording of the Convention of 1832. Because this Tejano document followed legal form, Músquiz had no choice but to forward it to the Mexican Congress. Although Músquiz publicly supported the Tejano petition, he privately attached a note to the governor of Coahuila y Tejas questioning Texian motives and warning that the Convention of 1832 might be the first step along a path that led to open rebellion.

The results of the Convention of 1832—or, rather, the lack of them— disillusioned many Texian settlers who criticized the impenetrable nature of Mexican politics. They resolved that more forceful measures might be necessary.

The Rise of the War Party

The distinguished Victorian jurist, James Fitzjames Stephen observed: "The minority gives way not because it is convinced that it is wrong, but because it is convinced that it is a minority." The so-called "War Party" seemed to have been an exception to this rule. Its members were fully aware that their political rivals greatly outnumbered them, but they were entirely indifferent to it. Their numbers varied but never exceeded two dozen. And although they cut across the grain of public opinion, they never doubted the righteousness—and the eventual success—of their cause. War Party militants simply took it for granted that the majority would eventually catch up with *them*. They never called themselves by the name, War Party (at times, even "War Dogs"); both were epithets that their political rivals devised.

Here again, labels can be confusing. The War Party was never a real political establishment like the Democrats or Whigs. David B. Edward, a contemporary, called it the "war faction," but even that designation fails to fully explain its function. Truthfully, it was a radical association, a band of dissidents joined in a covert scheme to advance their private views. More often than not, they used intrigue to achieve their ends; few outside their circle were privy to their means.

But what were those ends? Their opposition to Stephen F. Austin's policy of patient accommodation defined the members of this group. In

Roads to Texas, 1824–1835

Map by Donald S. Frazier, Ph.D.

its stead, they called for—nay, *demanded*—an uncompromising posture in transactions with Saltillo and Mexico City. Because so many of them were speculators, they pushed for a more liberal land policy. All favored a disconnection from Coahuila. If Mexican officials refused to sanction the separation, the War Party would compel the break. The clique promoted cultural and political pluralism, a circumstance in which Texas would be a self-governing commonwealth. Indeed, nearly all Texians— even those of a more moderate stripe—believed that the Constitution of 1824 had pledged such an arrangement. What the War Party desired was loose affiliation with Mexico, but not adherence to its laws, traditions, and values. If citizens of, say, Jalisco wished to accept the injunctions of Mexico City, fine. But Texians would live as they pleased—as they and their forebears always had. As early as 1832, some of the more radical War Party firebrands were already plotting to seize Texas from Mexico and annex it to the United States.

The War Party may have never numbered more than twenty-four men, but they were twenty-four of the most persuasive, eloquent, and unwavering individuals in Texas. They were for the most part youthful, unmarried, fervently pro-slavery, and frequently ill mannered. A Texian of a more judicious temperament recorded his impression of the ring: "There has been—*now is*—and I fear will be, such men in Texas as are governed by very improper motives, and who have, by their headlong conduct, brought on serious consequences, besides prejudicing the minds of many a Mexican, which time and the best of conduct can hardly eradicate." No doubt his description was accurate, but it has always proven difficult for young men in a hurry to embrace restraint.

The partners in the War Party hailed from various backgrounds, but a disdain for the Mexican government and their patriotic zeal united them. The Wharton brothers, William H. and John A., were the heart of the fraternity, so much so, that many Texians called it the "Wharton faction." A native of Virginia, William moved to Texas in 1826; John joined him there later, arriving between 1829 and 1833. Unlike most of his War Party fellows, William was a married man—and he had married well. He won the hand of Sarah Ann Groce, the daughter of Jared Groce, who was the most prosperous planter in Texas and presented the happy couple with four leagues of land as a wedding present.

Among other prominent War Party participants was Branch T. Archer. Also a son of Virginia, Archer had killed his cousin in a pistol duel in 1828. Arriving in Texas in 1831, he lived in Brazoria, where he was instrumental in organizing a Masonic lodge.

At the age of fifteen, Georgian Robert McAlpin Williamson contracted tuberculous arthritis. The disease caused his right leg to permanently bend at a ninety-degree angle, but physicians fastened a wooden leg to his knee, allowing him to stomp about. Subsequently, he acquired the nickname "Three-Legged-Willie." He did not allow his disability to hinder him; at the tender age of nineteen, he passed the Georgia bar and practiced law for one year in his home state. In June 1827, Williamson arrived in San

Felipe de Austin. A talented journalist, he cofounded the newspaper *The Cotton Plant* in 1829. Shortly thereafter, he became the first prosecuting attorney for San Felipe. But printing ink was in his blood; next he edited the newspapers *The Texas Gazette* and *The Mexican Citizen.* His fiery editorials against the Mexican government earned him acclaim as the "Patrick Henry of Texas."

When he came to Texas in 1830, James Bowie was already famous (some said *notorious*) for his exploits; some of which involved his gargantuan knife. Bowie became a Mexican citizen and, like his friend William H. Wharton, married up. On April 25, 1831, the thirty-five-year-old Bowie wed the nineteen-year-old Maria Ursula de Veramendi, the daughter of the province's vice governor and head of one of the leading Béxar families. Bowie spoke fluent Spanish and seemed to admire the Tejano culture and people, but he could not abide the Mexican government. In 1832, he involved himself in the Battle of Nacogdoches and established himself as a leader in the War Party.

When he landed in Texas in May 1831, William Barret Travis listed his marital status as "single." The truth was, however, that he had fled Alabama just ahead of the debt collector. In the process, he abandoned his infant son and his wife who was pregnant with his daughter. He opened a law practice in Anahuac and helped organize a militia company to oppose centralist rule. In 1832, he became a central figure in the violent uprising in Anahuac. His actions earned him the ire of Texian moderates, and he later had to print a public apology for his involvement in the carnage. Yet, in his heart, he remained unrepentant. As he explained to a cohort: "We must wait patiently for the moving of the waters. . . . The course of events will inevitably tend to the right point, and the people will understand their rights, yea, and assert them too."

In fall 1832, the most famous member of the War Party had not yet arrived in Texas. Highly respected as a hero of the Creek War, Sam Houston won election as Tennessee's youngest executive in 1827. In 1829, following the disintegration of his first marriage, he resigned as governor and relocated to Arkansas Territory, where he became infamous among his Cherokee friends as "Big Drunk." In 1832, Houston, on a Washington D.C. boulevard, publicly whipped a U.S. congressman who had slandered him. A judge found Houston guilty of assault. If Houston had risen to great heights, he had fallen even further.

For many U.S. immigrants, Texas had been the "land of beginning again," and John A. Wharton supposed that Houston might be in need of such a haven. In June 1832, he wrote the discredited champion urging him to shift to the troubled province:

> I gave Dr Branch T. Archer of Virginia a letter of introduction to you; Dr Archer has been in Texas for upwards of twelve months, is intimately acquainted with matters and things there, and is in the confidence of all their leading men. He is of the opinion that there will be some fighting there next fall, and that a fine country will be gained without much bloodshed, he is very desirous that you should go there, and believes that you can be of more service than any other man. Texas does undoubtedly present a fine field for fame, enterprise, and usefulness, and whenever they are ready for action, I will be with them. . . . You can let Mr. Jackson and our friends (such as you wish) see this letter.

"Mr. Jackson" was, of course, U.S. President Andrew Jackson.

Seduced by the solicitation, Houston left for Texas in December 1832. He arrived as an agent provocateur and immediately threw in with the Wharton faction. And it would be as its delegate that he would represent Nacogdoches in the Convention of 1833.

The Convention of 1833

During Sam Houston's brawl with Congressman William Stanbery, the Ohio legislator drew a pistol, stuck the muzzle into Houston's ribs, and squeezed the trigger. The weapon misfired. Had Stanbery been more attentive to his flint, he might have greatly altered course of Texas—and U.S.—history. Judge William Cranch subsequently fined Houston five hundred dollars for walloping Stanbery with a walking stick. "Big Drunk" never paid the judgment. Instead, he turned his back on the fuss and intrigue of U.S. politics, spurred his horse toward the setting sun, and pitched into the fuss and intrigue of Mexican politics.

During his journey, Houston enjoyed the company of his friend Elias Rector. Just before Houston crossed the Red River, Rector offered his friend a token of his regard but was ashamed that he had nothing to give him but his old razor. Houston accepted the souvenir with good grace, replying: "Rector, I accept your fine gift, and mark my words, if I have luck this razor will someday shave the chin of a president of a republic." Houston had never set eyes on Texas, but already he nurtured dreams of becoming the head of a republic that existed only in his mind.

His timing was impeccable. The same month that Houston lit out for Texas—December 1832—Anastasio Bustamante tumbled from power in Mexico City. His influence had been dwindling and, not wishing to end up on the business end of a firing squad, he reached out to his federalist rival offering a truce. Antonio López de Santa Anna acquiesced. Late in December, Bustamante, Santa Anna, and Manuel Gómez Pedraza, signed the Agreements of Zavaleta. Although Gómez Pedraza was a centralist, Santa Anna insisted that he assume the presidency. He had, after all, won the election in 1828. Honoring his part of the deal, Bustamante went into a quiet exile. Mexicans once more lauded Santa Anna for his sense of fairness and lack of ambition. They may have forgotten that Gómez Pedraza's term expired the following April, and no matter who sat astride the presidential saddle, Santa Anna gripped the reins.

Back in Texas, December was also an eventful month. Right before Christmas, the central committee appointed during the October conclave called another convention to convene in San Felipe on April 1. With Bustamante removed, the committee was confident that Mexico City would be more amenable to what most delegates believed were perfectly sensible requests. Yet, many *Tejanos*, and even some temperate Texians, blasted the committee's defiance; one colonist denounced the caucus as the "Junta of San Felipe." Had they learned nothing from the refutation of the Convention of 1832? Texian delegates ignored the grumbling. Next time, they swore, no minor Mexican minion would thwart their endeavors.

Texas municipalities dispatched fifty-six delegates to the April convention, where they addressed the same concerns of the previous October. The two meetings would, however, differ greatly in their tone. This time, the president of the convention was not the accommodating Stephen F. Austin, but the provocative William H. Wharton. Unlike the previous conclave, San Antonio de Béxar also sent delegates, including James Bowie, one of the ringleaders of the Battle of Nacogdoches. Cheering on Wharton were other malcontents, including little brother John, New Jersey native and former filibuster David G. Burnet, and—representing Nacogdoches residents—the newly arrived Sam Houston. The citizens of that Redlands community thought themselves fortunate to have a former Tennessee governor attending their interests; the Wharton brothers also appreciated having such a resourceful accomplice.

Representatives at the 1833 Convention again insisted on the separation of Coahuila and Texas. Amazingly obliging, they went so far as to draft a constitution for the as yet unsanctioned state. None other than Houston chaired the committee to draft the new charter. In his letter of the previous June, the one summoning Houston to Texas, John A. Wharton had been remarkably prophetic. As far as the War Party was concerned, Houston truly did supply "more service than any other man."

Delegates again demanded that government officials rescind the injunction against U.S. immigration and revoke customs duties. They also entreated supplementary guards against Indian raids and further required that administrators install a more effectual method of mail delivery. Houston's committee carved into the state's constitution a pledge of free public education. Conventioneers also drew up a twenty-seven-article Bill of Rights. That document's language parroted the first eight amendments to the U.S. Constitution. In his characterization of the *norteamericanos*, Manuel de Mier y Terán had been spot on. Apparently, they really did "go about with their constitution in their pocket"—complete with the Bill of Rights.

Recollecting the outcome of the Convention of 1832, the Wharton faction called for the immediate and unilateral enactment of the propositions. Austin and the moderates (now branded the "Peace Party") voted down that proposal, and the majority decided to offer their new petition to the Mexican Congress for its consideration. Stung by their defeat on this issue, agents of the War Party forced a pledge that, if the Mexican Congress refused their demands, the body would take autonomous action. Finally, delegates elected Austin, Erasmo Seguín, and Dr. James Miller to convey their appeals to Mexico City. Although the influential Seguín had not been present at the conference, delegates trusted that Austin could prevail upon Seguín to join him on the long and difficult journey. The involvement of a token Tejano might help convince Congress that native-born Mexicans also supported the recommendations of the 1833 Convention, which most did not.

As it happened, Seguín wanted no part of the proceedings, and Dr. Miller begged off to contend with a cholera epidemic, leaving Austin to make the journey alone. Although the petition's confrontational tenor horrified the *empresario*, he believed he had no alternative but to represent the will of his constituents. Austin understood he was under the microscope. One of the established Anglo colonists neatly summed up Austin's predicament: "He is closely watched, and his future prospects depend greatly upon his Conduct in this matter. If he succeeds, he will do well for himself, and, if for the want of proper Exertion on his part, the application should fail, Col. Austin will be a Ruined man in Texas."

As Austin spurred his mule toward Mexico City, the eyes of Texas were upon him.

The Convention of 1833:
Texian Demands

The differences between the Convention of 1832 and the Convention of 1833 were those of personnel and tone. Angered by Ramón Músquiz's fussiness, 1833 delegates assumed a more strident attitude and more associated with the so-called "War Party." In 1832, Texian settlers made request; in 1833, they made demands.

Among these were:

- Complete political separation from Coahuila,
- Repeal of the anti-immigration clause of the Law of April 6, 1830.
- Lifting of customs duties.
- A more effective mail delivery system.
- Increased government defense against raiding Indians.
- Prohibition of the African slave traffic into Texas.
- Judicial reform.
- Trial by jury.
- Habeas corpus.
- Freedom of the press.
- Universal male suffrage (excluding, of course, males who happened to be Indians or African American).

Although the Mexican Congress had not yet agreed to separate Tejas from Coahuila, a committee headed by Sam Houston prepared a constitution—complete with a Bill of Rights—for the detached state just in case it did. Such actions were premature, insolent, and ill-advised. Notwithstanding his reservations concerning the brazen document that the delegates drafted, Stephen F. Austin agreed to present it to authorities in Mexico City.

Austin Goes to Mexico City

O n March 1, 1833, Antonio López de Santa Anna became president of Mexico. Texians received the news with considerable enthusiasm. A federalist, a liberal, and a champion of the Constitution of 1824, he represented their idea of everything a Mexican official should be. Texians anticipated that the "Savior of Mexico" would receive their petition favorably—especially when such a distinguished delegate presented it.

At first, Stephen F. Austin seemed an odd choice. Why did the Wharton faction, so opposed to his patient accommodation, entrust him with such a vital assignment? In the first place, they well knew their own reputation among Mexican politicians. They were more likely to accommodate a man noted for his moderation than anyone tainted by militant associations. Furthermore, Austin spoke Spanish fluently and could articulate the Texian position better than any other man. The final reason may have been more Machiavellian in its motives. With the leader of the Peace Party removed from Texas for months, War Party agents might take advantage of his absence to agitate, propagandize, and (they hoped) swing public opinion.

In an effort to gain at least some *Tejano* support for the petition, on April 22, 1833, Austin departed San Felipe and booted his trusty mule toward San Antonio de Béxar. Once there, only Erasmo Seguín would endorse the document but stated that personal concerns prevented him

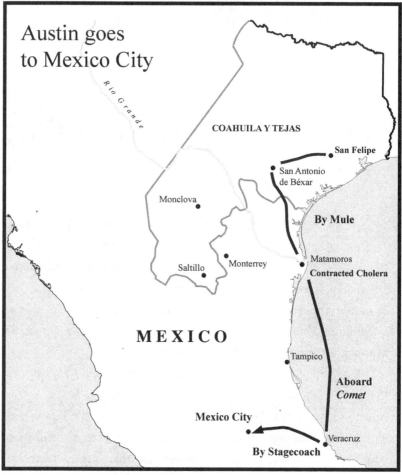

Austin goes
to Mexico City

Rio Grande

COAHUILA Y TEJAS

San Felipe

San Antonio
de Béxar

Monclova

By Mule

Saltillo   Monterrey   Matamoros
Contracted Cholera

M E X I C O

Tampico

Aboard
Comet

Mexico City

Veracruz

By Stagecoach

Map by Donald S. Frazier, Ph.D.

from traveling with Austin to Mexico City. Riding to Goliad, Austin
could muster even less support from Tejanos there. The *empresario* dreaded
the long and lonely journey. As he explained to his cousin, Mary Austin
Holley: "I am on the *wing* for twelve hundred miles, on a mule's back (not
a pegasus) over plains and mountains, to the City of Montezuma, farther
from farm and home than I ever was."

His apprehension was justified. From Goliad, Austin rode south
to Matamoros. Once there, he came down with cholera. Although he

recovered, Austin was too weak to continue overland. He detested sea travel, but nonetheless, booked passage aboard a schooner bound for Veracruz. The winds did not favor the good ship *Comet*. Belying the ship's name, its voyage (scheduled for a week) instead required a full month; Austin was seasick the entire time. Once again on dry land at Veracruz, he faced additional obstacles. Centralists had launched a coup against Santa Anna's liberal regime. Consequently, Austin found a war zone between Veracruz and the capital. On July 18, following thirteen days of difficult, sometimes dangerous, travel by stagecoach, Austin finally arrived in the capital city.

Austin discovered that President Santa Anna had abandoned the capital to suppress the rebellion, leaving in his stead Vice President Valentín Gómez Farías. If Santa Anna was a liberal, his vice president was a radical. He led the faction of extremist federalists called the *puros*, who were in the tradition of Vicente Guerrero. Gómez Farías employed his temporary authority to push liberal reforms through Congress. He seemed to go out of his way to alienate members of the army and the Roman Catholic Church. He did away with the *fueros* of the church and army, which had permitted them to stand trial in their own courts. He secularized education, heretofore the exclusive province of the clergy. If that were not enough, he also attempted to challenge the church economic domination. The acting president's extremism outraged many segments of Mexican society, but it suited Austin's purposes. He reported that Gómez Farías had given him a "kind and friendly" reception.

Yet, in Austin's dealings with Mexican officials, it was always one step forward and two steps back. Initially, he made considerable headway, but then his applications encountered resistance in the Mexican Congress. Worse still, a cholera epidemic in the city brought all business to a standstill. The infection that had stricken him in Matamoros now returned with a vengeance. This time, Austin almost died. He learned that the disease had also ravaged Texas, taking several of his dearest friends and family. Feeling abandoned and alone, Austin succumbed to a bout of depression. His near-death experience weakened him in both body and spirit.

Normally, Austin was the most prudent of men, but on October 2 he behaved in a most irresponsible manner. Writing to the Béxar *ayuntamiento*, he gave his frustrations full vent:

> The happening of the civil war have frustrated all the public business, so that until now nothing has been done, and, in my opinion, nothing will be done. Therefore I hope that you will not lose one moment in sending a communication to all the Ayuntamientos of Texas, urging them unite in a measure to organize a local government independent of Coahuila, even though the general government withholds its consent.

In his distressed state of mind, Austin may not have realized the implications of his letter. By pressing the Tejanos and Texians to act in defiance of the central government, he had committed sedition.

Soon after Austin fired off that incendiary missive, his fortunes took a positive turn. President Santa Anna returned to Mexico City, resumed his duties, and took two meetings with the empresario. Those meetings went extremely well. The Mexican Congress had voted to repeal Article 11 of the Law of April 6, 1830, the clause that prohibited further immigration into Texas from the United States. Santa Anna approved the retraction but stipulated that its implementation would occur in six months. Austin found the president obliging. Writing to his brother-in-law, he gushed: "He speaks very friendly about Texas. I am of the opinion that if you all keep quiet and obey the state laws that the *substance* of all Texas wants will be granted. The appearance of things is much better than it was a month or even two weeks ago."

By the end of November, Austin had spent four months in the capital. During that time he had achieved much. Mexican officials had reestablished the empresario system. They also seemed amenable to judicial reform and tariff relief. Although Santa Anna and Gómez Farías had given Austin a respectful hearing, they and the Mexican Congress still seemed unwilling to separate Texas from Coahuila. Austin understood, however, that it had always been unlikely—at least in the short term. He had accomplished all that he could in Mexico City. On November 26, he wrote his friend and business partner Samuel May Williams: "Texas matters are all right. Nothing is wanted but *quiet.* It is now very important to harmonise with Bexar. Keep this in view. I shall be home soon."

Such predictions were to prove unduly optimistic.

Austin Goes to Jail

It had almost killed him, but Stephen F. Austin felt good about his mission to Mexico City. Although he had been unable to separate Texas from Coahuila, he did strike off other items on his checklist. Mexican authorities revoked the anti-immigration clause of the Law of April 6, endorsed the *empresario* system, and even promised judicial reform and tariff relief. More importantly, he had met President Antonio López de Santa Anna and forged a personal association. Austin believed that the president was *simpatico* with his goals for Texas and that many additional reforms would spring from his office. He also thought that the journey's successes validated his methods. Mexicans were, as he had always said, reasonable people and one could reason with them; a person really could catch more flies with sugar than vinegar. He had saved face with and, satisfied his obligation to, his colonists.

On December 10, 1833, Austin departed the capital and began his return trip to Texas. Not wishing to subject himself again to the rigors of a sea voyage, he shared a carriage with Congressman Luis de la Rosa and two other traveling companions. Ten years previously he had traveled the same road. During that time, conditions in his colonies had greatly improved. Yet, here in the Mexican interior, circumstances remained the same or had even grown worse. Representative government had not produced the advantages that he expected it would a decade before. The Constitution of 1824 had been in place for nine years, but many

75

Mexico City's central plaza as it would have looked during Austin's imprisonment. *Author's collection.*

Mexicans still opposed its basic tenets. Austin concluded that the policies and practices of the Roman Catholic Church retarded Mexico's political, economic, legal, and intellectual development. He recorded these views in his travel diary:

> What a pity that Rome did not set down as a dogma, that the man who should leave his property to open roads, canals, to establish schools, foment agriculture & the arts, should go straight to heaven as soon as dead. Rome! Rome! Until the Mexican people shake off thy superstitions & wicked sects, they can neither be a republican, nor a moral people.

Austin may have spoken Spanish like a native; he may have wished the best for the Mexican government; and he may have even urged his colonists to obey Mexican laws, but his worldview remained American, Protestant, and frankly, somewhat priggish.

At Lagos de Moreno, Austin bid his friends goodbye, abandoned the carriage, hired a servant, and mounted a horse to continue his journey north. Riding hard, he arrived in San Luis Potosí on December 24, celebrating Christmas Day there. On January 2, 1834, he arrived in Saltillo. The following day, Austin entered the office of Pedro Lemus, who had recently won appointment to General Manuel de Mier y Terán's old position as Commandant General of the Eastern Interior Provinces. Austin had met Lemus in Mexico City and considered him a friend. The empresario was, therefore, completely surprised when Lemus informed him that he was under arrest.

Austin's indignant letter of October 2—or, rather the sentiments expressed in it—had returned to haunt him. His "exceedingly rash" suggestion that the Béxar *ayuntamiento* should form an independent state government without federal sanction shocked members of that council. Not wishing to appear complicit, they forwarded the missive to the state capital, which had only recently been transferred to Monclova. Once there, it became a ticking time bomb. The acting governor, Francisco Vidaurri y Villaseñor read the letter and issued an arrest warrant for Austin. The governor then informed the federal authorities of Austin's transgression. Predictably, the letter infuriated Valentín Gómez Farías, who also ordered Austin's arrest and his return to Mexico City. An armed guard ushered him back to the capital where, in February 1834, they delivered him to cell fifteen in Inquisition Prison.

Austin now began the worst period of his life. For three months, Austin occupied a 16- by 13-foot cell. Its tiny skylight admitted reading light only from 10 AM to 3 PM. Initially his only visitors were his lawyer and Father Michael Muldoon, a priest who had served in Texas before. Boredom was Austin's greatest enemy. He shared crumbs with a prison mouse, which eventually became so tame he could pet it. His rodent companion supplied a welcomed diversion because his jailers denied him books. The circumstances of his confinement improved slightly when Austin "loaned" thirty pesos to the prison's commandant and ten more to a guard. If they ever repaid the advance, Austin never mentioned it. The empresario assumed that War Party machinations were behind his arrest and castigated its members as "inflammatory men, political fanatics, political adventurers, would-be-great-men, vain talkers, and visionary fools."

In April 1834, Santa Anna took control of the executive office and released Austin from solitary confinement. In June, probably on Santa Anna's instructions, officials transferred Austin to Acordada Prison, a vast improvement over the Inquisition's dank cell. In his new digs, Austin now enjoyed a larger, brighter room that sported a small balcony overlooking a busy street. Later, authorities transferred him again, this time to the Prison of Deputation on the city's main plaza. Its accommodations were no better than those in Acordada Prison, but its centralized location enabled more visitors and easier access to news.

Austin's case flummoxed the Mexican legal system. For months his hearings bounded from one court to another. Each time, the judge ruled the case outside his jurisdiction. Eight months following his arrest, it seemed clear that Austin had violated *some* law, but Mexican judges could not agree on exactly which law he had broken. In the end, it seemed easier to decide not to decide. Meanwhile, while the authorities dithered, Austin remained caged.

On October 15, Texas lawyers Spencer H. Jack and Peter W. Grayson, arrived in the capital to provide council and assistance. Realizing that the case might take months, even years, to play out in the courts, Jack and Grayson devoted their labors to securing bail for their client. Grayson used obscure language to describe the process: "This could only be effected by the exertion of personal influence with the Judge. It is needless to detail here, the various efforts that were made to influence the Judge to grant bail to the prisoner." Or, to state it more directly, the legal team employed the one procedure that always seemed to work with Mexican officials: they bribed the judge. On December 25, 1834, Austin posted bond and walked out of the Prison of Deputation. It was the best Christmas present he could possibly receive.

Austin was out of prison but was not a free man. The bail terms demanded that he remain in the city until the courts determined what to do with him. Still, Austin did not suffer excessively. He celebrated the New Year in high style. He lodged in a lavish hotel; he attended operas, masquerades, and even a ball hosted by the British minister. Austin also spent time with a "very sprightly young lady," with whom, he admitted, he was "particularly pleased." In July 1835, a Mexican court brought both his tribulations and amusements to a close. It ruled that Austin fell under the terms of a general amnesty law for political prisoners. After eighteen month's detention, the empresario was truly free. His first instinct was to return to Texas.

Yet, he returned a radically different man than the one who left San Felipe in 1833. Given all that he had endured, how could he have been otherwise?

Trouble in Anahuac–
Again!

While Stephen F. Austin sat in prison, events continued to unfold; surprisingly, many of them were positive. The incarceration of their chief *empresario*, naturally dismayed Anglo American colonists. Nevertheless, they applauded the liberal legislation emanating from the state and national capitals. The federalist government in Monclova, for example, instituted measures that divided Texas into three departments and, as requested by the Convention of 1833, reshaped judicial procedures. Moreover, the legislature raised the Texas representation in the state congress. In May 1834, the repeal of the anti-immigration clause of the Law of April 6 became effective. A torrent of settlers poured across the Red and Sabine rivers. Although accurate records did not survive, anecdotal evidence suggested that hundreds of settlers swept in during the following year. Few, if any, of these newcomers had any connections with, or regard for, the Mexican government. Their only interest lay in Mexican land.

As pleased as they were with the federalists reforms, Texians voiced concern over rumblings from Mexico City. Mexican politics could twirl on a dime, and in January 1835, they took a sharp U-turn. The new Congress assembled, but on this occasion the majority consisted of centralists. Antonio López de Santa Anna had quietly packed that body with his proxies representing the clergy and military. The reforms Valentín Gómez Farías enacted had insulted and incensed both of those communities and, now back in power, they brought out their knives. They immediately set about nullifying the acting president's liberal amendments. They organized a standing national army to replace state militias. With this maneuver, Santa Anna transferred the loyalty of most professional soldiers from their state capitals to Mexico City—or rather, to him. At the same time, congressmen drastically scaled back the size and scope of state militias, proclaiming them superfluous and a potential threat to authority: centralist authority.

Many federalists resisted this blatant power grab. Citizens of Oaxaca, Zacatecas, and other states swore to fight for their rights guaranteed under the Constitution of 1824. Resistance proved futile. Santa Anna personally led the National Army into Zacatecas. Demonstrating his characteristic ruthlessness and efficiency, he crushed Zactecan militia in a two-hour battle on May 11, 1835. Then the real horror began. To reward his solders, their general allowed them to pillage Zacatecas for forty-eight hours. Throughout Mexico, citizens observed the "Sack of Zacatecas" with terror and trepidation—exactly as Santa Anna had intended.

Once its champion, Santa Anna now discarded federalism. He, and most other prominent Mexicans, resolved that only a formidable central government could exercise hegemony and thwart the regional recalcitrance that stymied national progress and stability. Traditional Texas historians paint Santa Anna as the villain of their narratives, and to be sure, his methods were reprehensible. Yet, he was not entirely wrong. Thomas Jefferson himself had reflected, "If a nation expects to be ignorant and free in a state of civilization, it expects what never was and never will be." Truthfully, the illiterate majority was not ready for representative government, and the nation could never function as a loose amalgamation of semi-autonomous states. Mexican federalism suffered all the inadequacies of the Articles of Confederation with none of the correctives of the Constitution of 1787. After taking care of business in Zacatecas, Santa Anna returned to Mexico City, disavowed the Farías reforms and flung his former associate into exile. Poor Farías,

Santa Anna had played him like a two-peso fiddle. Once again, the general assumed the mantle of national "savior," upholding religion and traditional values.

The centralist Congress again dispatched tax collectors to Texas. Many U.S. settlers had recently immigrated into the area around Anahuac and resented the presence of the newly established military garrison. In a replay of 1832, a radical group—the so-called "Citizens of Texas"—protested what they considered discriminatory taxation. Mississippi native Andrew Briscoe, a local merchant and ship's captain, complained that Mexican officials had levied taxes mercurially from port to port. In other words, corrupt officials were taking their cut. Briscoe intentionally taunted the new commander, Captain Antonio Tenorio, by loading his ship with nothing but ballast. An indignant Tenorio placed Briscoe and his business partner DeWitt Clinton Harris under arrest for their insolence. Just as prisoners William Barret Travis and Patrick Jack had been the catalyst for the violence in 1832, the detention of Briscoe and Harris would spur hostility in 1835.

When news of the Anahuac turbulence reached San Felipe in June 1835, it enraged Texian citizens, especially the War Party activists. Political chief Peter Miller authorized Travis—the same man who had been at the center of the Anahuac uprising in 1832—to call out the local militia company. This twenty-five-man unit, hauling a cannon, arrived in Anahuac and demanded the surrender of the centralist garrison, which then numbered more than forty soldiers. Tenorio meekly agreed to terms, ordered his men to hand over their weapons, and pledged to take his men out of Texas.

Unlike the Anahuac Disturbances of 1832, the Anahuac Disturbances of 1835 spilled little blood. It did, however, highlight an increasing polarization of the Texian population. The majority still clung to Austin's policy of peaceful adjustment. Even so, more and more Texians were quickly losing patience with capricious Mexico City politics. Shortly before he marched on Anahuac, Travis had grumbled:

I have as much to lose by a revolution as most men in the country. Yet, I wish to know, for whom do I labor—whether for myself or a plundering, robbing, autocratical, jumbled up government, which is in fact no government at all—one day a republic—one day a fanatical heptarchy, the next a military despotism—then a mixture of evil qualities of all.

Witnessing the actions of Santa Anna's regime, most Texians shared Travis's exasperation, including Austin.

Austin Comes Home

On July 11, 1835, Stephen F. Austin received his passport, boarded a stagecoach, and left Mexico City bound for Veracruz. Although he still detested sea travel, it was the quickest way to place distance between himself and all the misery and frustration of the past year. On July 23, he boarded the brig *Wanderer* and sat sail from the port of Veracruz; Austin surely noted the aptness of the ship's name. *Wanderer*'s destination was not a Texas port, but rather a city on which Texians depended more than any other: New Orleans.

Austin was grateful that the voyage did not repeat his 1833 ordeal while aboard *Comet*; the calm passage allowed him to process all that had happened to him. He might have expected the centralists to arrest him, but not the federalists—they were supposed to be his friends. Yet, bitter experience had taught him that federalists could be as distrustful, vindictive, and incompetent as the centralists were. He had criticized the doctrines of the Roman Catholic Church, but one of the few people to visit him in prison was Father Muldoon, a priest. He had lashed out at members of the War Party, but Spencer H. Jack—a vehement War Dog, and many claimed, the first Texian colonist to actually spill centralist blood in 1832—had traveled all the way to Mexico City to secure Austin's freedom. He learned that petty prejudices and sweeping generalities did not survive contact with everyday experiences. Henceforth, Austin would be less rigid in his pronouncements and his thinking. It was a testament to his character and resilience that he left prison a wiser and better man.

Austin enjoyed his layover in New Orleans. During his time there, he took advantage of the Crescent City's hotels, restaurants, theaters, and bookstores—especially the bookstores. Always a bibliophile, Austin avowed that the cruelest part of his incarceration had been the lack of books. He possessed many fond memories of the place where he had studied law as a young man. At forty-one years of age, however, Austin hardly recognized the eager student he had been. His experiences had altered him. He had always preached loyalty to Mexico, but now in his letters to his cousin Mary Austin Holley, he almost sounded like a War Dog:

> A large immigration will prepare us, give us strength, resources, everything. A great immigration from Kentucky, Tennessee etc., each man with his rifle or musket, would be of great use to us—very great indeed. For fourteen years I have had a hard time of it, but nothing shall daunt my courage or abate my exertions to complete the main object of my labors—to Americanize Texas. This fall, and winter, will fix our fate—a great immigration will settle the question.

On August 25, Austin took passage aboard the schooner *San Felipe*; its destination was Brazoria. On September 1, *San Felipe* and the river steamer *Laura* encountered the Mexican revenue cutter *Correo de México* and captured the vessel following an exchange of cannon fire. During the fighting, the Texian crews deposited Austin and their cargo of munitions ashore because they considered both too valuable to risk. Austin predicted that this episode, along with June's Anahuac embarrassment, would incite Antonio López de Santa Anna into some kind of punitive action. His prediction was correct.

Actually, the centralists were already ahead of him. On August 1, General Martín Perfecto de Cos, recently appointed as Commandant General of the Eastern Interior Provinces and headquartered in

Map by Donald S. Frazier, Ph.D.

Matamoros, issued arrest warrants for "the ungrateful and bad citizen W. B. Travis," R. M. "Three-Legged Willie" Williamson, and several other known rabble-rousers. William Barret Travis took the threat seriously and immediately went into hiding. Texians affiliated with the Peace Party may have thought the War Dogs reckless blockheads, but they detested military despotism even more. They swore they would never surrender fellow Texians to Cos or any other centralist toady.

Responding to these new threats, Texians organized committees of safety and correspondence. On August 15, the Columbia committee issued a general call for the Anglo municipalities to elect delegates for a General Consultation at the Town of Washington (present-day Washington-on-

87

the-Brazos) in October. Such a conclave appeared a precursor for out-and-out rebellion. Many yearned for Austin's experience and wise council.

They soon got their wish. Austin landed in Texas during the first week of September and word spread through the colonies like wildfire. On September 8, the citizens of Brazoria hosted a lavish reception to celebrate the return of their prodigal son. Moses Austin Bryan, Austin's nephew, described the emotions of the proceedings: "No man ever received a warmer greeting and no one ever appreciated such greeting more."

Rumors arrived that General Cos was heading toward Texas at the head of a centralist army. On September 19, Austin declared that Cos intended to "destroy and break up foreign settlements in Texas." Then, throwing aside all restraint, he proclaimed: "Conciliatory measures with General Cos and the military at Bexar are hopeless. WAR is our only resource." And this from the head of the Peace Party? Truthfully, by then, what remained of the Peace Party had faded off the scene. Travis was almost beside himself with joy: "Huzza for Liberty, and the rights of man! Texas is herself again. The Tories are dying a violent death. I feel the triumph we have gained, and I glory in it." It was as the Wharton brothers, Houston, Travis, and the rest had always predicted. Their time had arrived. At last, the majority had caught up with *them*.

And not a moment too soon. On September 20, General Cos landed at Copano Bay with five hundred centralist *soldados*. He intended to disarm the Texian militia companies and take leading militants into custody before they could provoke a rebellion. Yet, his presence on Texas soil had already done that. Anglo colonists now united against Santa Anna and his centralist minions. Just weeks before, Travis had crowed: "We shall give them hell if they come here." And now, Texians of every stripe were preparing to do just that.

By the end of September, Texas was a powder keg. A single cinder could ignite the whole. As it happened, the explosion erupted from the most unlikely of places.

REVOLUTION
October 1835–April 1836

COME AND TAKE IT!

In August 1825, *Empresario* Green DeWitt established the capital of his colony on Kerr Creek. In a show of friendship and gratitude, DeWitt named the fledgling community after Rafael Gonzáles, acting governor of Coahuila y Tejas. Two separate Indian raids devastated the settlement and forced DeWitt to question the wisdom of such a vulnerable location. In 1826, settlers abandoned the original site. The following year, they rebuilt the town near the junction of the Guadalupe and San Marcos rivers. With the raiding Indians still a threat, DeWitt wrote Political Chief Ramón Músquiz in San Antonio de Béxar on January 1, 1831, requesting a cannon for the town's defense. DeWitt stipulated in his initial letter that the cannon was on loan and that he would return the piece if the authorities ever needed it. On March 10, 1831, James Tumlinson, Jr., a DeWitt colonist and teamster, traveled to Béxar to pick up the barrel, which period documents identified as a bronze six-pounder—that is to say, a cannon firing a six-pound ball. Tumlinson delivered the ordnance to DeWitt, who signed a receipt for it.

This transaction was typical because DeWitt's colonists enjoyed a warm and loyal affiliation with Mexican officials. Far removed from San Felipe and Anahuac, they had nothing to do with the militant activity that had roiled those settlements. Nor did they have any sympathy for the War Party, for which they expressed utter contempt. As late as July 7, 1835, Commissioner Edward Critten wrote Colonel Domingo de Ugartechea,

Texian rebels shout defiance at Lieutenant Francisco de Castañeda and his centralist troopers. Gonzales citizens were indisposed to surrender their cannon but were more than willing to share its contents. *Charles Shaw, illustrator. Courtesy of the San Jacinto Museum of History.*

military commandant of the forces at Presidio San Antonio de Béxar, reporting that the Texian colonists earnestly desired peace. Nonetheless, he counseled that centralist officers not dispatch soldiers to Texas. That same day, Gonzales settlers approved a resolution pledging their continued loyalty to the Mexican government. Indeed, relations were so good that on August 29, Ugartechea requested that Gonzales citizens assist his soldiers in pursuing Indians who had raided the region.

An unpleasant incident soured relations. On September 9, a company of centralist soldiers entered Gonzales and occupied local merchant Adam Zumwalt's general store. Unaware of their presence, Gonzales citizen Jesse McCoy attempted to enter the establishment. Without warning, a centralist sentry pushed McCoy back, then butt-stroked him with the heavy wooden stock of his Brown Bess musket. McCoy collapsed nursing a painful head wound. The *Acalde* Andrew Ponton wrote Ugartechea to protest the unprovoked assault, but even then, his language was deferential: "This representation is not made to your Excellency for the purpose of obtaining satisfaction or revenge for the outrage and insult offered to one of our citizens but to prevent misrepresentation and consequently misunderstanding which might arise between the authorities and the people of this Municipality." How did Ugartechea reply? He dispatched soldiers to retrieve the borrowed cannon. Given all that had transpired over the summer, he now believed U.S. settlers—even those in Gonzales—to be more of a threat than Indians. By the time the soldiers arrived, the DeWitt settlers, once so loyal, had undergone a complete transformation. They resolved that the War Party fanatics were, perhaps, not so fanatical after all.

The previous May, DeWitt had died, so Gonzales citizens were probably unaware of his pledge to return the cannon whenever requested. Thus, they swore to keep it. Not because the gun was so vital to their defense; they never appeared to have fired it in anger or, for that matter, even bothered to mount the tube on a carriage. They decided to preserve it on principle. The object became symbolic. The soldiers had entered their town uninvited, violated their hospitality, and behaved discourteously. They were, therefore, simply undeserving of the consideration normally accorded to gentlemen.

Consequently, when Lieutenant Francisco de Castañeda and a one-hundred-man squadron of presidial dragoons arrived on September 29, they discovered that Gonzales citizens had burned the welcome mat. Settlers had removed all boats and the ferry from the Guadalupe River. On the Gonzales side of the flooded river stood eighteen armed Texians—later famed as the "Old Eighteen." Albert Martin, captain of the Gonzales militia, apprised Castañeda that Ponton was away, and until his return, the centralists must remain on the river's west bank. Because Castañeda could not ford the river, he had no choice but to acquiesce.

Castañeda pitched camp atop DeWitt's Mound, a slight hill some three hundred yards from the river. To be prudent, Gonzales townsmen buried their cannon in George W. Davis's peach orchard. Then, they dispatched couriers to surrounding settlements requesting reinforcements. More than eighty neighbors responded to the call, which created an organizational dilemma. Independent Texians insisted on electing their leaders and the newcomers appeared unwilling to serve under Martin, a man they did not know. They chose instead John Henry Moore of Fayette to lead the combined unit, with Joseph Washington Elliot Wallace and Edward Burleson, both of Columbus, second and third in command.

On the afternoon of September 30, a Coushatta Indian informed Castañeda that the Texian force had swelled to 140 men and 300 more were reportedly on the march to join them. Disliking those odds, he ordered a withdrawal toward Béxar. In Gonzales, the assembled militia companies held a council of war. The volunteers decided that if the centralists refused to cross the river and attack them, they would cross the river and attack the centralists. It was time to dig up the cannon.

Texians spent the evening of October 1 crossing the river and marched through the night in pursuit of the centralists. Around 3 AM on October 2, Moore's command stumbled into Castaneda's camp, which lay about seven miles from the river crossing. Because it was too dark to fight, both sides fell back to await the dawn.

The rising sun revealed that the centralists had taken position on a slight rise some three hundred yards from the rebel position. The Texians had fashioned a white banner with an image of the cannon painted in black, which they now hoisted above the six-pounder—also emblazoned on the banner was a challenge to the centralists to: "COME AND TAKE IT." The Texians actually boasted two artillery pieces that day: the six-pound "Come-and-Take-It" cannon and another that Castaneda described as an "*esmeril*"—a diminutive gun firing a ball that weighed about one-fourth of a pound.

Veteran artilleryman James Clinton Neill touched off the six-pounder. The riflemen fired a volley and swept up the slope in a headlong, screaming charge. Someone (no one bothered to record his name) even popped off the esmeril. The two sides never closed. Seeing that he was outnumbered and outgunned, Castañeda ordered a hasty retreat toward Béxar. The centralists lost two men and several horses killed.

The skirmish had resembled a schoolyard shoving match more than a battle, yet its political significance was immeasurable. The long-anticipated rebellion had begun. Centralist soldiers had *come* to Gonzales, but all they had *taken* was a beating.

"On to Béxar!"

As word of the "Come-and-Take-It" fight spread across Texas, other volunteers entered the fray. George M. Collinsworth, the commander of the Matagorda militia, received reports that General Martín Perfect de Cos was planning to pass through Goliad and prepared to confront him there. Yet, the centralist commander marched quickly, passing through the town ahead of Collinsworth and leaving behind a skeleton force located inside the Presidio La Bahía. In Victoria, Collinsworth learned that his prize had eluded him, but his men nonetheless voted to attack the outpost. On October 9, they marched all day and most of the night, reaching the fort an hour before midnight. With axes provided by local *Tejanos*, they cut through the gate, overwhelmed the seventeen-man garrison, and accepted its surrender. During the firefight, three centralist soldiers suffered wounds and one lost his life. The Texians had one man wounded: Samuel McCullough, a free man of color.

The capture of Goliad proved a strategic coup. Not only did the Texians gain a large cache of much-needed military supplies, but they also denied the centralists access to gulf ports.

Cos arrived in Béxar with about 400 men. Other centralist units arrived from Coahuila, boosting his command to some 1200 effectives. Still, cut off from the coast, he knew that additional reinforcements must take the long and torturous overland route from the Mexican interior. Finally, he decided to fortify the town and stand on the defensive.

Mississippi Volunteer. Recruits like this fellow proved terrors to the local civilians as well as their officers. Headstrong, independent, and proud, they made fine fighters but poor soldiers. *Gary Zaboly, illustrator, from* Texian Iliad: A Military History of the Texas Revolution. *Author's collection.*

As Collinsworth moved against Goliad, hundreds of Texian volunteers flocked to Gonzales. Once there, however, the various militia captains began to jostle for overall command. Because each company championed its own captain, none could win a majority. Fortunately for the Texian cause, Stephen F. Austin, the one man who possessed absolute moral authority, arrived in camp. John A Warton, leader of the War Party and Austin's former nemesis, placed the *empresario's* name into nomination. Moses Austin Bryan recalled that his uncle was a reluctant leader, who accepted the proposal only following "earnest entreaty." The assembled throng elected Austin as commander in chief—unanimously. He had always had a delicate constitution, and his time in prison had wrecked his health. Even so, he understood that no other man could provide a sense of unity at this critical time. Like George Washington before him, Austin became the "indispensable man." He made no effort to hide his shaky health. He even referenced it in a speech to the men: "I will wear myself out by inches rather than submit to Santa Anna's arbitrary rule." This, of course, made his soldiers respect him that much more. Demonstrating his characteristic flair for order, he organized the men into companies and selected a general staff. Soon he could hear the men shouting, "On to Béxar!"

Taking the offensive against Cos made strategic sense. Time was on his side. The longer the Texians dawdled the more likely it became that the centralist commander would receive reinforcements from the Mexican interior. Once he had sufficient forces, he would undoubtedly launch an offensive against the Texian settlements. The best way to prevent that nightmare scenario was to attack—and defeat—him first. On October 12, "The Volunteer Army of the People of Texas" departed Gonzales and began their march toward enemy-held Béxar.

What the volunteers lacked in marshal splendor they supplied in gusto. Volunteer Noah Smithwick, described the appearance of the rebel legion on the march:

> It certainly bore little resemblance to the army of my childhood dreams. Buckskin breeches were the nearest approach to uniform, and there was wide diversity even there. Boots being an unknown quantity; some wore shoes and some moccasins. Here a broad-brimmed sombrero overshadowed the military cap at its side; there a tall "beegum" rode familiarly beside a coonskin cap, with the tail hanging down behind, as all well-regulated tails should do. A fantastic military array to a casual observer, but the one great purpose animating every heart clothed us in a uniform more perfect in our eyes than was ever donned by regulars on dress parade.

When Austin's army reached the outskirts of Béxar, the full extent of his tactical challenge came into sharper focus. From Camp Salado, five miles east of San Antonio, Austin could make out the Mexican fortifications. To assault enemy breastworks with his inferior numbers would be foolish; to do so without artillery would be suicidal.

But hopeful signs also appeared. On October 15, Victoria *Alcalde* Plácido Benavides joined the federalist cause with about thirty mounted *rancheros*. On October 22, Tejano Juan Seguín rode into camp with intelligence that many Mexican citizens of Béxar—*Bexareños*—supported the revolt, and some were even eager to join Texian ranks. Austin appointed Seguín a captain and authorized him to raise a company of *vaqueros* who provided "essential service" as mounted troopers. For Anglo American colonists out of their geographical and cultural element, such assistance was critical.

Even with Tejano support, Austin considered a frontal assault to be out of the question; a slow strangling siege seemed the only option. On October 26, Austin wrote to Goliad commander Philip Dimitt expressing his intentions to "commence such operations on the town as to shut in the force now there so that it will be obliged to surrender for want of provisions." To carry out his plans, Austin marched the Army of the People far below the town and established his camp and headquarter near the Mission San Francisco de la Espada.

The actual cause for which they were fighting remained unclear. Smithwick recollected: "Some were for independence, some were for the Constitution of 1824; and some were for anything, just so long it was a row." While Austin's volunteer army grappled with tactical problems outside San Antonio, Texas delegates assembled in San Felipe to organize something resembling a government and provide justification for the war that had already begun.

A Provisional Government

P rovisional governments are much like first drafts. Each is a work in progress; all is in flux. In times of crisis, stop-gap measures prevail only until an orderly political process can establish a new and permanent regime. Likewise, initial drafts are mere shadows of polished, final, and improved compositions. Consequently, few are the folks who pay much heed to either first drafts or provisional administrations.

The days and weeks following the "Come-and-Take-It" fight certainly qualified as a time of crisis. Delegates to the announced Consultation of 1835 dribbled into San Felipe. On October 11, 1835, the committee of safety proclaimed an interim government. This body administered civil affairs until a quorum arrived in town. Boldly styled the *Permanent* Council, it lasted but twenty days before the requisite number of delegates arrived and the Consultation supplanted it. Yet, they were twenty decidedly productive days. Enlisting Kentucky-born merchant Thomas F. McKinney (who enjoyed excellent credit in New Orleans), the council secured a $100,000 loan, procured provisions for the army, contracted privateers, established a postal system, bade the land offices closed and further surveying halted, and broadcast calls for volunteers in the "old states."

On November 3, Consultation members began their deliberations. Delegates elected Branch T. Archer, War Party militant, cousin killer, and the man who in 1832 had invited Sam Houston to Texas, as president

San Felipe de Austin as it would have appeared when the Texas provisional
government assembled there in 1835 and 1836. *Charles Shaw, illustrator. Courtesy of
the San Jacinto Museum of History.*

of the assembly. The first, and most pressing, order of business was to
determine the justification for a war that was already raging. Texians all
agreed on what (and who) they were fighting against, but they could
not concur on exactly what they were fighting for. To no one's surprise,
Archer and his fellow War Party delegates John A. Wharton and Henry
Smith urged outright and immediate independence from Mexico. Led
by Vermont native Don Carlos Barrett, moderate delegates deemed such
abrupt action premature and countered that it served only to alienate
Mexican federalists, who might serve as useful allies. General Stephen
F. Austin dispatched a long letter advocating a measured course. Stymied
in his independence endeavors (at least temporarily), Archer proposed
that the Consultation proclaim Texas a state in the toppled Mexican
Republic and declare common cause with those Mexican federalists who
still opposed Antonio López de Santa Anna and his centralist despotism.

Following two and a half days of deliberation, delegates voted on the
central issue of independence. On November 6, fourteen voted for the
proposition, but thirty-three rejected it. With that critical question settled,
they quickly proceeded to draft a declaration of causes to validate the conflict.
The next day, the group issued the "Declaration of the People of Texas." The
document asserted that the Texians had resorted to violence only because,

"General Antonio Lopez de Santa Anna and other Military Chieftains have, by force of arms, overthrown the Federal Institutions of Mexico, and dissolved the Social Compact which existed between Texas and the other Members of the Mexican Confederacy."The authors further explained,

> they hold it to be their right, during the disorganization of the Federal System and the reign of despotism, to withdraw from the Union, to establish an independent Government, or to adopt such measures as they may deem best calculated to protect their rights and liberties; but that they will continue faithful to the Mexican Government so long as that nation is governed by the Constitution and Laws that were formed for the government of the Political Association.

In other words, Texians were fighting (officially at least) as federalist Mexicans to restore the Constitution of 1824. Unofficially, Archer, Wharton, Smith, Houston, and other War Partiers bided their time, trusting, as they always had, that the majority would eventually catch up with them. They would not have to wait long.

Delegates then shifted their attention to the construction of an organizational structure. In accordance to the so-called "Organic Law," a governor, a lieutenant governor, and a general council, composed of a representative from each Texian municipality, were to supervise the transactions of the provisional government. The emissaries elected Kentucky native and War Party promoter Henry Smith governor and Indiana lawyer James W. Robinson lieutenant governor. It was a calamitous choice. While the delegates pledged their support for Mexican federalism, they elected an executive officer who ached for independence. Even worse, they neglected to define the powers of the executive and legislative branches. Members of the general council possessed no legislative authority unless "in their opinion the emergency of the country requires" it. The legislation allowed them to impose import duties but no domestic taxes. It further granted Smith "full and ample" executive authority that included command of revolutionary military units. Moreover, the council might grant the governor unspecified powers if its members deemed them necessary. The lack of a clear description of the authority and limits of government officers was an omission that planted the seeds of political pandemonium.

Next, the delegates pondered the formation of a regular army. Already the limitations of an all-volunteer military force were becoming apparent. On November 3, General Austin wrote to urge the "absolute necessity of organizing a regular army and inviting a Military man of known and tried Talents to Command it." Houston had just such a man in mind: Sam Houston. His fellow legislators agreed. He won unanimous election as commander of the regular army, with the rank of major general. As commander, Houston in theory took control of "all the forces called into public service during the war." Nevertheless, his fellow delegates explained in no uncertain terms, that he had no authority—absolutely none— over the volunteers already serving under Austin's command. Houston was commander of the regular army. The only catch being that such a force only existed in the fertile imaginations of San Felipe politicians. If Houston wanted to command a regular army, he would first have to raise and organize one. Yet, notwithstanding his specific instructions, he thought that it would be much easier to simply "borrow" Austin's army.

Austin, the one man who possessed the moral authority to head any Texas government, was commanding the Army of the People; his unique talents probably would have been of more use in a civilian capacity. Other political operatives—Archer, Smith, and Houston—attempted to assume Austin's traditional role, but none of them quite filled the bill. The willingness of the War Party delegates to accept a more moderate course allowed the Consultation to function, at least for the short term. Even so, because of its transitory nature, few Texians (and even fewer Tejanos) expressed any confidence in the governance, rationale, or organization of the provisional government. Most Texians behaved as they always had: they flouted political pronouncements and did as they pleased.

Meanwhile, outside Béxar, General Austin and the Texian Army faced problems of their own.

"Who Will Follow Old Ben Milam?"

With courage, confidence, and resolve (fortified by generous amounts of corn liquor) the Texian "Army of the People" marched on San Antonio de Béxar. Yet, when Stephen F. Austin's forces reached the outskirts of town, the full extent of their task came into sharper focus. General Martín Perfecto de Cos had dug in, erecting barricades and planting artillery. A siege seemed the only option.

Austin swung far to the south, establishing a basecamp near the Mission Espada. Deploying his forces below Béxar placed a bulwark between Cos and any reinforcements marching from the Mexican interior. Espada proved too far from town to detect Mexican movements, so the general dispatched a reconnaissance-in-force under James Bowie and James W. Fannin up the San Antonio River to discover a better campsite. Near sundown on October 27, 1836, they located the perfect spot. It was in a horseshoe bend of the river near the Mission Concepción. The location was close enough to Béxar to allow the Texians to better conduct their siege, but that tight proximity also made it dangerous for Bowie and Fannin's men. Nonetheless, they decided to pitch camp and await the arrival of Austin and the army.

Cos had learned of the Texian reconnaissance and hoped to crush it early the next morning. Accordingly, on October 28 in the predawn darkness, 270 centralist soldiers under Colonel Domingo de Ugartechea marched out to surprise the isolated Texian force, which numbered only

On October 28, 1835, a Texian reconnaissance-in-force tangled with centralist soldiers at the Battle of Concepción. Here, James Bowie leads a charge to capture a centralist field piece. *Courtesy of Gary Zaboly, illustrator,* An Altar for Their Sons: The Alamo and the Texas Revolution in Contemporary Newspaper Accounts.

90 men. Bowie, however, had placed sentries who heard the approaching assault force and alerted their comrades. Bowie ordered his men to take up defensive positions under the steep bank of the river, which formed a natural trench line.

The centralist troops opened fire with two cannon, but their fire was ineffectual; the river's bank sheltered the Texians. Ugartechea's infantry then advanced into the cul-de-sac. Accurate rifle fire halted three charges; it required only thirty minutes for the Texian marksmen to strike down a majority of the centralist infantry and artillerymen. Observing the enemy forces falling back, Bowie ordered a countercharge that commandeered one of the field pieces.

Austin and the main Texian army arrived on the field in time to see the enemy forces withdrawing toward Béxar. He ordered a cavalry charge that accomplished little more than to prod the retreating centralists.

Texas in Revolt, 1835

THE UNITED STATES OF AMERICA

Nacogdoches

Natchitoches

Fort Jesup

CHIHUAHUA

Town of Washington

BATTLE OF GONZALES OCTOBER 2

San Felipe   Anahuac

Río Bravo del Norte (Río Grande)

STORMING OF BÉXAR December 5–9

Gonzales   Harrisburg   ANAHUAC JUNE 20, 1835

COAHUILA Y TEXAS

Béxar

CAPTURE OF GOLIAD OCTOBER 9   Velasco

Presidio del Río Grande

Goliad

Refugio

Copano

Monclova

LIPANTITLÁN NOVEMBER 3–4   San Patricio

Laredo

Gulf of Mexico

COS

Monterrey

Saltillo   Matamoros   MEXÍA

NUEVO LEÓN

DURANGO

Tampico Expedition

TAMAULIPAS

ZACATECAS May 11 ★

SANTA ANNA   San Luis Potosí

☆ *Texan - Federalist victory*

SAN LUIS POTOSÍ   TAMPICO November 13-15 ★

★ *Centralist victory*

Map by Donald S. Frazier, Ph.D.

During the fighting, the centralists suffered fourteen killed and thirty-nine wounded; some of whom subsequently died. Texas losses included one killed—Richard Andrews, the first Texian fatality of the war—and one wounded. The victory at Concepción, won against such long odds, greatly boosted Texian morale.

105

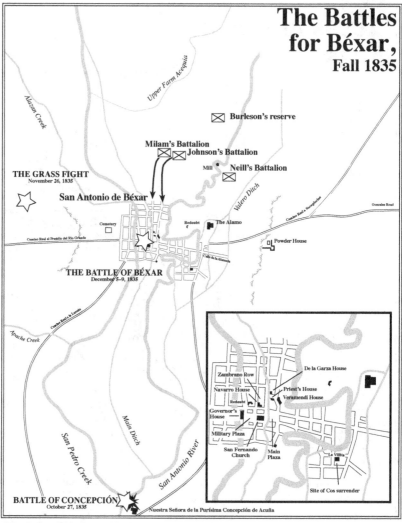

Map by Donald S. Frazier, Ph.D.

Following Concepción, the Siege of Béxar lapsed into dreary routine. Austin kept a tight noose around the town; Cos watched his troops consume dwindling supplies. Blockade warfare rankled Texian volunteers. They had signed on to fight the centralists, not to watch them starve. Troops began to wander off. Those who remained sought relief from their boredom at the bottom of a brown jug. Austin implored the San Felipe officials: "In the name of almighty God, send no more ardent spirits into this camp—if any is on the way turn it back, or have the head [of the barrel] knocked out."

With the onset of cold weather, illness swept the Texian camp, compounding current problems. Even the general fell victim. On November 8, he wrote: "I believe that my worn out constitution is not adapted to a military command, neither have I ever pretended to be a military man."

The politicians in San Felipe agreed. Austin received word that Texian officials had named him an agent to the United States, an assignment better suited to his temperament and well-being. Still, he wished to tie up loose ends in Béxar before he left. On November 21, Austin ordered an assault on the town, but the bulk of the men refused to participate. On November 24, a disgusted Austin called the army together to inquire if they even wanted to continue the siege. The men affirmed they did, if— and only if—they could elect their new commander. Austin acquiesced to their demands. The volunteers elected Edward Burleson their new commander, and a weary Austin rode out of camp north toward San Felipe and the United States.

On November 26, a skirmish broke the monotony. The Texians spied a centralist mule train approaching the town. Rumors spread that the beasts carried silver to pay the besieged garrison. Led by James Bowie, the Texians attacked and captured the supply column. Tearing open the packs, they discovered no riches—only grass cut to feed the starving cavalry horses stabled in San Antonio. With much self-derision, the Texians wryly labeled the affair, the "Grass Fight."

On December 1, General Burleson announced an assault for the following day. Once again, however, a majority of the volunteers announced that they were unwilling to attack the heavily fortified town. On December 4, with his army melting around him, Burleson announced his decision to abandon the siege and go into winter quarters at Goliad.

Soldier of fortune and former *empresario*, Ben Milam had other ideas. He could not believe his ears: Why after weeks of siege, now break it with nothing to show for it? Making no effort to conceal his anger, he confronted General Burleson. The pair reached an agreement. Milam could call for volunteers willing to storm the town. If a sufficient number responded, Burleson would hold the remainder in camp to cover a retreat in case the attack failed. Milam stormed through camp bellowing, "Who will follow old Ben Milam into San Antonio?" Of the more than five hundred Texians who remained in camp, some three hundred answered the call. Milam figured that was enough.

Under Milam's dynamic leadership, what had been the "Siege of Béxar" shifted into a five-day slug fest: the "Storming of Béxar." He divided his force into two units; he commanded one, and Virginia native Francis W. "Frank" Johnson led the other. Under cover of the early-morning gloom of December 5, the Texians assault troops snuck into town. By the time the centralists detected their presence, Milam's men had already established a toehold. What followed was five days of bitter house-to-house—at times room-to-room—fighting. On the third day of the assault, December 7, a centralist sniper shot Ben Milam neatly through the head. He died instantly, the first martyr to Texas liberty. His death incensed the Texians, who redoubled their efforts. "Old Ben" had not died in vain. On December 5, General Cos hoisted a white flag and requested terms.

Cos agreed to take his surviving soldiers to a point below the Rio Grande and promised that neither he, nor they, would ever again take arms against the Constitution of 1824.

With that, many Texians believed the war won. The following year's events proved them overly optimistic.

Matamoros Fever

ollowing the capture of Béxar, most Texian soldiers returned
home to celebrate Christmas with kith and kin; without
friends or family in Texas, the U.S. volunteers were at loose
ends. From their tedium, grew the scheme for the Matamoros
Expedition—an episode that demonstrated that idle hands really were
the Devil's workshop. Notwithstanding the strategic advantage that
Texians would enjoy if they did manage to capture the town, the excursion
ultimately produced the collapse of the Texas provisional government and
the near annihilation of the Texian army.

Matamoros was a tantalizing prize. By the late 1820s, the town
served as the financial and trade hub in the south–north trade routes
between the Mexican interior and Texas. The upriver settlements, or
villas del Norte, deposited their goods there before placing them on
oceangoing vessels. The port of Matamoros was northern Mexico's
gateway to the rest of the world. Likewise, it was the world's gateway
to northern Mexico. Tremendous revenue streams flowed through the
area as the consequence of escalating European trade. Commerce from
the United States—especially that generated out of New Orleans—
further contributed to the bounty. Matamoros merchants, by virtue of
their location, acumen, and industry, had forged lasting and lucrative
links between northern Mexico and the grasping merchants of the
United States.

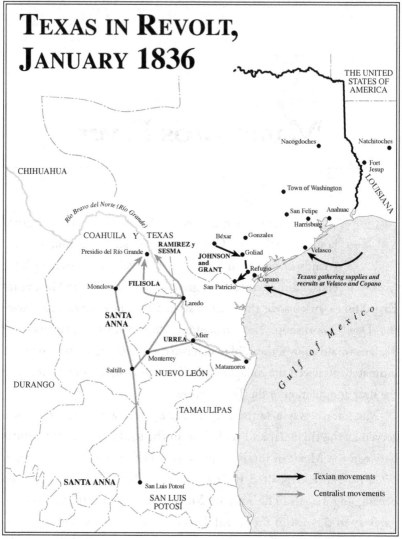

TEXAS IN REVOLT, JANUARY 1836

Map by Donald S. Frazier, Ph.D.

To many Texians, Matamoros seemed a rich plum ripe for the picking. Not only would it give the unruly U.S. volunteer units something to do, but the port was also an essential source of much-needed income. If Texian forces were able to lay hands on the town's proceeds, they might then employ them to discharge the mounting war debt. Some forward-thinking individuals argued that if the centralists should launch another campaign into Texas, rebels could employ the town's strategic location to repel the enemy's advance. If, moreover, Matamoros were under Texian control, they could use it as a base of operations to mount their own offensive into the Mexican interior.

Those caught up in the heat of what General Sam Houston called "Matamoros fever" seldom considered the many obstacles standing the way of their unrealistic scheme. During the Siege of Béxar, Texian officials had found it almost impossible to supply their fighting men. But now the victors of San Antonio were calling for an offensive against the Mexican port on the far bank of the Rio Grande. Exactly how the government would equip a Texian army at such distance did not seem to have been an issue of concern.

Although Governor Henry Smith and the council favored the broad notion, they could not agree on a commander. General Houston was a Smith crony but believed (correctly) that the council would not endorse his candidacy. Houston offered command to James Bowie, the victor of Concepción, but he turned Houston down. The council appointed Francis W. "Frank" Johnson, who first rode to San Felipe seeking sanction for the excursion. Upon receiving an ironclad endorsement, he began to have second thoughts. While Johnson dithered, council members tapped James W. Fannin to command, but he was unable to attract a sufficient number of volunteers. Houston and Johnson again offered their services, seeking the consent of both Governor Smith and the council. Yet, like a recurring nightmare, neither prospective leader could recruit enough men. Dismayed with the backbiting and ineptitude, Houston withdrew his name from consideration and accepted an appointment as commissioner to the Cherokees. Smith and the council were at loggerheads.

Soldiers in the field awaited instructions from officials who appeared incapable of making any decision. Johnson camped at San Patricio with some one hundred volunteers, while Fannin took up winter quarters at Refugio.

On January 6, 1836, Houston informed Smith that Johnson, before retiring to San Patricio, had stripped the Béxar garrison of vital supplies. In Houston's opinion, gallant soldiers, many of them still bearing the wounds from the December fighting, had suffered depredations at the hands of one who was little better than a bandit chief:

> The brave men who have been wounded in the battles of Texas, and the sick from exposure in her cause, without blankets or supplies, are left neglected in her hospitals; while the needful stores and supplies are diverted from them, without authority by self-created officers, who do not acknowledge the only government known to Texas and the world.

A source of contention and confusion at the time, the so-called Matamoros Expedition remains perplexing. In truth, there never was a Matamoros Expedition, inasmuch as a Texian force never marched a mile toward Matamoros. All San Felipe officials could do was argue about it. It would be more accurate to call it the *proposed* Matamoros Expedition.

No matter what one chooses to label it, the machinations surrounding the design would have destructive and lasting consequences. Upon receiving Houston's letter, Governor Smith could hardly control his anger. He convinced himself that the council had been in cahoots with Johnson, approving of his sack of Béxar while keeping all concealed from him. In clear and forceful terms, the governor determined to confront the members of the council.

His actions were about to topple the provisional government.

Political Chaos

Governor Henry Smith determined that it was time for a showdown. On January 9, 1836, he addressed a scalding missive to council members, accusing them of fomenting an unlawful filibustering mission and appointing their own "Generalissimo" to command it. He further charged councilmen with sacrificing Texas on a "shrine of plunder."

As if that were not inflammatory enough, Smith then allowed his rhetoric to run rampant. His anger flowed over the council members like lava:

> Look around upon your flock, your discernment will easily detect the scoundrels. The complaint; contraction of the eyes; the gape of the mouth; the vacant stare; the head hung; the restless fidgety disposition; the sneaking sycophantic look; a natural meanness of countenance; an unguarded shrug of the shoulders; a sympathetic tickling and contraction of the muscles of the neck anticipating the rope; a restless uneasiness to adjourn, dreading to face the storm [they] themselves have raised.

This was but a prelude to the substance of his tirade. Smith explained that the council's services where no longer needed. He avowed that he would, "continue to discharge my duties as Commander-in-Chief of the army and navy, and see that the laws are executed."

Smith had thrown down the gauntlet, and the council took it up. Two days later, members reviewed their rancorous relationship with the

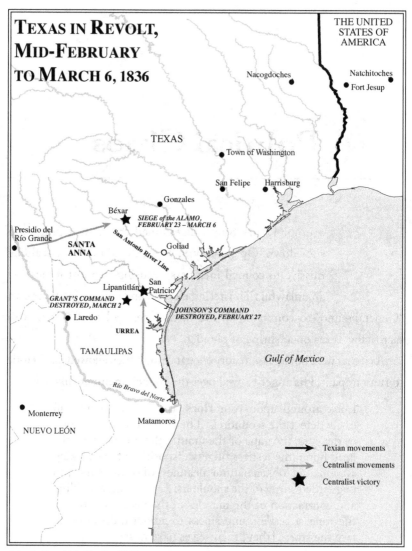

TEXAS IN REVOLT,
MID-FEBRUARY
TO MARCH 6, 1836

Map by Donald S. Frazier, Ph.D.

governor. In their proclamation to the "People of Texas," councilmen insisted that Smith's behavior had left them but one alternative. They levied charges of impeachment against him for the "manifest injuries and difficulties he has endeavored to bring upon this country." Smith fired the council; the council fired him right back.

At that juncture, the political climate became genuinely anarchic. For a while, Texas was blessed with *two* governments, each at odds with the other. The council declared Smith's lieutenant governor, James W. Robinson, to be "acting governor." Moreover, military commanders in the field, agents in the United States, and all Texian officials were to report to him. On January 18, Smith declared that the council "did not make, nor can they break me." He still insisted that he was the rightful governor and refused to hand over the archives. For its part, the General Council ignored Smith and continued to meet sporadically.

As for the people of Texas, they were uncertain who possessed the legal authority and few seemed to care. Everyone knew that a convention was to meet in the Town of Washington on March 1, at which time delegates would organize a permanent government anyway. Truthfully, few were the Texians who had ever paid much attention to the actions of the provisional government. Even fewer mourned its breakdown.

One who did was Colonel James Clinton Neill. At Béxar were some twenty-one artillery pieces of various caliber. Because of his artillery experience and his regular army commission, Neill was a logical choice to command. Throughout January he did his best to fortify the old mission on the outskirts of town. If the centralists launched another offensive into Texas, Neill and his men constituted the first line of defense. Far from the bulk of Texas settlements, the garrison suffered from a lack of even basic provisions. On January 14, Neill wrote Sam Houston that his people were in a "torpid, defenseless condition."

By January 17, Houston had begun to question the wisdom of maintaining the Béxar garrison. On that date he informed Governor Smith that Colonel James Bowie and a company of volunteers had left Goliad for San Antonio. On January 19, Bowie rode into the Alamo compound. What he saw impressed him. As a result of much hard work, the mission had begun to look like a real fort. Neill, who well knew the consequences of leaving *el camino real* unguarded, convinced Bowie that the Alamo was the only defensive stronghold between the enemy and Anglo settlements.

Neill's arguments and his leadership electrified Bowie. As he explained to Governor Smith: "I cannot eulogize the conduct & character of Col. Neill too highly, no other man in the army could have kept men at this post, under the neglect they have experienced." On February 2, Bowie wrote Smith that he and Neill had resolved to "die in these ditches" before they would surrender the post.

The letter confirmed Smith's understanding of controlling factors. He had concluded that the Texian rebels must hold San Antonio. Rejecting Houston's advice, Smith prepared to funnel additional troops and provisions to the town. In brief, Houston had asked for permission to abandon the post; Smith considered his request, and the answer was no.

If the Alamo were to function as an early-warning station, Neill had to have outriders. Smith directed Lieutenant Colonel William B. Travis's "Legion of Cavalry" to report to San Antonio. Travis resisted, but at length, he rode toward Béxar with only thirty horsemen. Reinforcements began to trickle in. On February 3, Travis's cavalrymen reached the Alamo. Like Bowie, he soon became committed to Neill and the fort, which he began to describe as the "key to Texas." About February 8, former U.S. Congressman David Crockett arrived with a group of U.S. volunteers.

On February 14, Neill departed on furlough. He learned that illness had struck his family and that they desperately needed him back in Mina. He promised that he would resume command when circumstances permitted, certainly within twenty days, and left Travis in charge as acting post commander. Neill had not intended to slight the older and more experienced Bowie, but Travis, like Neill, held a regular army commission.

Travis received reports that Antonio López de Santa Anna's centralist army had crossed the Rio Grande. Travis believed that "His Excellency" could not reach Béxar until at least March 15. His arrival in San Antonio on February 23 convinced him otherwise.

Travis and Bowie understood that they could not hold the town with their skeleton force and so took refuge in the former mission across the

San Antonio River. The plan had always been that the picket garrisons at Béxar and Goliad would alert the government upon the enemy's approach. Then rebel forces would assemble at those vital choke points and halt the centralists before they drove into the heart of the Texian settlements. The Alamo garrison could hold for a while, but not indefinitely. Their fate now rested with the General Council in San Felipe, James W. Fannin at Goliad, and other Texan volunteers who might rush to assist the beleaguered garrison.

Ominously, the provisional government that would have coordinated those relief efforts had ceased to exist.

Thirteen Days:
The Siege of the Alamo

O n February 23, 1836, the same day he arrived in Béxar, Generalissimo Antonio López de Santa Anna dispatched a courier to demand the Alamo garrison's surrender. William Barret Travis replied with a cannonball. There could be no mistaking such a concise response. Santa Anna retorted by hoisting a red flag of no quarter atop the bell tower of San Fernando Church. Centralist artillerymen then planted their batteries and directed their fire against the fort. Once the heavy pounding breached the walls, those inside would have to surrender in the face of overwhelming odds. Bottled up, the defenders had only one hope: that Texian reinforcements would break the siege.

On the second day of the siege, February 24, Travis assumed full command when Colonel James Bowie fell victim to a mysterious malady variously described as "hasty consumption" or "typhoid pneumonia." As commander, Travis penned his celebrated letter to the "people of Texas & all Americans in the world," in which he recounted that the fort had "sustained a continual Bombardment and cannonade for 24 hours." He pledged that he would "never surrender or retreat" and swore "Victory or Death." The predominant message, however, was an entreaty for help: "I call on you in the name of Liberty, of patriotism & everything dear to the American character, to come to our aid, with all dispatch." Far from being bent on self-sacrifice, Travis and his men honestly believed that they could hold the fort—at least until reinforcements arrived. That had, after all, always been the strategy.

119

On February 24, 1836—the second day of the siege—Colonel Juan Almonte noted the following: "Very early this morning a new battery was commenced on the bank of the river, about 350 yards from the Alamo." This highly detailed illustration shows that battery in action. Note that the artilleryman in the left foreground is hoisting a red-hot solid shot from a field furnace. The gunners hoped that these "hot shots" would ignite dry lumber or thatched roofs inside the enemy compound. If they were extremely lucky, they might even explode the rebel powder magazine. *Courtesy of Gary Zaboly, illustrator,* An Altar for Their Sons: The Alamo and the Texas Revolution in Contemporary Newspaper Accounts.

A few responded to his entreaties. On March 1, thirty-two troops attached to Lieutenant George C. Kimbell's Gonzales ranging company made their way through the enemy cordon and into the compound. The irrepressible David Crockett celebrated their arrival by serenading the garrison with his fiddle; Scotsman John McGregor joined in on his bagpipes. In one of his letters to Sam Houston, Travis described how "the honorable David Crockett was seen at all points, animating the men to their duty." Even the stricken Bowie had his cot brought out in the open, where he encouraged the men from his sickbed. Morale remained high, and Travis was grateful for the Gonzales reinforcements, but he knew they would not be enough. He needed more.

Yet, days dragged by and no more help arrived. The centralists continued their cannonading, and the defenders observed that the enemy artillery edged ever closer to the walls. Travis could not imagine why Colonel James W. Fannin and his four hundred men had not arrived. It had been nine days since he and Bowie had summoned him, plenty of time for the ninety-five-mile journey. The Alamo commander knew that his couriers were getting through enemy lines. Why were the "people of Texas & all Americans in the world" paying his letters no heed?

And where was General Houston? With the collapse of the provisional government, he held no official authority. But Texians had scheduled a new convention to meet at the Town of Washington on the Brazos River to create a permanent government and (Travis hoped) declare independence from Mexico once and for all. Predictably, Houston rushed there to confirm his position. While he and the other Texian politicos dithered, Santa Anna's cannonballs hammered the walls of the Alamo. Travis and his men would just have to fend as best they could.

By March 3, the determination and defiance of his February 24 letter had begun to give way to anger and despair. Travis wrote to the Washington delegates that he had lost all faith in Colonel Fannin. "I look to the colonies alone for aid; unless it arrives soon, I shall have to fight the enemy on his own terms." He grew increasingly bitter that his fellow Texians seemed blind to his plight. In a letter to a friend, Travis revealed his frustration: "If my countrymen do not rally to my relief, I am determined to perish in the defense of this place, and my bones shall reproach my country for her neglect."

Why did Texian leaders ignore Travis's repeated calls for assistance? Modern Texans dislike admitting it, but the provisional government that should have—and could have—organized relief efforts had fallen apart because of its bickering, dissention, and discord. When the Washington delegates finally assembled to organize a permanent government, they did not have sufficient time or resources to rescue the men trapped inside the Alamo. Having received pledges that "every possible effort is making to strengthen, supply and provision the Garrison," Travis found it difficult to accept that his superiors had placed him and his men in harm's way only to forsake them through sheer ineptness. Had he lived longer, the twenty-six-year-old Travis might have learned to place less trust in the promises of politicians.

The worsening situation wholly justified Travis's growing melancholy. The constant pounding had weakened the walls. By day eleven of the siege, centralist engineers had planted a battery within "musket shot" of the north wall. At that range, they did not require heavy siege guns; each shot bashed and battered until the wall was on the verge of collapse. Green Jameson, the Kentucky lawyer turned Alamo engineer, directed work parties throughout the night, buttressing the wall with odd pieces of timber. But both he and Travis realized that this was only a stopgap measure. In the event of a determined assault, the north wall could not hold.

On Friday, March 4—day eleven of the siege—Santa Anna called a council of war and announced a predawn assault for the following Sunday. This sudden declaration stunned his officers. The enemy's walls were crumbling. No Texian relief column had appeared. When the provisions ran out, surrender would remain the rebels' only option. There was simply no military justification for the costly attack on a stronghold bristling with artillery. But ignoring these reasonable objections, Santa Anna stubbornly insisted on storming the Alamo.

His Excellency's attack order of Saturday, March 5, scheduled the onslaught for five o'clock the following morning. The centralists' cannon fell silent toward the end of the day. Santa Anna hoped the weary rebels would take advantage of the lull to catch up on their sleep. If his *soldados* approached silently under the cover of darkness, they might be over the walls before the bleary-eyed defenders reached their posts.

The plan worked. For twelve days the Alamo garrison had endured almost constant bombardment. Now, near the end of their tether, they collapsed in exhausted heaps. Travis posted a few picket guards, but they too seemed to have nodded off.

All was silent inside the compound as the stroke of midnight heralded day thirteen of the siege—March 6, 1836.

Meanwhile, Back at the Convention . . .

I n Béxar, those inside the Alamo dodged shells and scanned the horizon for reinforcements. At the same time, at the Town of Washington, delegates from the various Texian municipalities gathered to create a new government and settle the issue of independence from Mexico. Indeed, on February 7, the Béxar garrison had elected Sam Maverick and Jesse Badgett to represent them at the pending conclave. The vast majority went whole-hog for independence. War Party hotspur, William Barret Travis, had, of course, long supported that ambition. In a March 3 letter to the convention, he affirmed: "If independence is not declared, I shall lay down my arms and so will the men under my command. But under the flag of independence we are ready to peril our lives a hundred times a day."

All this talk of independence will mystify attentive readers. Back in November 1835, Texian representatives had voted to support Mexican federalism and the Constitution of 1824. Now, less than four months later, many of the same delegates were clamoring for independence. What had changed? Actually, a lot had.

Texas leaders understood that they could not win the war alone. If Mexican federalists would not lend a hand, they must enlist assistance from the United States. Texians claimed thousands of acres of disposable land, but they were cash poor. To win this war, they first had to fight it. That required troops, weapons, and provisions and all those cost money

This haunting photograph reveals the interior of the reconstructed Independence Hall at Washington-on-the-Brazos State Park. A copy of the 1836 Declaration of Independence lies on the table. *Courtesy of Texas Parks and Wildlife.*

—mountains of it. U.S. President Andrew Jackson was unlikely to risk an international incident by *openly* supporting the Texas rebels against Mexico. Texians sought instead the support of individual Americans who championed their cause. The provisional government dispatched Stephen F. Austin as an agent to the United States. Once in the "old states" the *empresario* appealed to supporters to provide volunteers, funds, and supplies. He and other Texas agents visited U.S. banks to secure loans for the rebel effort.

There, however, they encountered a dilemma. Banks in the north would not consider supporting a cause that might ultimately bring another slave state into the union. Southern bankers, although more sympathetic, refused to lend their money so long as the war remained a Mexican domestic dispute. They might be interested if—and only if—Texians declared their complete separation from Mexico.

Why this Southern support for independence? Those living below the Mason-Dixon Line anticipated that Texas would remain independent for, say, six months before entering the Union as a slave state. In 1836, the United States had an equal number of free and slave states. Because both factions voted as a block, they created a legislative gridlock. Southerners believed that adding Texas to the list of slave states would tip the congressional balance of power in their favor.

In a letter on January 7, 1836, Austin neatly summed up the state of affairs:

> I go for Independence for I have no doubt we shall get aid, as much as we need and perhaps more—and what is of equal importance—the information from Mexico up to late in December says that the Federal party has united with Santa Anna against us, owing to what has already been said and done in Texas in favor of Independence so that our present position under the constitution of 1824, does us no good with the Federalists, and is doing us harm in this country, by keeping away the kind of men we most need.

It was meaningful that even Austin—who had always preached cooperation and accommodation with Mexico—now urged complete independence. The day that the War Party members had prayed for had arrived; the majority of Texians had finally come round. By March 1, nearly all of the delegates judged that their best hope rested on separation from Mexico. Consequently, declaring independence was not so much an act of political conviction as it was an exercise in expedience.

At the time, Texians did not consider a declaration of independence an especially momentous occasion. Most representatives arrived at the Washington convention knowing full well that independence was a forgone conclusion. Tennessee native George C. Childress called the convention to order and introduced a resolution authorizing a five-man committee to draft a Declaration of Independence. The delegates adopted the resolution and named Childress as chairman. The committee completed a rough copy in one day; many claimed that Childress had arrived in the Town of Washington on the Brazos River with a draft in his saddlebags. Virginia observer William Fairfax Gray captured the casual nature of the proceedings in his diary, but they impressed him so little that he did not even record author Childress's name correctly:

> The Convention met pursuant to adjournment. Mr. Childers [*sic*], from the committee, reported

a Declaration of Independence, which he read in this place. It was received by the house, committed to a committee of the whole, reported without amendment, and unanimously adopted, in less than one hour from its first and only reading. It underwent on discipline, and no attempt was made to amend it. The only speech made upon it was a somewhat declamatory address in committee to the whole by General Houston.

And it was done. Henceforth, the war was no longer one to sustain the federalist Constitution of 1824, but rather sought to uphold the sovereign Republic of Texas. The delegates assembled on March 1 and declared independence on March 2. It was not a highly deliberative process. Never had so many politicians weighed so quickly a question of such momentous importance.

Childress's prose may have lacked the elegance of Thomas Jefferson's but he at least followed his template. Jefferson's 1776 document was a litany of complaints against George III and Parliament; Childress's enumerated Texian grievances against Antonio López de Santa Anna and his centralist regime.

Thus, in the midst of commotion, conflict, and chaos, did fifty-nine representatives sign into existence the Republic of Texas and ushered in a decade of autonomy singular in the annals of U.S. history. Although Travis and his men inside the Alamo never learned of the declaration, the knowledge that they were now fighting for a sovereign nation would have thrilled them.

They might have been less pleased to know what they were about to sacrifice to preserve that fledgling country.

Grievances Listed in the
Texas Declaration of Independence

- Antonio López de Santa Anna's overthrow of the Constitution of 1824 and his establishment of a dictatorship
- The centralist government's subjugation of Texas to Coahuila, which lessened Texian representation
- The centralist regime's refusal of the colonists' right to trial by jury, the right to religious freedom, and the right of colonists to bear arms in their own defense
- The centralist regime's neglect in establishing an education system for the people of Texas
- Santa Anna's employment of the army, rather than civilian courts, to enforce Mexican laws
- The centralist regime's efforts to incite hostile Indians to attack Texas settlers
- Santa Anna's deployment of foreign mercenaries, who were even then marching to annihilate Texian colonists

March 6, 1836: Assault

At midnight, the centralist camp came alive. Officers and noncommissioned officers inspected the soldiers and scrutinized their weapons. Antonio López de Santa Anna's order had been ominous: "The arms, principally the bayonets, should be in perfect order."

By 3 AM all were ready. The predawn hours were frosty, and many troops stood shivering for hours. Column commanders informed "His Excellency" that their men were losing their edge. Finally, at 5:30, he signaled the advance.

All proceeded smoothly as four columns pressed forward under a vivid moon—one column for each quadrant of the compass. Some 1,700 veteran infantrymen assembled for the assault. Santa Anna also posted 369 cavalrymen along the perimeter of the battlefield to "prevent the possibility of escape."

All remained quiet inside the Alamo as the columns moved within range. The tension finally became more than one *soldado* could bear. "*¡Viva Santa Anna!*" he roared. "*¡Viva la Republica!*" screamed another. Then, hundreds of voices shattered the stillness.

The racket alerted the defenders. Groggy, they roused themselves and scurried to their posts. William Barret Travis sprang from his cot, grabbed his shotgun, and rushed to his north wall battery. He shouted to his men: "Come on, boys, the Mexicans are upon us and we'll give them Hell!"

131

A bird's-eye view of the Mexican assault. Santa Anna's troops have penetrated the outer walls and pour into the fort. The men of the Alamo are doomed. *Courtesy of Gary Zaboly, illustrator,* An Altar for Their Sons: The Alamo and the Texas Revolution in Contemporary Newspaper Accounts.

Gunners discharged their cannon, disgorging fragments of horseshoes, links of chain, nails, door hinges, any trace of rusty scrap they could scrounge. Packed bodies soaked up the force of the scatter shot. Jagged shards slammed home, gashed as they plowed through the ranks, and finally stopped—lodged in flesh.

But the assault troops were now returning fire. Travis had just unloaded both barrels of his shotgun into the onrushing mass when a slug slammed through his forehead and into his brain. He had sworn to "never surrender or retreat." He did neither.

The fire savaged centralist ranks. It ripped columns asunder, but still they drove forward. Assault troops who pressed themselves flush against the north wall were under the guns. There, they were relatively safe from Texian fire. Knowing that, other soldados pushed forward seeking to share this haven. Too many bodies struggled for too little space. In their panic, the stronger and larger shoved aside the smaller and weaker. Yet, more continued to thrust forward. It became a cruel choice—to be shot by the rebels or crushed by comrades.

Another option was to scale the wall and kill their tormenters. Back at his command post, Santa Anna influenced that decision. Watching the attack bog down, he ordered in reserves—engineers, the elite *Zapadores*. Driving within range, they unleashed a volley toward the few defenders atop the north wall. But most rounds fell short, wounding and killing their comrades hunched below. Thus, this "friendly fire" gave the huddled mass impetus to scale the wall. But they needed someone to lead them; the attack was faltering.

General Juan Amador began the grueling twelve-foot ascent and called on the soldados to follow him. His audacity shamed them to action. Ultimately, despair and sheer weight of numbers replaced all of Santa Anna's careful planning. Unit integrity broke down. Even so, each soldado knew what he must do: scale the wall and perhaps survive or perish where he crouched.

So they climbed. To reach the enemy, they had to heave and elbow a path over their friends. Amador grappled up and over the parapet and fell into the courtyard below. His men dropped in behind him. For now, regardless to what units they belonged, they were *his* men. Amador and the first soldados inside the fort located a small door in one of the west wall rooms and swung it open. Their comrades flooded through. From that moment, the outcome of the assault was beyond doubt.

Defenders abandoned the north wall. After that, events unfolded quickly. At the southwest corner, centralist riflemen picked off the Texian gunners manning the eighteen-pounder, scaled the wall, and poured into the compound. Some defiant defenders endeavored to make a stand in the plaza but found themselves caught between the fire of assault troops streaming in from the south and that of Amador's men pouring in from the north. Defenders fell back into the long barracks. David Crockett and his riflemen took cover inside the church.

Others, however, concluded that the Alamo had become a deathtrap. As many as seventy-five darted over the walls and sought cover in the chaparral. Santa Anna had anticipated their dash for safety and posted lancers to intercept them. General Joaquín Ramirez y Sesma had to twice dispatch reinforcements to quell these rebels who were "ready to sell their lives at a very high price." But soon all of them had perished on the points of the vicious lances.

Inside the fort, the defenders prepared to make their final stand. The Texians had abandoned the outer perimeter in such haste that they had neglected to spike their guns. Now, the centralists hauled them into the courtyard and methodically blasted each door into the long barracks. Soldados tore through shattered entryways to finish the work begun by the captured cannon. There in the darkness, adversaries grappled with bayonet and butcher knife. Breaking into a room on the south wall, assault troops discovered one rebel too faint and delirious to rise from his sick bed. By that point, soldados were beyond pity, they killed him where he lay; but pity was never a sentiment that James Bowie had especially valued.

The Alamo church was the last to fall. Employing an abandoned cannon, the centralists knocked aside the sandbags blocking the main door and rammed through. They overwhelmed and slaughtered all but six or seven of the defenders inside. The Mexicans were victorious; there was no need for more senseless bloodshed. General Don Manuel Castrillón ordered his soldados to spare these defenseless adversaries.

With the fighting finished, Santa Anna entered the fort. As he assessed the carnage, Castrillón presented his prisoners. He urged humane treatment for these hapless individuals, but His Excellency countered with a "gesture of indignation" and ordered their deaths. Gallant soldiers, those who had actually fought in the battle, hesitated to perform such a distasteful duty. But staff officers anxious to curry favor with their commander fell on the unarmed prisoners and hacked them to pieces with their swords. José Enrique de la Peña recalled that the butchered men, "died moaning but without humiliating themselves before their torturers." He minced no words when he identified one of the murdered men as the "famous American naturalist," David Crockett. Not all Mexicans condoned such barbarity. Captain Fernando Urissa recalled: "Castrillón turned aside with tears in his eyes, and my heart was too full to speak." With that last shameful act, all the Texian combatants—some 250 of them—lay dead.

The Alamo had fallen but, even as the blood dried on those shattered stones, its myth was being born.

Indecision and Calamity

On March 4, 1836, delegates of the Independence Convention appointed Sam Houston major general and instructed him to organize the republic's military forces. They had previously received William Barret Travis's letters from the Alamo pleading for reinforcements. One faction led by Nacogdoches representative Robert Potter called for the convention to adjourn and for all to rush to the aide of the besieged Béxar garrison. Houston slammed the scheme as "madness." Delegates would do better, he insisted, to remain in the Town of Washington on the Brazos River and draft a constitution for the new nation whose existence they had just proclaimed. As for the Alamo defenders, he pledged all "mortal power" to save them. Accompanied by his aides-de-camp, Houston departed the Town of Washington on the evening of March 6. He had no way of knowing, of course, that the Alamo had fallen that morning.

What Houston discovered when he arrived in Gonzales on March 11 did nothing to boost his confidence. On February 11, Alamo commander James Clinton Neill had gone on furlough to care for his ailing family. He left Travis in temporary command of the garrison until his return. But on February 23, Antonio López de Santa Anna arrived and besieged the Alamo. Consequently, Neill could not make his way back to assume command. He did, however, raise a relief column of some 374 men in Gonzales—men who became the core of Houston's San Jacinto army.

At the height of the Goliad Massacre, one of Fannin's men sprints for his life. Only twenty-eight Texians escaped the slaughter. *Gary Zaboly, illustrator. From* Texian Macabre: The Melancholy Tale of a Hanging in Early Houston. *Author's collection.*

Soon after Houston's appearance, two *Bexareños* under Juan Seguin's command galloped into town with news that the Alamo had fallen. Houston had little reason to doubt their report but was fearful of the panic it might generate. He, therefore, arrested the two couriers as spies. Although he *publicly* disparaged their information, the general *privately* admitted in a letter to Colonel James W. Fannin that he feared that "a melancholy portion of it will be found too true." Houston immediately dispatched orders to Fannin in Goliad to blow up the Presidio La Bahía and fall back to Victoria with all possible haste. Houston knew he could not defend Gonzales with 374 untrained volunteers and thus made plans to retire to the Colorado River where he intended to rendezvous with Fannin's command. He had no inkling what was going on further south.

In Goliad, Fannin commanded more than four hundred troops—the largest Texian unit under arms—inside the Presidio La Bahía, which the Texians had renamed Fort Defiance. On February 13, Mexican General José de Urrea began a lightning march toward San Patricio, en route ultimately to Refugio, Goliad, Victoria, and Brazoria, to gain control of crucial Texas ports.

Fannin learned of the enemy's advance but still dispatched units to Refugio to evacuate Texian settlers only to have Urrea's command swallow them up.

The Goliad garrison finally abandoned Fort Defiance on the morning of March 19, bound for Victoria. Fannin even stopped at midday to rest. Captain Jack Shackleford inquired why he would halt on an open prairie devoid of natural cover. Fannin replied that the Mexicans would never attack a corps as large as his. Yet soon afterward, Urrea's cavalry appeared in hot pursuit. Fannin ordered his men to head for a slight rise, but an ammunition wagon broke down. The rebels had no choice but to form a square formation around the stricken wagon and stand their ground. Urrea's cavalry kept the rebels pinned in place while his infantry moved forward to engage.

During the subsequent Battle of Coleto Creek, the Texians fought bravely throughout the afternoon and into the evening. That night they dug entrenchments and suffered from thirst. Dawn on March 20 revealed that Urrea had received reinforcements during the night. Now armed with a howitzer, Mexican artillerymen could stand beyond rifle range and blast the rebel square to bits. If the Texians broke their formation and ran for cover, Urrea's lancers stood ready to ride them down. Realizing the hopelessness of his situation, Fannin surrendered.

Urrea marched the defeated Texians back to the Presidio La Bahía; few of the prisoners would have now had the heart to call it Fort Defiance. For a week Mexican soldiers held Fannin's men in close confinement. During that time the captive rebels, especially the wounded, suffered terribly. General Urrea continued his campaign, leaving Lieutenant Colonel José Nicolás de la Portilla in command at La Bahía. It proved an unhappy assignment.

On March 26, Portilla received direct orders from Santa Anna to execute all of his prisoners. Later that same day, a countermanding order arrived from Urrea. In a quandary, Portilla concluded that he had no choice but to follow the instructions of the supreme commander.

The following day, March 27, 1836—Palm Sunday—Mexican soldiers led between 425 and 445 Texian prisoners out of the fort. They marched in three columns between two rows of Mexican soldiers. The prisoners were in high spirits. Enjoying the fresh air for the first time in a week, they also believed that they were traveling to the coast where they would board ships to return them to the United States. Yet, when the three groups had marched about a mile from the presidio, their guards halted the columns and opened fire at point-blank range. Charles B. Shain, one of the prisoners who escaped the carnage, later recounted, "They were within three or four feet of us when they fired." *Soldados* finished off those not immediately killed by musket fire with bayonets, lances, and butcher knives.

Forty prisoners were wounded so badly that they could not march out with the others. Captain Carolino Huerta oversaw the murder of these helpless men. Because Mexicans required trained physicians, he spared Captain Jack Shackelford. Portilla also concocted reasons to spare numerous Texians who practiced useful occupations—mechanics, carpenters, and the like. Fannin was the last to face death, knowing that most of his command had preceded him on their final journey. Mexican soldiers placed him in a chair in consideration of his painful leg wound received at the Battle of Coleto Creek. As a final request, Fannin asked that the officer commanding the firing squad send his personal possessions to his family, that the firing party aim for his heart, and that his body should receive a Christian burial. The soldados pocketed his belongings, shot him in the face, and tossed his body on a common funeral pyre.

Twenty-eight men escaped what Texians would forever recall as the Goliad Massacre, but some 342 others fell victim to Santa Anna's malice. He could have acted with discretion but chose otherwise. He would have done better to dump an army of defeated and demoralized volunteers on U.S. shores. Their tales of Mexican compassion and Texian neglect might have dissuaded others from flocking to join the conflict. He could have gained the moral high ground; instead the world came to view him as a bloodthirsty butcher. Fannin and his men, moreover, joined the Alamo garrison as martyrs whose blood called out for vengeance. Sam Houston's ragged soldiers—all that remained of the Texian army—were eager to answer that call.

Provisions of the 1836 Constitution of the Republic of Texas

On March 1, 1836, fifty-nine delegates assembled at the Town of Washington to declare independence from Mexico and draft a constitution for the Republic of Texas. They constituted a remarkably diverse group. Most were Southerners younger than forty years of age. Nine were from Virginia, but others hailed from places as far-flung as England, Wales, Canada, Mexico, Ohio, Connecticut, and New York. Notwithstanding the various origins of delegates, the document stressed the Southern view on slavery. The "peculiar institution" was part of the toxic stew that led to the Texas Revolution, but not the principal ingredient. Even so, provisions of the Constitution of 1836 assured that the Republic of Texas would become "an empire for slavery."

- The delegates created a unitary republic, rather than a federal one as defined in the U.S. Constitution.

- Presidential terms were three years. Chief executives could not succeed themselves but might serve any number of nonconsecutive terms. Delegates modeled this feature after provisions in the Mexican Constitution.

- The Constitution protected the right of citizens to own slaves.

- The Constitution established the three branches of government: Legislative, Executive, and Judicial.

- The Constitution limited the powers of Congress but authorized it to tax, borrow money, and provide for the republic's general welfare. Congress also regulated commerce and maintained a navy. Only Congress could declare war.

- The first elected president would serve only two years. Subsequent presidents were to serve three-year terms.

- The Constitution established the judiciary and a Supreme Court. It authorized Congress to establish lower courts. There were to be no less than three and no more than eight judicial districts.

- The Constitution forbade ministers of the gospel from holding office. Delegates reasoned that such service distracted them from their sacred obligations.

- The president would serve as commander-in-chief of the army and navy but would not personally command them unless authorized by Congress.

- Any citizen who was twenty-one years of age and had resided in Texas for six months was eligible to vote. Indians and African Americans could never be citizens.

- Convicted criminals could not hold public office, vote, or serve on juries.

- The Constitution demanded that Congress establish and fund a system of public education.

- Slaves who were brought into Texas were to remain the property of the one who brought them in. Their masters could not free them without the consent of Congress.

- The Constitution forbade Congress from crafting laws that threatened the slave trade, nor could it ever proclaim the emancipation of bonded persons.

- The Constitution forbade free persons of color from living within the boundaries of the republic without the consent of Congress.

- The Constitution authorized each head of a family one league and labor of land. Every man who was at least seventeen years of age could claim one third of a league of land.

- The Constitution granted all white men equal rights, but it denied all women the right to vote.

- The Constitution awarded no preference to any religious denomination but did recognize the freedom of citizens to worship (or not) as they pleased.

- The Constitution granted freedom of speech and expression to all citizens. Congress could never pass laws interfering with that solemn right.

- Of the fifty-nine delegates to the 1836 Convention, only two (José Antonio Navarro and José Francisco Ruiz) had been born in Texas. Only one was a member of Stephen F. Austin's Old Three Hundred original settlers. Only ten had lived in Texas for more than six years. Seventeen of them had been in Texas less than six months.

Texian Exodus

O n March 13, 1836, Texian scout Erastus "Deaf" Smith arrived in Gonzales with Susanna Dickinson in tow. She had been inside the Alamo throughout the thirteen-day siege and final assault during which her husband Almeron had died. Although she confirmed reports that *Tejano* scouts had delivered two days before, General Sam Houston could not conveniently lock her away. The Dickinsons were residents of Gonzales and had many friends and neighbors there. Accompanied by her infant daughter and Joe, William Barret Travis's body servant, the widow Dickinson delivered a message from Antonio López de Santa Anna: All who opposed him would suffer the fate of the Alamo garrison. After learning of Mrs. Dickinson's ordeal, Houston—that hard-drinking, loud-swearing frontier veteran—wept like a little boy.

News of the Alamo defeat stunned Texas, but nowhere was the grief greater than in Gonzales. There the loss of life was intensely personal. Every family mourned the loss of a friend or relative. At least twenty women, many with small children, found themselves widows. John Sharpe, a Texian officer, recalled the scene on the night of March 13: "For several hours after the receipt of the intelligence, not a sound was heard, save the wild shrieks of the women, and the heartrending screams of the fatherless children."

The terror in Gonzales spread throughout Texas. Even in Nacogdoches, far from the Mexican threat, residents convinced themselves that the Cherokees had allied with the enemy and were coming to massacre them. Frightened out

145

During the Runaway Scrape, a motley gathering of Texian civilians make their way toward the border. A mounted courier brings news of the San Jacinto victory. *Charles Shaw, illustrator. Courtesy of the San Jacinto Museum of History.*

of their wits, Anglo settlers fled in disorder toward the Sabine River. Colonist John A. Quitman recorded: "The panic had done its work. The houses are all deserted. There are several thousands of women and children in the woods on both sides of the Sabine, without supplies or money."

Texians remembered the rush to the Louisiana border as the "Runaway Scrape," the "Great Runaway," or the "Sabine Shoot." Whatever they called it, the wild exodus was a nightmare of terror and suffering for the civilians. On April 15, Quitman observed: "We must have met at least 100 women and children, and every where along the road were wagons, furniture, and provisions abandoned."

The volatile Texas weather contributed to the misery. The spring rains of 1836 were the heaviest in memory. Roads, still little more that trails, became swamps. One of Houston's recruits described conditions:

> Delicate women trudged . . . from day to day until their shoes were literally worn out, then continued the journey with bare feet, lacerated and bleeding at almost every step. Their clothes were scant, and with no means of shelter from frequent drenching rains and bitter winds, they traveled on through the long days in wet and bedraggled apparel. . . . The Wet earth and angry sky offered no relief.

146

One woman and her two small children rode a horse that bolted at a swollen creek and plummeted into the torrent. Horrified refugees on the opposite bank could only watch as the deadly current swept under horse, mother, and youngsters.

Even when their operators worked around the clock, the few ferries could not accommodate the large volume of traffic. Dilue Rose, a young girl at the time, recalled, "fully five thousand people at [Lynch's] ferry. . . . Every one was trying to cross first and it was almost a riot."

At many streams women had to cross without the benefit of ferries. Settler S. F. Sparks recalled,

> the bottomlands were from a foot to waist deep in water. The younger and stouter women would take the feeble ones on their backs and shoulders and wade through water to dry land, set them down, and go back for another load, and continued until all were over.

It seemed only natural that slaves would take advantage of the turmoil and escape. Certainly contemporary accounts reveal that whites feared slave uprisings. Those same accounts, however, pay homage to those who stood by their masters. Rose recalled that although blacks outnumbered whites in her contingent, "there was no insubordination among them; they were loyal to their owners." In one crisis, "Uncle" Ned, an elderly black man, took charge: "He put white women and children in his wagon. It was large and had a canvas cover. The negro women and children he put in the [open] carts. Then he guarded the whole party until morning."

Tejanas also took part in the Sabine Shoot. Most were neutral, looking after their families and striving to keep out of harm's way until the storm subsided. But those married to Tejanos known to have cooperated with rebellious Texians had good reason to fear the wrath of Antonio López de Santa Anna. "Deaf" Smith's Tejana wife took to the road with her daughters because they were no longer safe in their San Antonio home. Neither was Josepha Seguín, wife of Erasmo and mother to Juan Seguín; she was the matriarch of one of Béxar's leading families. From the early days of Stephen F. Austin's first colony, she and her husband had been loyal friends of the Anglo settlers. During the 1835 Siege of Béxar, the Seguíns had supplied four thousand dollars' worth of food and provisions to the insurgent army. The family paid for its friendship in 1836 when Santa Anna's troops ransacked their ranch. Josepha and Erasmo fled northeastward with Texian civilians; Juan led a Tejano company in Houston's army. Following a long and perilous journey, during which Mexican soldiers appropriated most of their livestock, Doña Josepha and her family took refuge in San Augustine.

The Runaway Scrape proved even harder on Tejanas than on most. Escaping to the Anglo regions of East Texas, they entered a land that was geographically and culturally foreign to them, a land where few understood their language, and where—despite their contributions to the struggle—many despised them as "greasers."

The non-combatants endured dangers and hardships as harsh as those of the soldiers. The dearth of reliable records makes it impossible to know how many civilians fell victim to disease, mishap, or exposure during the Runaway Scrape, but the number must be in the hundreds. Texian Secretary of War Thomas Jefferson Rusk extoled the women who held their families together during the crisis:

> The men of Texas deserve much credit, but more was due the women. Armed men facing a foe could not but be brave; but the women, with their little children around them, without means of defense or power to resist, faced danger and death with unflinching courage.

The plight of civilian refugees both angered and inspired the men of Houston's army—wives and loved ones would lodge heavy in their minds as they prepared to unleash a full measure of revenge on the Mexicans.

The Road to Lynch's Ferry

Knowing he could not hold Gonzales with his meager forces, Sam Houston ordered the town burned and withdrew toward the Colorado River. He evacuated civilians from the settlement and then instructed his soldiers to leave no roof "large enough to shelter a Mexican's head."

On March 17, Houston reached Burnham's Ferry. The general soon realized, however, the site was indefensible. Instead, Houston burned the ferry and marched down the Colorado's east bank until reaching Beason's Crossing on March 19.

On March 21, Mexican General Joaquín Ramírez y Sesma's division pitched camp opposite Beason's Crossing. Texian volunteers urged Houston to attack the enemy across the river. But for six days Houston waited and watched. Ramírez y Sesma, unable to ford the swollen Colorado, did the same. Houston had recently received reinforcements, and his scouts reported that Ramírez y Sesma had about the same numbers that the rebels did. Texians eagerly awaited a fight, and Houston hinted that one was in the offing.

Then, on March 23, Houston received news that upset all his plans. Writing Secretary of War Thomas Jefferson Rusk, he bemoaned: "You know that I am not easily depressed, but before my God, since we parted, I have found the darkest hours of my past life." Houston wrote this on learning of James W. Fannin's defeat and capture. Accurately describing the indecisive

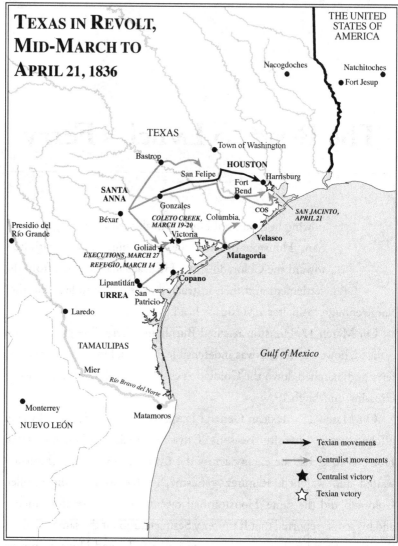

Map by Donald S. Frazier, Ph.D.

Goliad commander, the general lamented: "He is an ill-fated man." Houston ordered a withdrawal to San Felipe de Austin on the Brazos River.

The rebel army reached San Felipe on March 28. But spending only one night there, Houston ordered a retreat to Jared Groce's plantation some twenty miles upriver. The abandonment of San Felipe created a tempest in the ranks because it was the hub of Stephen F. Austin's original colony, and many believed it the most important point in Texas—one that Houston should defend at all cost. Instead, Houston burned it down.

Houston spent the following two weeks at the boggy campsite across the Brazos River from Groce's plantation; it proved the Valley Forge of the Texas Revolution. Groce turned his fine plantation house over to the army's surgeons for a hospital. Following weeks of constant exposure to the elements, many soldiers had fallen prey to various illnesses.

The army employed the time at Groce's to heal and learn the basics of linear combat. On April 11, two cannon arrived in camp, a gift from the citizens of Cincinnati, Ohio; the men dubbed them the "Twin Sisters." As the men drilled and regained their health, their confidence returned, but not their faith in Houston. All he had done was retreat. Would he ever stand and fight?

The interim Texas government was also losing patience with its timorous general. President David G. Burnet dispatched Secretary of War Rusk to deliver a scathing letter to Houston: "Sir: The enemy are laughing you to scorn. You must fight them. You must retreat no further. The country expects you to fight. The salvation of the country depends on your doing so."

On April 12, Houston broke camp at Groce's, crossed the Brazos, and headed eastward. He did not deign to reveal the army's destination. Many soldiers speculated that they were traveling toward the enemy; others suspected that they were bound for the Sabine River and shameful safety. Houston said nothing and rode on.

Historians have long pondered the question: What was Houston thinking? U.S. General Edmund P. Gaines had established Fort Jessup and Camp Sabine on the east bank of the Sabine River. Houston maintained communications with Gaines and apprised him of his movements and intentions. U.S. President Andrew Jackson had authorized Gaines to engage if Antonio López de Santa Anna crossed the Neches River. Houston became intent on retreating into East Texas. If he could lure Santa Anna across the Neches, it would trigger U.S. intervention and guarantee victory. This is what I have termed Houston's "American Strategy."

In 1845, Houston admitted the following:

> In the course of two days [at Gonzales] I received the lamentable information that Colonel Travis and his noble compatriots had succumbed to overwhelming numbers and had been brutally slaughtered. I immediately sent a courier to Colonel Fannin ordering him to destroy all his artillery that he could not remove and retreat to Victoria, and informed him of the fall of the Alamo. Deaf Smith having returned from a scout reported the enemy advancing. I then determined to retreat and get as near to Andrew Jackson and the old flag as I could.

Note that Houston made his determination at Gonzales. He obviously never intended to fight on the Colorado or on the Brazos. Did Houston lie to his men and government officials when he repeatedly reported that he intended to defend the Texian settlements? Yes, what other conclusion can one reasonably draw?

But let's not be too hard on Houston. Given his men's inexperience and ill-discipline, the enemy's numerical superiority, the lack of vital supplies, and his desire to add Texas to the federal union, the American Strategy probably was the most prudent option. But Houston failed to consider the fighting spirit of the rank-and-file. Texians had no intention of doing nothing while a Mexican dictator laid waste to all it had taken them fifteen years to build.

On April 16, the army continued to march eastward. The soldiers were abuzz for they approached a major crossroads—both literally and metaphorically. At the "Forks of the Road," one prong led north toward "Andrew Jackson and the old flag." The other led south toward Harrisburg and the enemy.

That night Secretary of War Rusk informed Houston that the following day the army would take the southern fork. Crestfallen, Houston ordered his staff to inform company commanders of Rusk's decision and that "in so doing he yielded to his own judgment in obedience to his superior."

On April 18, the rebel army arrived at a location across Buffalo Bayou from a smoldering Harrisburg. The Mexicans had just burned the settlement. Later that day, scouts Erastus "Deaf" Smith and Henry Karnes brought in a Mexican courier. He had carried documents that revealed that Santa Anna personally commanded a small detachment that was nearby. This was an opportunity too juicy to ignore.

Discovering Santa Anna's whereabouts, Houston also knew his adversary must travel via Lynch's Ferry to join his main force. If the rebels could arrive first, they might surprise His Excellency. At mid-morning on April 20, Houston's nine-hundred-man army reached Lynch's Ferry. No Mexican soldiers were in sight.

Houston had won the race and could choose his ground.

San Jacinto

When Antonio López de Santa Anna arrived at Lynch's Ferry on April 20, 1836, he received the shock of his life. The rebel army—the same rebel army he thought camped at Groce's Plantation—barred his route of march. Notwithstanding the objections of many of his subordinates, Santa Anna pitched camp on a boggy plain at the juncture of Buffalo Bayou and the San Jacinto River. His Excellency well knew the spot he was in. He dispatched a courier to General Martín Perfecto de Cos at Fort Bend with orders to bring with reinforcements with all possible speed. Dense woods bordered his position on one side, a marsh and lake enclosed the other. Less than five hundred yards separated the opposing forces—a grassy plain containing a deep basin lay between them. Moreover, Sam Houston had about nine hundred men; Santa Anna, seven hundred. For the first time, Texians enjoyed numerical superority.

Most of the Texian soldiers wished to press their advantage and urged Houston to attack immediately. Yet, the circumspect general only authorized a reconnaissance-in-force. Mounted Texian riflemen forced a small squadron of Mexican dragoons to withdraw. A larger force of Mexican cavalry returned the favor, forcing the Texian horses to retire. During the skirmish, the Mexicans almost captured Texas Secretary of War Thomas Jefferson Rusk, but Mirabeau B. Lamar boldly charged through to rescue him. Disobeying Houston's direct orders,

During the Battle of San Jacinto, *Tejanos* of Juan Seguín's company vault the Mexican barricades intent on revenge. *Courtesy of Gary Zaboly, illustrator,* An Altar for Their Sons: The Alamo and the Texas Revolution in Contemporary Newspaper Accounts.

several companies of rebel infantry rushed to support their beleaguered horsemen, who fell back under the fire of the Texian foot. The skirmish of April 20 accomplished little. Many of the Texians believed that Houston had been perfectly willing to leave his horsemen to their fate. As night fell, they wondered what the morrow would bring. Houston's inactivity appalled them. What would it require to force this weakling to fight?

On April 21, most Texians expected to attack at first light, but General Houston ordered that no one should disturb him and slept late that morning. About 9 AM, Cos arrived with 540 reinforcements, swelling Mexican ranks to 1,200 men. Houston's lethargy had squandered the numerical advantage. Watching the enemy reinforcements arrive on the field, the rebels were beside themselves with anger. How many more Mexicans would Houston allow to arrive before he unleashed them?

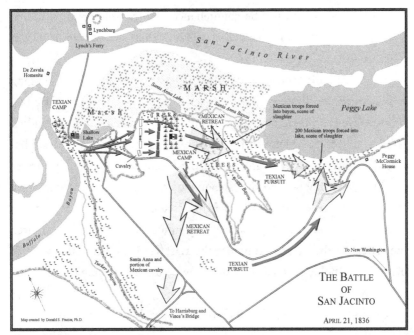

Map by Donald S. Frazier, Ph.D.

Later that morning, Houston met with his scouts who advised the destruction of Vince's Bridge over Sim's Bayou. Cos's reinforcements had previously used it to reach Santa Anna's camp. The Mexicans already outnumbered the rebels, and it was a safe bet that more were on the way. The demolition of the bridge would, the scouts hoped, hamper the arrival of those enemy units. Houston duly issued orders for the dismantling of the bridge, and Erastus "Deaf" Smith and a squad of volunteers carried them out with alacrity.

Bridges were much on Houston's mind that day. Around noon, he called a council of war. During that meeting, the general urged the construction of a "floating bridge" across Buffalo Bayou to enable the army's retreat. The proposition utterly flabbergasted his lieutenants. They were here; Santa Anna was here, and although the Texians no longer enjoyed numerical superiority, these were the best odds they were likely to have. The other council members insisted that Houston "must fight, that a further delay would not be countenanced by the soldiers or officers." Finally, the dejected commander spat, "Fight then and be damned!" Not exactly words to inspire confidence.

What explains Houston's diffident behavior? He was likely clinging to his American Strategy, realizing that a battle on the banks of Buffalo Bayou—even if a victory—would not accomplish his long-standing political objective, which was to bring Texas into the United States. That would require a battle fought east of the Neches River. The advance of the Mexican army beyond that stream would trigger the participation of General Edward P. Gaines's U.S. Army, assure Mexican defeat, confirm Texas independence, and guarantee early annexation. But all that required the retreat of the Texian army into the East Texas timber country. With his political hopes dashed, Houston bowed to the inevitable and called the army to arms.

By 4:30, the time that the rebels began their advance toward the enemy camp, the long shadows of late afternoon fell across the field. The delay paid unexpected dividends. In the Mexican camp, many of Santa Anna's officers complained that their men were dead on their feet. The *soldados* of Santa Anna's detachment had been up all night erecting barricades and standing guard against a night attack; Cos's men had marched all night and were all but spent. The Mexicans had stood on the alert all day. They had expected an attack a first light, then mid-morning, then noon. But they detected no movement in the rebel camp. If Houston had not attacked by now, it was unlikely he would do so late in the day with so little daylight left. Santa Anna ordered his men to stand down. Exhausted, they collapsed into their bedrolls.

Across the field, the rebels advanced in a two-column formation, with the Twin Sisters in the middle and mounted riflemen screened behind an oak grove on the Mexican left. Nineteen *Tejanos* led by Béxar native Juan Seguín marched alongside their Anglos comrades. In their hatbands they had placed pieces of cardboard least in the heat of battle Texians mistake them for the enemy. The Texian cavalry now boasted a new commander.

Lamar, a private the day before, had so distinguished himself that Houston awarded him with the cavalry command.

Topography favored the Texians. As they marched toward the Mexican camp, they sank into the large basin that concealed them from view. Climbing out of the depression, they quickly formed into a battle line. The training at Groce's camp was paying off. Even then, the tall prairie grass blocked them from view. The rebels advanced within musket range of the makeshift barricades before the Mexicans saw them.

Disoriented soldados stumbled to their feet, but already the rebels were among them. Surprise was complete. One of their officers described his men as a "panic-stricken herd." Shouting their battle cry, "Remember the Alamo—Remember Goliad," the Texians swept the Mexican camp. The actual battle lasted only eighteen minutes, but the slaughter lasted much longer.

Avenging the defeats at the Alamo and Goliad, Texas soldiers committed atrocities as reprehensible as those of the Mexicans. Soldados cast down their muskets and threw up their hands, all the while shouting "Me no Alamo; Me no Goliad." It availed them nothing, the Texians gunned them down. Ashamed, Texian surgeon Nicholas Labadie bemoaned that he had "witnessed acts of cruelty which I forbear to recount."

The bloodletting continued. Texas rebels killed until they were too exhausted to kill anymore. Some 650 Mexicans fell victim to their rage. About 700 escaped the carnage, only to fall captive later. Miraculously, Texian casualties were nine killed and thirty wounded. Among the wounded was General Houston—a canister round had smashed his ankle to powder.

Texians soldiers searched franticly among the prisoners for Santa Anna, but found nothing. Nor could they identify his body among the slain. "His Excellency," it seemed, had escaped.

The Treaties of Velasco

A ntonio López de Santa Anna galloped off the field at San Jacinto on the fastest horse he could find. His destination was Vince's Bridge, which Erastus "Deaf" Smith and his fellow scouts had demolished previously that day. Unable to cross Sims's Bayou—"His Excellency" could not swim and was deathly afraid of water—he abandoned his horse and spent a miserable night hovering in the swamp.

On April 22, rebel search parties scoured the countryside for Mexican soldiers who had escaped the battle. One of these discovered Santa Anna crouching in the weeds and took him into custody. Because he had been careful to strip himself of all signs of status, the members of the search party did not know their prisoner's identity. Not until they observed other Mexican prisoners paying him deference, did the Texians realize that they had captured a high-ranking officer. Only later did they learn that they had bagged the highest-ranking Mexican of them all.

Texian soldiers hauled Santa Anna before the wounded Sam Houston. Through an interpreter, Santa Anna complimented his rival: "That man may consider himself born to no common destiny who has conquered the Napoleon of the West. And now it remains for him to be generous to the vanquished."

Houston snarled: "You should have remembered that at the Alamo." He, however, did not execute Santa Anna—although, to be sure, many of his soldiers urged him to. Ever the politician, he realized that a

161

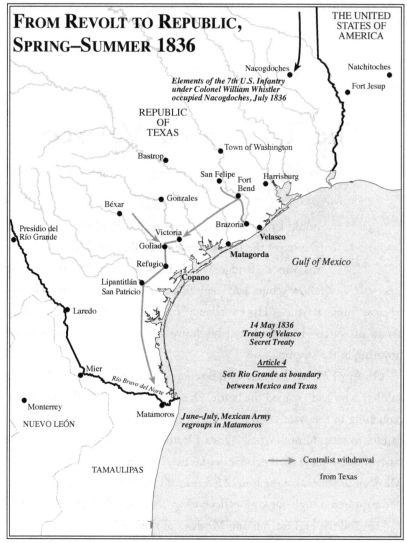

FROM REVOLT TO REPUBLIC,
SPRING–SUMMER 1836

THE UNITED STATES OF AMERICA

Nacogdoches

Elements of the 7th U.S. Infantry
under Colonel William Whistler
occupied Nacogdoches, July 1836

Natchitoches

Fort Jesup

REPUBLIC
OF
TEXAS

Town of Washington

Bastrop

San Felipe   Harrisburg
        Fort
        Bend

Béxar   Gonzales

Presidio del
Río Grande

Victoria   Brazoria

Goliad   Velasco

Refugio   Matagorda

Lipantitlán   Copano
San Patricio

Gulf of Mexico

Laredo

14 May 1836
Treaty of Velasco
Secret Treaty

Article 4
Sets Rio Grande as boundary
between Mexico and Texas

Mier   Río Bravo del Norte

Monterrey

NUEVO LEÓN

Matamoros   June–July, Mexican Army
regroups in Matamoros

TAMAULIPAS

Centralist withdrawal
from Texas

Map by Donald S. Frazier, Ph.D.

captive tyrant could be a powerful diplomatic card. Furthermore, Houston
feared that Generals Vicente Filisola and José de Urrea, who still greatly
outnumbered his force, might launch their own attacks. Texians has achieved
a minor miracle; their general doubted they could do it twice. In return for
his life, Santa Anna dispatched orders for Filisola to retire to Victoria.

In consultation with his subordinates, Filisola had already made that decision independent of Santa Anna's orders. On April 23, news of Santa Anna's defeat and capture reached Filisola at Old Fort. On April 25, he called a council of war at Elizabeth Powell's tavern. Urrea and the other generals present agreed to establish communications with the Mexican government. At that juncture, the movement was a strategic withdrawal. Filisola had every intention of continuing the campaign after the army had regrouped and refitted at Victoria.

Now that the Mexican army was in full withdrawal, Texas officials could take advantage of the opportunity that having the Mexican dictator in their clutches provided. On May 14, 1836, ad interim president David G. Burnet and Santa Anna signed two treaties at Velasco. The parties agreed to release the public treaty immediately. The other, a secret covenant, would go into effect only when both sides had satisfied the terms of the public treaty.

On May 26, Filisola, in accordance with the public treaty, began the retreat of the Mexican army toward Victoria. Yet, what awaited the Mexican *soldados* was worse than anything they had experienced. During the march, it began to rain. By the time they reached the San Bernard River, the boggy ground made any kind of travel all but impossible. The Mexicans recalled the area as the *"Mar de Lodo"*—the Sea of Mud. Men sank to their knees; each step became an ordeal. The men began to unload everything that weighed them down: shells, round shot, canister, and even entire boxes of nails. To make matter worse, many came down with dysentery. The Mar de Lodo sapped what morale the army had left. Filisola always maintained that it was not the rebels who defeated the once-proud Army of Operations, but the "inclemency of the season . . . made still more unattractive by the rigor of the climate and the character of the land." Consequently, Filisola retreated not only to Victoria, but also across the Rio Grande. Many in the army condemned his actions, but there was little doubt that he had made the prudent choice.

Fearing that President Burnet might release Santa Anna, rogue elements of the Texas army took the dictator into their own custody—all of this against the orders of Burnet and his cabinet. The army steadfastly refused to follow the commands of the civilian authorities. It became a real possibility that a military gang might soon take control of the government. The actions of theses firebrands prevented Burnet and his officials from carrying out the terms of the secret treaty.

But it was a moot point. On May 20, the Mexican Congress declared all of Santa Anna's acts done while a captive null and void. Both governments violated the Velasco treaties. Notwithstanding Santa Anna's hasty assurances, the government of Mexico refused to recognize the independence of Texas Republic, nor acknowledge its southern border as the Rio Grande. As far as Mexicans officials were concerned, San Jacinto was merely an unfortunate setback. Tejas was, they asserted, still part of the Mexican federation. A state in rebellion perhaps, but nonetheless one they would reconquer as soon as circumstances permitted. The war was over—at least for the moment—but hostilities were not.

The independence of the Texas Republic was far from secure.

Outline of the Treaties of Velasco

The public treaty specified that:

- hostilities would cease;
- Santa Anna would never again take up arms against Texas;
- Mexican forces would retire to a point south of the Rio Grande;
- Mexicans would return all Texian property they had confiscated;
- the belligerents would exchange prisoners on an equal basis;
- officials of the Republic of Texas would return Santa Anna to Mexico with all convenient speed;
- and, the Texas army would not approach closer than five leagues to the retreating Mexicans.

The secret treaty specified that:

- the Texas government assure the immediate release of Santa Anna with the understanding that he attempt to procure acknowledgment of Texas independence from the Mexican government;
- Santa Anna swear never again to make war against Texas;
- Santa Anna give orders for withdrawal of Mexican troops from Texas;
- Santa Anna work to have the Mexican cabinet receive a Texas mission favorably;
- and, Santa Anna would work for a treaty of commerce and limits specifying that the Texas boundary not lie south of the Rio Grande.

REPUBLIC

May 1836 – February 1846

Starting Over

ollowing the victory at San Jacinto, many who had damned Sam Houston as a cowardly drunk now praised him as the savior of Texas. Even so, the triumph on Buffalo Bayou displeased widow Peggy McCormick, who owned the land where the soldiers had clashed. She believed the presence of hundreds of decomposing enemy corpses devalued her property. A few days after the battle, she demanded that Houston remove the putrefied bodies. To appease the angry matron, the general appealed to her sense of posterity.

"Madam, your land will be famed in history as the classic spot upon which the glorious victory of San Jacinto was gained."

She was not impressed.

"To the devil with your glorious history! Take off your stinking Mexicans."

Her demands, however, went unheeded, and for years afterward, the sun-bleached bones of unburied Mexican *soldados* littered the McCormick homestead.

Although McCormick was less than thrilled about one result of the victory at San Jacinto, the news left most other Texians exultant. Mary S. Helm, a painfully proper Episcopalian-turned-refugee, remarked that the members of her party were so excited that they "all turned shouting Methodist." She recalled that people reacted differently: "some danced; some laughed; some clapped their hands." For fellow wanderer Mary Ann

For many Runaway Scrape evacuees, the trip back home proved the greatest ordeal. In this grim image, an alligator attacks and kills Texian settler Grey B. King while his family watches in horror. *Courtesy of Gary Zaboly, illustrator,* An Altar for Their Sons: The Alamo and the Texas Revolution in Contemporary Newspaper Accounts.

Zuber the notification that her son, William, had fallen at San Jacinto dampened her enthusiasm. Her grief was so severe she could not force herself to begin the trip home. The next day another messenger arrived fresh from the battlefield. The first report had been false; William was alive and well. A relieved and euphoric mother quickly joined in the celebrations.

After San Jacinto, Texian families could indeed make their way home, but their troubles were far from over. The Mexicans were no longer a threat but nature remained unrelenting. For many, the return trip was the hardest. Fearing Antonio López de Santa Anna's vengeance, Erasmo and Josepha Seguín had fled their San Antonio home. Receiving reports of the victory at San Jacinto, they traveled from San Augustine to Nacogdoches where they fell victim to fever. Far from home, without friends, and "prostrated on their couches," the lack of cash compelled the Seguíns "to part, little by little, with their valuables and articles of clothing." When at last they reached home, they found that the Mexicans had sacked their ranch and pilfered or scattered their cattle.

Likewise, the settlers of Gonzales returned to burned homes and ravaged fields. Robert Hall was among the first to return to the gutted town site and recorded the scene: "The town of Gonzales had been almost entirely destroyed; there was only one little house remaining. I looked into an old corn crib, and there laid a dead man. He had been killed with arrows." Clearly, Mexicans were not the only enemies. On the frontier, hostile Indians frequently moved in to ransack settlements as soon as residents moved out. People returning to their homes needed to be wary to avoid the fate of the unidentified man Hall found in the corn crib.

The King family of San Felipe traveled through the treacherous East Texas swamps. Quicksand was a constant danger, and when the wind rose, the refugees were buffeted by high waves. Worst of all, the waters were infested with alligators. Grey B. King, having secured his wife and children on dry land, swam back to retrieve the horses. Twelve-year-old Dilue Rose described what happened next:

> He had gotten nearly across, when a large alligator appeared. Mrs. King saw it first above the water and screamed. The alligator struck her husband with its tail and he went under water. There were several men present, and they fired their guns at the animal, but it did no good. It was not in their power to rescue Mr. King.

After a short stay at Harrisburg, the widow King and her three children moved to Galveston.

Few sacrificed as much as Fanny Menefee Sutherland did. With her husband George with the army and her eldest son dead inside the Alamo, she had to fend for herself and four young children. She never felt abandoned, however, explaining: "the Lord supported me and was on our side for I may boldly say the Lord fought our battles. . . . Mr. Sutherland's horse was killed under him [at San Jacinto], but the Lord preserved his life and brought him back to his family." Following a frantic search, George Sutherland finally located his wife and children among other Runaway Scrape refugees at the mouth of the Sabine River and took his family home.

But their homecoming produced only more heartache. Like many Texas families, the Sutherlands returned to discover much of what they had left behind gone or destroyed. Retreating soldiers had burned the family warehouse and one of their residences.

Texas independence cost many settlers virtually everything—homes, crops, animals, and loved ones. Nevertheless, in the wake of San Jacinto, most looked toward the future with remarkable confidence. They accepted their losses with stoic resignation and a strong sense of Christian grace. Fanny Sutherland might have spoken for them all: "If we can have peace and can have preaching, I won't care for the loss of what property is gone."

Terror at Parker's Fort

A sense of mission drove Elder John Parker. He judged that God demanded that he create a new Zion in the wilderness, a place where about thirty family and followers could worship by their own lights. They had traveled far to find their Promised Land; first Virginia, then Tennessee, then Illinois. Wherever they wandered, however, the Parkers failed to fit in. Elder John, his sons, Benjamin, Silas, and James, along with their wives and children were members of the Pilgrim Predestinarian Baptist Church, a closed-communion, "hard-shell" sect. Elder John and his kin worshiped a loving God, but one who loved only those who comprehended the gospels exactly as they did. The rest, they preached, were bound for the fiery pit—a doctrine that did not endear them to their less-zealous neighbors.

The Parkers arrived in Texas in 1833. Elder John's clan finally settled near the headwaters of the Navasota River. There they constructed a stockade fort against hostile Indians. Completed in March 1834, Parker's Fort enclosed some four acres. Most of the residents were part of the extended family of Elder John and his wife, Sarah.

They did not participate in the Texas Revolution; their stern dogma did not allow them to fight for any cause other than their own. During the spring of 1836, when the Mexican army approached, they abandoned their fort. Yet, with news of San Jacinto, they quickly reclaimed their abode. Few Texians had settled the area; only two or three other families

173

"Comanches Coming out of Woods." Richard Petri, a German immigrant, was one of the few artists who painted native subjects from life. The warrior he depicted here would have resembled those who ravaged Fort Parker. *Courtesy of the Center for American History, University of Texas at Austin.*

inhabited the region. The Parkers were on their own, which was just the way they liked it.

But on the morning of May 19, 1836, the Parkers received unwelcomed callers. Most of the Parker men were working the fields, which lay out of sight of the fort. Six of the men and all the women and children remained inside the compound. Around midmorning, a large party of mounted Indians—perhaps as many as a hundred—suddenly appeared outside the gates. They were a mixed bunch, mostly young Comanche warriors, along with a few hostile Kitsais, Wichitas, and Caddos. Strangely, these warriors rode beneath a white flag of truce. Benjamin, Elder John's eldest son, dealt with them outside the walls.

Returning to the fort, Benjamin told his younger brother, Silas, that these Indians were antagonistic. They had demanded that the whites provide water and deliver a beef for them to slaughter. Outnumbered as they were, Benjamin and Silas agreed that their best chance lay in further negotiation. Although their wives and children begged them not to, Benjamin and Silas left the safety of the walls and returned to deliberate.

Benjamin evidently informed the raiders that he had no beeves to spare. Infuriated, several of the Comanches ran him through with their lances. Silas dashed for the fort, but the Indians rode him down and killed him. Two more men fought to defend the gates, but the warriors forced their way through and slaughtered them as well. The Indians then flooded into the compound.

Panic swept Parker's Fort. Elder John and his wife Sarah—who all the clan called "Granny"—attempted an escape. Mounted on fleet war ponies, Indians overtook them. They lanced Elder John Parker, scalped him, stripped off his trousers, and then cut off his genitals. Capturing "Granny" Parker, the Indians stripped her and pinned her to the ground with a lance. Then, they repeatedly gang-raped the elderly woman. Other women inside the fort received similar abuse.

Hearing the commotion back at the fort, the Parker men who had been tilling their fields came running, rifles in hand. Seeing armed reinforcements approaching, the Indians lashed their ponies and galloped away. In their wake, they left five dead men and several wounded women. Two of them would later die. Remarkably, one who did not was "Granny" Parker. With her own hands, she pried the lance from her flesh. She sprang from hardy stock. Defying all odds and predictions, the old woman survived.

The raiders absconded with five captives: seventeen-year-old Rachel Plummer and James, her infant son; the forty-year-old Elizabeth Kellogg; and the children of Silas and Lucy Parker, John and Cynthia Ann, ages six and nine.

The raiders pushed their ponies frantically until they were confident that they had outdistanced pursuers. They then enjoyed a midnight victory dance. Their raid had been a complete success. They would return to their camps brandishing scalps taken in battle, their status among their tribes enhanced. Most impressive, they had slain and raped while suffering no losses of their own. Following the ritual dancing, they stripped the two women captives and tortured them. This was a form of mental conditioning, what one authority called a "rite of total humiliation." It was the fate of the women to be slaves. If the Indians could terrorize them, break their spirit, and kill all hope, they would prove more pliable. Then, the raiders threw the screaming naked women to the ground and every raider took turns raping them. The ordeal of Plummer and Kellogg continued until daylight. The warriors were careful to rape the mothers in full view of their children. Again, this was simply part of the humiliation rite. If children learned that their mothers were helpless to defend either themselves or them, they would learn to rely on the tribe for all their needs. The youngsters suffered no harm; they were young enough assimilate fully into Comanche society. At dawn, in the time-honored practice of the Plains Indians, the raiding party split up and rode their separate ways.

Plummer suffered Comanche captivity for twenty-one months. During that time, she bore a child, but not wishing to bother with a newborn, the warriors killed it. Finally, an American living in Santa Fe ransomed her. She returned to Texas but died soon afterward. She never saw James again.

The Caddoans hauled Kellogg to the Red River. There they sold her to a band of Delaware Indians. In December 1836, that tribe sold her back to President Sam Houston for $150.00.

The raid on Parker's Fort was a vicious introduction. Although the Comanche Indians had terrorized Spanish and Mexican settlers for generations, this was the first time that Anglo Texians had encountered the "Lords of the South Plains." The foray was but the opening salvo, the first of hundreds just as destructive. For the next four decades, Texians and Comanches engaged in a bitter race war. Both sides fought without stint, without consideration for age or gender. White settlers came to dread full moons, when it became bright enough to ride and raid under the luminous glare of what they called a "Comanche Moon." At its beginning, the Republic of Texas inherited Indian wars. Given the social protocols of the combatants, it would be a fight to the finish, a vicious brawl that wrought the virtual destruction of the Comanches and the savage brutalization of the Texians.

Captain Burton and His "Horse Marines"

While Comanches terrorized Parker's Fort in the north, on the southern frontier, Mexicans remained a cause for concern. The wounded Major General Sam Houston convalesced in New Orleans. Texians were fortunate that a talented understudy waited in the wings. From May to October 1836, former Secretary of War Thomas Jefferson Rusk stood in as commander-in-chief and with it came the rank of brigadier general. He led the Republic's army southward, trailing—at a respectful distance—fleeing Mexican forces. Rusk was not keen for a fight but wanted to make certain that General Vicente Filisola kept his pledge to withdraw his troops south of the Rio Grande.

The Sea of Mud had wrung all the fight out of the Mexican Army, but Rusk knew that the Mexican privateers still remained a threat. He feared the enemy might launch an amphibious attack at some point along the Texas coastal bend. To guard against such a possibility, he dispatched thirty Texas Rangers under Captain Isaac Watts Burton on May 29, 1836, to patrol the zone between the mouth of the Guadalupe River and Mission Bay.

Burton's Rangers were keen to carry out their mission but were unfamiliar with the coastal region. They required help from locals who knew the lay of the land. General Rusk assigned three Refugio colonists to ride with the mounted squadron to act as guides. They were Nicholas Lambert, Walter Lambert, and John Keating.

177

On June 2, Captain Burton received reports that a suspicious schooner lay anchored in Copano Bay. Because the vessel flew no colors, he could not be sure which nation it served. The rangers mounted up and rode the twenty miles to the coast. Burton concealed his men behind the dunes and bushes and ordered that they build no campfires. Like the crew of the ship, he wanted to conceal his identity.

Through his spyglass, Burton made out the craft's name: *Watchman*. But for whom did it watch? Captain Burton had two of his men stow their weapons and make distress signals. Aboard the *Watchman*, sailors hoisted the star-spangled banner and the Texian star-and-stripes ensign. That struck Burton as incongruous. Normally, a ship would fly one national standard or the other—but *both*? The captain instructed his men to make no response. This seabird might be flying under false colors. Burton's wariness was warranted. Several moments passed. Then the deceptive banners came down and the Mexican tri-color ascended. The two signal men feigned excitement and motioned the crew to send a boat to save them.

The rangers lay in wait. The ship's launch crunched into beach sand, but the two distraught signalmen had disappeared. Puzzled, the *Watchman*'s captain and four crewmen made their way inland. Then, the rangers sprang from the brush, fell upon the startled seamen, beat them down, and took them prisoner. Because Burton had allowed the launch crew to journey so far ashore, those still aboard did not observe the capture of their shipmates.

The captain hatched a daring scheme. He ordered four of his men to guard their prisoners. Burton and sixteen rangers then boarded the launch and rowed toward the *Watchman*. Because the Mexican mariners were expecting their captain's prompt return, they suspected nothing out of the ordinary. The rangers pulled alongside, scrambled up the side, and overwhelmed the astonished crew. The Texians placed the Mexican captain and his crew in chains and confined them in the hold. Burton was delighted to find the ship heavily laden with supplies intended for the use of Santa Anna's army—provisions Texian soldiers sorely needed. The *Watchman* might now hoist the Texian ensign with no taint of deception.

When Texian officials learned of Burton's coup, they could hardly believe their good fortune. They dispatched orders for him to sail the schooner to Velasco. But at the onset of rough weather Captain Burton delayed his journey. He and his men were rangers, not sailors. Having captured a rich prize, he did not wish to lose it to the elements.

Burton's prudence proved a godsend. On June 19, two Mexican schooners, *Comanche* and *Fanny Butler*, dropped anchor in Copano Bay. If the ruse had succeeded once, the Mexicans might fall for it again. Raising the Mexican flag, Burton used impolite persuasion to convince the *Watchman's* captain to signal his fellow officers. Burton, acting through his prisoner, brazenly invited the Mexican captains aboard to "take a glass of grog." When they arrived on deck, Burton calmly took them prisoner, and then his rangers rowed out to take possession of their ships and crews—all that without firing a shot. Sadly, existing documents do not indicate whether the captains of the *Fanny Butler* and the *Comanche* ever received their glass of grog.

Like the *Watchman*, the other captured schooners were bursting with supplies. On June 22, all three ships departed Copano Bay bound for Velasco. Arriving safe in port, the vessels then sailed to Galveston Island for condemnation procedures. The cargo was a windfall for the penniless Texas regime. The total came to more than $25,000 worth of bread, beans, beef jerky, rice, and pickled pork. Perhaps even more beneficial, the bonanza also included cartridges, bayonets, gunpowder, and "Brown Bess" muskets. A grateful nation promoted Captain Burton to major.

Even in the United States, the exploits of Burton and his rangers thrilled and amused. A Kentucky native, Edward J. Wilson, had traveled to Texas to fight as a volunteer but now took up his pen to fire off an article for one of his state's leading newspapers. With tongue fixed firmly in cheek, he noted: "On yesterday [reports arrived] of the capture of three Mexican vessels by a troop of horses—these you will call 'Horse Marines' I suppose."

The moniker stuck. And although few remember them nowadays, Captain Burton and his "Horse Marines" helped set the standard for Texas courage and audacity.

Transition:
The Summer of 1836

uring the summer of 1836, Texas experienced something
approaching a demographic tidal wave. As news of San
Jacinto traveled across the Sabine River, many U.S.
citizens who had previously hesitated to immigrate now
flooded into the fledgling republic. Soon newcomers outnumbered
Stephen F. Austin's old contract colonists. The influx of U.S. settlers,
none of whom were beholden to Austin's vision, soon created a shift
in political power—one not entirely welcomed by established Texian
elites.

Overseeing this chaotic transition was Interim President David G.
Burnet. The people of Texas had not elected him. Rather, the delegates at
the Washington Independence Convention had selected him. Even then
his support was not overwhelming: the vote had been twenty-nine to
twenty-three. Burnet labored under no illusions. The front-runners for the
presidency, Stephen F. Austin, Sam Houston, and William H. Wharton,
were absent from the convention, which was the only reason delegates
had considered him in the first place. His legitimacy was insecure, his
mandate paper thin, and his status shaky.

Understanding the tenuousness of his position, Burnet advanced
no policies. He did not wish to repeat the mistakes of his predecessor,
Governor Henry Smith, and appear hungry for power. Instead, he handled
difficulties as they appeared.

181

During the summer of 1836, ad interim President David G. Burnett faced numerous challenges: an unruly Texian army, an empty treasury, questions concerning the fate of Santa Anna, and the lack of support from most Texian citizens. *Courtesy of the Prints and Photograph Collection, Center for American History, the University of Texas at Austin.*

He had plenty of those. Burnet's biggest problem was the disruptive elements inside the Texian army. Following San Jacinto, hundreds of U.S. volunteers flocked to Texas. To their annoyance, they discovered Antonio López de Santa Anna was a prisoner; the Mexican army had retreated; and the fighting, for the moment anyway, was finished. Even so, Texian leaders expected Mexicans to launch a new campaign and so welcomed the newcomers into their ranks.

By the Treaties of Velasco, Burnet had agreed to release Santa Anna. Yet, when Texians learned of the terms they became infuriated. They, along with some members of Burnet's own cabinet, called for the dictator's execution for atrocities he had committed at the Alamo and Goliad. Notwithstanding the hue and cry, Burnet booked Santa Anna a cabin aboard the *Invincible*, a Texas Navy ship bound for Veracruz. Before it could depart, however, 250 volunteers under Thomas Green arrived. Not only did they seize the ship, Green further demanded Burnet's immediate resignation. Fearing for his well-being, the *Invincible*'s captain refused to depart without Green's consent. Temporarily, stymied, Burnet ordered Santa Anna brought ashore and imprisoned at Quintana. Many Texas army officers threatened to execute Santa Anna on their own—the Treaties of Velasco be damned—and impeach Burnet for treason.

In July, Santa Anna called on U.S. President Andrew Jackson to intervene. Yet, the Mexican Congress had disavowed both Treaties of Velasco and given notice that it would never recognize any act Santa Anna made while a prisoner. Consequently, Jackson took no further action believing it would prove fruitless. Meanwhile, Santa Anna sat under close confinement, daily fearing that the insubordinate rabble might take matters into their own hands and string him up.

In addition to insubordinate soldiers who ignored civilian authorities, Texas faced financial ruin. The treasury was empty. Furthermore, the interim government had neglected to implement any system of taxation. The government defaulted on Burnet's salary. It became so bad that he could not provide for his family. To keep body and soul together, the embattled executive had to sell two of his household slaves. Hoping to earn some money to fill the nation's coffers, Burnet called upon this cabinet to sell land script in New York. Yet, when bids dropped to only one cent per acre, he abandoned the scheme.

The Texas Republic was in complete turmoil. The government could not pay its soldiers, who ran wild. Nor could it even reimburse its officials, who went hungry. Texian civilians, bunched in fetid river bottoms or plodding back to charred cabins, were in no mood to mind proclamations from a man who had proven utterly impotent to prevent the calamities that plagued them. In an attempt to gain some control over the army and prevent a military clique from overthrowing the civilian administration, Burnet dispatched Secretary of War Mirabeau B. Lamar to replace Thomas Jefferson Rusk. Felix Huston, a U.S. volunteer leader who had only just arrived in Texas, protested the administration's "interference." The soldiers saw no reason to obey the orders of mere politicians.

When Lamar arrived in camp, Rusk called for a popular vote. Despite the troops overwhelming support of Rusk, Lamar blithely continued to issue orders as commanding general. Just as blithely, the independent volunteers (by a vote of 1,500 to 179) chose to ignore him. Huston and other officers finally persuaded Lamar to step aside. It had been a humiliating spectacle for Lamar, Burnet, and the rule of law.

Burnet could read the handwriting on the wall. No one had any regard for him or the interim regime. Somewhat disingenuously given the state of affairs, he announced that his administration had restored order sufficiently for the people to establish a regular government—one actually elected by the people. On July 23, 1836, President Burnet issued a proclamation calling an election for the first Monday in September. Texians rejoiced. At last, they could boast a leader of their own choosing.

As for Burnet's departure? There was not a damp eye in all of Texas.

The First Monday in September 1836

Having enjoyed the dubious charms of provisional and ad interim governments, Texians greatly anticipated a regular government, one with elected representatives responsive to the will of the people. They viewed the September election as the first real manifestation of independence from Mexico. In addition to the election of officials, voters were to consider two other issues. Voters deliberated the question of granting authority to Congress to amend the Constitution—the one just six months old. Voters also weighed in on the issue of annexation to the United States. This last question was a straw poll, an unofficial ballot conducted as a test of opinion.

A slate of candidates quickly appeared. Henry Smith's friends placed the former governor's name in contention. It appeared that they did so in an effort to hide his activities under the provisional government. Even so, many could remember his tenure and the disasters it had wrought. Many mentioned William H. Wharton as a possible candidate, but he insisted he had no interest in running. His supporters tried to put Thomas Jefferson Rusk forward, but he would not hear of it. Branch T. Archer consented to have his name placed in the mix, but his heart was never in it; his was never a serious candidacy.

One could not say that of Stephen F. Austin. The old *empresario*, who had done so much to shape the destiny of Texas, made it clear that he remained eager to steer the ship of state. Notwithstanding his many

All of Sam Houston's portraits are staged and formal—except this one. Here is the candidate Texians saw on the stump. The wry grin, air of confidence, and twinkle in his eye combined to make him irresistible to voters. *Courtesy of the DRT Library Collection, San Antonio, Texas.*

services, a black cloud hung over his bid for office. In the eyes of many voters, his long association with his business partner and land speculator Samuel May Williams had sullied his public standing. Others charged that he had abandoned Texas during the Revolution and fled to safety, hardly fair in light of all the good service he had provided as an agent. One misinformed critic insisted that Austin had done nothing in the United States but "eat fine dinners and drink wine." Despite all of the abuse, Austin explained his motive for standing for office to Rusk: "I have consented to this for only one reason, which is that I believe I can be of material service in procuring the annexation of Texas to the U.S. should the people here wish it, as I have no doubt they do."

One candidate was prominent in his absence. In the wake of the almost-miraculous victory at San Jacinto, Sam Houston was easily the most popular person in Texas. But he remained in New Orleans, recovering from the serious ankle wound that he received on April 21. Many predicted that he would never recover. Moreover, the general had expressed no interest in throwing his hat into the ring. Austin emerged as the only significant contender.

Unusually, party loyalties played no part in the race. The Declaration of Independence in March and victory at San Jacinto in April had rendered the old War and Peace parties entirely irrelevant. Before the war, Austin and Wharton were bitter rivals. Yet, when Austin became an advocate of independence, the source of their antagonism vanished. Working together as agents, the former adversaries actually became fast friends. As events unfolded, the reconciliation between Austin and Wharton greatly influenced the tenor of Texas politics.

But then, Houston surprised Austin as much as he had Antonio López de Santa Anna. A mere eleven days before the balloting, he entered the race. Historians still contemplate his change of heart. They know he had written Rusk, who assured him of his support. It is unlikely, however, that Rusk's patronage in and of itself would have convinced Houston to run.

On the first Monday in September, Texians turned out to cast their ballots in record numbers. In the returns, "Ol' Sam Jacinto" polled 5,119 votes (77%) to 743 (13%) for Smith and 587 (10%) for Austin. Austin must have felt humiliated; Smith had formally withdrawn from the race, but he still garnered more votes than the empresario. Archer received a few votes here and there, but not enough to mention or matter. Austin's era had passed.

President-elect Houston sought unity. In an effort to achieve it, he appointed Austin as secretary of state and Smith as secretary of the treasury. Mirabeau B. Lamar won the post of vice president with little opposition. Rusk received placement as secretary of war, James Pinckney Henderson served as attorney general, and Rhoads Fisher won appointment as secretary of the navy.

Texians ratified the Constitution, but denied Congress the power to amend it. These were people who were highly suspicious of government, even one of their own. As for the straw poll regarding the question of U.S. annexation, voters approved the notion 3,277 to 91.

What a difference a year made. Had the election taken place in September 1835 instead of September 1836, Austin would have won in a landslide. Yet, in the interim he had been gone from Texas performing service as an agent; he had led no glorious charges astride a white stallion. It was a classic case of out of sight, out of mind. Although he lamented the outcome, David G. Burnet well understood the reason for Houston's victory:

> Genl. Houston is beyond all question the President elect, he has beat my worthy friend, Austin, the pioneer of pioneers in Texas, as much as the splendor of military fame (no matter how acquired) excels the mild luster of meditative and intellectual worth.

The constitution stipulated that the victor of September's election would not assume the executive office until December. On October 3, ad interim President Burnet, now a lame duck, called the first session of the Texas Congress to order in Columbia. On October 9, President-elect Houston arrived at the session. Congressmen coerced Burnet to resign so that Houston might immediately take the reins. Bowing to the pressure, Burnet agreed to resign on October 22, and the following day, interim Vice-President Lorenzo de Zavala also submitted his resignation.

Elias Rector's tarnished razor now shaved the chin of a president of a republic. Likely, Houston never doubted that it would.

The Patriarch Departs

H is defeat in the presidential election of 1836 had been a bitter pill for Stephen F. Austin to swallow. Just a year before, all of Texas had rejoiced upon his return from Mexican detention. Citizens had hosted barbecues in his honor, sought his advice, and praised his dedication. But now even some of the old contract colonists doubted his integrity and withheld their votes. As for the flood of U.S. newcomers, the name *Austin* meant nothing to them. Apparently the only brands they knew were "Houston" and "San Jacinto."

Even so, a gentleman as always, Austin exhibited no rancor toward the victor. Only once did his resentment reveal itself and then with but one word. He bemoaned the "blindness" of old Texians who had forsaken him. He shared a gloomy reflection with his favorite cousin, Mary Austin Holley:

> A successful military chieftain is hailed with admiration and applause, but the bloodless pioneer of the wilderness, like the corn and cotton he causes to spring where it never grew before, attracts no notice. No slaughtered thousands or smoking cities attest his devotion to the cause of human happiness, and he is regarded by the mass of the word as a humble instrument to pave the way for others.

189

At the time of his death Stephen F. Austin was virtually penniless. He died on a pallet placed on the floor of a borrowed cabin. He sacrificed everything—his fortune, his happiness, his hopes for a family, his health, and ultimately his life—for the dream of an independent Texas. *Courtesy of the Prints and Photograph Collection, the Center for American History, University of Texas at Austin.*

Nonetheless, the old optimism never faded. The week of Houston's inauguration, he wrote his brother-in-law: "I think that matters will go on well and smoothly in both the Executive and Legislative departments. There evidently is a disposition to harmonise in all persons."

On October 28, 1836, President Houston informed Austin that the senate had approved his nomination as secretary of state. This was a generous gesture on Houston's part, who wished to honor his former rival and ensure political harmony. Yet, there were also more pragmatic considerations. The new president needed a steady hand at the state department—and whose hand was steadier than Austin's?

President Houston may have meant well, but he did Austin no favors. The former *empresario* was in wretched health. He had always possessed a delicate constitution. He had almost died on his last trip to Mexico City, and his stint in prison had all but broken his health. Returning to Texas, he had accepted the command of the Army of the People but had been so weak during the 1835 campaign that he required Simon, his body servant, to help him mount his horse. Traveling to the United States, Austin had worked unstintingly as an agent promoting the cause of Texas. Then, he returned to Texas to campaign for the executive office. Now, in October 1836, Austin was near the end of his tether—and he knew it. He wrote the president:

> Your Excellency is fully aware of the debilitated state of
> my constitution and health, and also of the labors which
> devolve upon me in the land department. I however
> accept of the appointment and am ready to enter upon
> the duties of the office, with the understanding that I be
> allowed the privilege of retiring should my health and
> situation require it.

Most other men would have simply said no, but Austin was unlike
other men. Nowadays, one might describe him as a "workaholic."
Austin would have found it difficult to grasp that term. Time was short
and there was still much to do; how could one ever work too much?
A profound sense of obligation was his northern star. He would have
agreed with the English novelist Jane Austen when she observed, "It
isn't what we say or think that defines us, but what we do." Austin would
have described himself as—and this is a word contemporary people
seldom hear—dutiful.

He should have taken the time to recover his health, but true to his
nature, Austin pitched into his new responsibilities heart and soul. He
had much to do. At last, he concluded preparations for Antonio López
de Santa Anna's release. Both the president and the secretary of state
desired that the captive dictator quietly depart Texas and travel to the
U.S. capital on the Potomac River. Once there he would huddle with
President Andrew Jackson, before returning to Mexico. Surely his mere
presence in that benighted country would prove troublesome enough
to relieve pressure from the breakaway republic. Other particulars
on Austin's to-do list included a prisoner exchange from the recent
revolution and the promulgation of a decree against the African slave
trade.

The Texas capital had migrated from the Town of Washington,
to Harrisburg, to Galveston, to Velasco, and finally Columbia. Austin
followed the government. He lived in a rented "shed room," without
stove or hearth. For all of his labors and dedication, Austin had little
estate. As he explained:

> I have no house, not a roof in all Texas, that I can call
> my own. The only one I had was burnt at San Felipe
> during the late invasion of the enemy. I make my home
> where the business of the country calls me. I have no
> farm, no cotton plantation, no income, no money, no
> comforts. I have spent the prime of my life and worn out
> my constitution in trying to colonize this country.

He had worked as hard as anyone ever had, but despite all that he feared he would meet the same fate as his father—dying penniless.

Right before Christmas in 1836, a blue norther swept across Texas. Shivering in his unheated shack, Austin caught a cold. It would have been a minor malady for anyone with a vigorous immune system, but by now no one could describe any part of him as vigorous—except, perhaps, his intellect. The cold settled into his lungs and became pneumonia. No bed was available, so doctors placed him atop a pallet on the hard wooden floor.

On December 27, Austin seemed a bit more coherent. During the day, he drifted in and out of perception. At one point, he woke and in a voice so faint that visitors could barely hear it, uttered: "The independence of Texas is recognized! Don't you see it in the papers? Dr. Archer told me so." With that, he lapsed back into slumber and faded away.

Ironically, it fell to President Houston, Austin's old nemesis, to notify the nation. His public notice read in part: "The Father of Texas is no more! The first pioneer of the wilderness has departed!"

And so he had. The patriarch had not lived to see the end of that pivotal year in Texas history—one that included the Alamo, Goliad, San Jacinto, the capture of Santa Anna, and the election of Houston. Nor did he live to see most of his ambitions and dreams fulfilled, the same ambitions and dreams which he made possible for so many others.

Texans, his spiritual children, continue to live Austin's dreams for him.

The Capital at Houston City: "The Most Miserable Place in the World"

President Sam Houston took his oath of office at Columbia, but that location suited few Texian officials. House and Senate committees met and deliberated but could reach no consensus regarding the location for a new governmental seat. A number of towns were in the running: Matagorda, Fort Bend, Washington, Columbia, Nacogdoches, and Houston. The representatives could not reach an agreement and decided to locate the capital by a vote of both houses of Congress.

At that juncture, the Brothers Allen, Augustus C. and John K., instigated their machinations. They had acquired land on Buffalo Bayou, just five miles north of the ravaged Harrisburg. They swore that their new town was "handsome and beautifully elevated, salubrious and well watered, and now in the very heart or center of population." Moreover, the devious brothers offered the politicians many inducements. The brothers promised to build and pay for a capitol building. They also offered the congressmen private lodgings and complimentary town lots. Enticed by all the honeyed payoffs, on December 15, 1836, the people's representatives passed legislation transferring the seat of government to Houston until the end of the legislative session, 1840.

By year's end, Texians began to make their way to Houston City; what they found shocked and surprised them. The town did not exist—only a town site. Despite the Allen brothers lavish descriptions, Houston was

The splendor of Houston's upper crust clashes with the squalor of the Rowdy Loafers. The street litter and animal carcasses in the street justify one citizen's description of the capitol as the "most miserable place in the world." *Gary Zaboly, illustrator. From* Texian Macabre: The Melancholy Tale of a Hanging in Early Houston. *Author's collection.*

nothing more than marks on a chart and stakes in the ground. Arriving on New Year's Day 1837, merchant Francis R. Lubbock witnessed a few citizens constructing frame buildings on newly acquired lots. Other enterprising Houstonians, unable to afford lumber, pitched tents and conducted business under canvas. Prophetically, one of the larger tents functioned as a saloon; Houston City had already begun to assume its distinctive character.

By April 28, 1837, the capital had grown by leaps and bounds. On that date, President Houston, the city's namesake, boasted:

> On the 20th of January, a small log cabin & 12 persons were all that distinguished it from the adjacent forest, and now there are upwards of 100 houses finished, and going up rapidly (some of them fine frame buildings) and 1500 people, all actively engaged in their respective pursuits. It is remarkable to observe the sobriety and industry like we see in the North—I have not seen a drunken man since my arrival.

This last aspect would not last. Soon the city would provide the president with the opportunity to view more tosspots than even he would have thought possible. By November 19, when Methodist minister Littleton Fowler arrived in Houston, his impression was far different: "Here I find much vice, gaming, drunkenness, and profanity the commonest."

By 1838, the Allen brothers' dream had become a nightmare. What began as an impromptu hamlet had morphed into a makeshift metropolis, and it suffered all the ills of haphazard development. Even the most zealous booster had to admit that much of the year Houston City was a contaminated cesspit. In the summer, swarms of flies carried the bacteria that caused dysentery. Winter brought typhus, influenza, cholera, and tuberculosis. Almost yearly yellow fever epidemics swept the city claiming vast numbers of victims.

One official was dead on target when he referred to "this detested, self-polluted, isolated mud hole of a city." Dr. John Washington Lockhart described Houston thoroughfares: "The avenues were very muddy, and it was not an unusual thing then and long afterward to see ox wagons bogged down on the principal streets." Dr. Lockhart further recalled that he had seen "the roads lined with carcasses." Frequent rains liquefied the black dirt and horse droppings. Wagon wheels whipped the mixture into a putrid slime. Add raw sewage and the stench was nauseating. The place smelled less like a town than a charnel house.

Houstonians suffered a dazzling assortment of vermin, but rats were the worst. As soon as they snuffed their candles, the skitter of the repulsive pests lulled them into slumber. Gustav Dresel, a young German immigrant, described the scourge of these loathsome creatures:

> Thousands of these troublesome guests made sport by night, and nothing could be brought to safety from them. All the provisions were soon begnawed by them, and the best rat dog became tired of destroying them because

their numbers never decreased. Human corpses had to be watched during the whole night because otherwise these fiends ate their way into them. The finger of a little child who lay alone in the cradle for a few hours was half eaten away. This I saw myself. Rats often dashed across me by the half-dozens at night. In the beginning this proves annoying; of course, later one gets accustomed to it.

One might accuse Dresel of hyperbole if others had not corroborated his observations. Settler C. C. Cox confirmed:

I cannot convey an idea of the multitude of Rats in Houston at that time. They were almost as large as prairie dogs and when night came on, the streets and houses were literally alive with these animals. Such running and squealing throughout the night, to say nothing of the fear of losing a toe or your nose, if you chanced to fall asleep, created such an apprehension that together with the attention that had to be given our other companions made sleep well nigh impossible.

The "other companions" to which Cox referred were fleas.

Nacogdoches Representative Kelsey H. Douglass had nothing good to say about the capital. Shamefaced, he admitted in a letter to his wife: "We liv like hogs." More than a few shared his belief that Houston City was, "the most misera[b]le place in the world."

Houston versus Huston

A mong the numerous challenges facing President Sam Houston, those revolving around the Republic's army were the toughest. During summer 1836, hundreds of U.S. volunteers flocked to Texas seeking adventure, glory, and plunder. So it was that the cast of the army transformed from settlers fighting for hearth and home to one three times as large, consisting primarily of U.S. volunteers with few ties to the republic they had sworn to defend. And the most fractious of these was Felix Huston.

And what a piece of work he was. A native of Mississippi, he had arrived in Texas on July 4, 1836. Almost immediately he embroiled himself with local politics, aligning himself against ad interim President David G. Burnet. On December 20, 1836, President Houston appointed him junior brigadier general and *temporary* commander of the army. Houston never intended to retain Huston, a newcomer with scant military experience, in command. Nevertheless, shortly thereafter Huston started speaking of "*my* army."

From the instant he took temporary command, Huston demonstrated that his ambition leapt far beyond his ability. Impatient to realize his dreams of conquest, he proposed an invasion of Mexico that would culminate in the capture of Matamoros. The volunteers nicknamed their thirty-six-year-old chief "Old Leather-Breeches," denoting his rough and rowdy manner. How could his men fail to love him? In his rebellion, insolence, and sedition, Huston was a mirror image of themselves.

Attorney, opportunist, and would-be conqueror, Felix Huston was an insubordinate thorn in President Houston's flesh. Texas historian Eugene C. Barker accurately observed that Huston's Texas service was "more obstreperous than effective." *From Henderson King Yoakum, History of Texas from Its First Settlement in 1685 to Its Annexation to the United States in 1846 (1855).*

President Houston decided that General Huston had to go. On January 31, 1837, West Point graduate Albert Sidney Johnston won appointment as senior brigadier general in command of the army. Yet, on February 4, when Johnston arrived in camp to take lawful command of the army, Huston refused to stand down. Instead, citing his refusal to be "over-slaughed under humiliating circumstances," he challenged his replacement to a duel. The two men exchanged six shots. Huston's last bullet tore through Johnston's hip, rendering him unable to assume command.

Besides, Huston was now more popular than ever. When he returned to camp following the duel, "a thousand soldiers rushed forward to congratulate him." The raucous throng would never have abided his removal. Both General Huston and the mutable, rank-scented mob he led had spun wildly out of control. Neither appeared willing to follow the mandates of the duly elected civilian authorities.

The president had no choice but to retain Huston. He may have been a fighting fool, but he was the only man the volunteers seemed willing to obey. There were also political considerations. The president required the support of the "army party" to preserve control of the government.

Most of his opposition came from those with army ties or who harbored military aspirations. Consequently, Houston had to bide his time and give General Huston just enough rope to hang himself.

Following the duel, conditions deteriorated even further. President Houston received reports that bands of soldiers were ransacking supplies from citizens without offering even the promise of compensation. As he explained: "My object is to have the Army supplied regularly and prevent all future impressments of supplies or anything else which may belong to the citizens." Such may have been the president's object, but at least in the short term, it was far beyond the capability of the government. One frustrated Texian officer complained in a letter to Houston: "I am a doing evry thing in my power for to disiplin my command . . . [but] it is very hard for to command men that is bear footed and naked and hongry." The volunteers not only failed to observe the regulation and routine of military organization, but openly mocked such notions. Many citizens came to believe that the Texian army was more of a threat to their peace, security, and civil liberties that the Mexican army was.

The wily Houston advocated placing a portion of the army on what amounted to a permanent liberty. The president authorized Secretary of War William S. Fisher to grant leaves to as many of the troops as he deemed appropriate.

When Fisher arrived in camp he was "assailed by crowds of applicants for furlough." The volunteers seemed to have had enough of hunger, inactivity, and the rigors of camp life. Even before Fisher's arrival, most of the troops were feeling run down. It was time to move on. Many of them were drifters anyway—gamblers, thimble riggers, or men on the make for the next big score. The majority, who joined up anticipating a quick coup, now realized that military life offered nothing of what they craved. The vision of wealth, fame, and glory had proven a mirage. It was manifest: they would not fulfill their destiny in the Texas army.

On May 24, Fisher wrote Houston asserting it "would be good policy to furlough all but military men and . . . new recruits. This would leave in the field a force of 600 men." The president immediately approved Fisher's proposition and in one stroke reduced the army from some 3,600 to a manageable number. In time, those troops that remained served out their enlistments, received their furloughs, or deserted. Future governor Francis R. Lubbock, a man involved in Texas politics for more than sixty years, later stated the "furloughing of the army of the Republic in 1837 was one of the most marked evidences of statecraft" he had ever witnessed.

And what of General Huston? With his army reduced to six hundred men, he knew that he could not conduct a campaign against Matamoros and abandoned his dreams of conquest. Thus, the army of the Texas Republic became less of a burden—and less of a threat—to its citizens.

The Rowdy Loafers

President Sam Houston had resolved one crisis only to create another. Suddenly, hundreds of soldiers were free as the air and loose on the countryside. Because most were Americans, some booked passage back to the United States never to return. Many, however, had nothing waiting for them back home and cast their lot with the Texians. The furloughed soldiers were young men, who, for the most part, lacked money, skills, or connections. But following months of want and inactivity, they did have a thirst to quench, steam to blow off, and wild oats to sow. Houston sounded like their kind of town.

The discharged warriors descended on the new capital like a plague of locusts. In most cases, however, it was they who found themselves stripped clean. Unscrupulous civilians were eager to exploit the desperation and gullibility of these young men. Many were young and unwordly; suddenly they found themselves among hard-nosed men of business with their feet on the ground and their hands in a bumpkin's pocket.

Houston's upper-crust citizens soon began describing the furloughed soldiers as "rowdy loafers." Vagabond volunteers were undesirables: "rowdy" because they were young men with too much time on their hands and "loafers" as a result of government policy.

Now that Texians no longer required U.S. volunteers, they had cast them out like a worn-out shoe. Soldiers had answered the call; they had suffered privation and want. Now, all they had to show for their service

A disagreement over a card game erupts into a lethal affray—a common occurrence in early Houston. *Gary Zaboly, illustrator, illustrator. From* Texian Macabre: The Melancholy Tale of a Hanging in Early Houston. *Author's collection.*

were worthless land scripts. Discharged warriors became estranged from the Texas establishment that, at least in their eyes, had bilked them. As Houston resident Francis R. Lubbock described their situation: "The army was being furloughed in the winter of 1837 and 1838, and finally disbanded. This brought a large number of soldiers to the city, consequently there was much dissipation, gambling, and fighting." Their behavior appalled Congressmen Kelsey H. Douglass, who complained: "Drinking, fighting, and rangling is the order of the day at this place."

So ubiquitous was a particular weapon that it became a sartorial requisite. According to English visitor Matilda Houstoun, most men she encountered in the Texas Republic sported a particular weapon: "The Texans, almost without exception, carry their national weapon, the Bowie knife, about them." Irish diplomat Francis C. Sheridan also corroborated that throughout the country the "use of the Bowie Knife is in general among high and low." Dr. John Washington Lockhart recollected, "It was very common to see men passing on the streets with from two to four pistols belted around them, with the addition of a large bowie knife."

Observing the brutality that constituted the capital's daily life, hundreds of prospective Houstonians opted to settle elsewhere. Town officials were willing to allow a degree of boisterous conduct, so long as revelers confined their shenanigans to prescribed areas. But that was the problem. Early Houston did not have a district set aside for gainful vice. It was, in every sense of the term, a "wide-open" town. As Constable Edward Stiff chronicled, "Pick-pockets and every description of bad characters abound here and are in promiscuous confusion mingled with the virtuous part of the community. So much is the case, that a man can scarcely divine when or where he is safe from their depredations." There was simply no way for respectable folk to dodge the bloodshed that could erupt on any street corner, at any time.

On March 28, 1838, city officials sought to curb the raucous passions of the loafers by stringing up two of them. A Houston court found two Texas army veterans guilty of murder and sentenced them to hang. The condemned were John Christopher Columbus Quick and David James Jones. The case of Jones was especially poignant; he had escaped the Goliad Massacre, only to perish at the end of a judicial rope. Between two and three thousand Houstonians watched the pair meet their Maker. One citizen found the execution of Quick and Jones an opportunity for edification: "Their fate suggests many solemn and awful reflections to the passionate and vicious."

Houston's upper crust hoped that a public execution would send a message to the other rowdy loafers plaguing the town. Yet, if the idlers ever received it, they soon forgot its contents. On May 11, 1839, a reporter for the *Morning Star* protested, "Loafers have increased, and are increasing, and ought to be diminished. District court in session—crimes and criminals are undergoing scrutiny—hope it will have some effect on the loafers." In the end, however the example of Quick and Jones made little or no impression on Houston's criminal underclass.

In 1839, the republic's officials moved the capital to Austin; the loafers, gamblers, and prostitutes remained. They soon forgot the "lessons of the gallows" and disproved one optimistic resident's prediction that the hangings would promote "the public peace." Ultimately, brawls, dissipation, or yellow fever ended the heyday of the rowdy loafers. But until then, public peace in Houston proved elusive.

Texas Rebuffed

esentment surrounding Governor Henry Smith's shenanigans influenced delegates drafting the 1836 Constitution. They had grown wary of chief executives who became hungry for power the moment they assumed office. To guard against such abuse, Article III stipulated that the first elected president would serve only a two-year term and never succeed himself in office. Later presidents would serve for three years, but neither could they serve successively. They might, however, serve any number of *nonconsecutive* terms. Texians wished to make sure that their chief magistrates did not wield too much power and never ensconce themselves in public office.

Sam Houston yearned to join Texas to the United States, but many hurdles blocked the path to statehood, and he had precious little time to clear them. Over the summer of 1836, U.S. President Andrew Jackson dispatched State Department clerk Henry M. Morfit as a special agent to Texas. Jackson tasked him with gathering statistics on the new republic, information the president could use to make an informed decision. Morfit submitted his findings in August. He approximated the population at 30,000 Anglo Americans; 3,478 *Tejanos*; 14,200 Indians; 5,000 slaves; and a handful of free blacks.

With so few inhabitants, Texas sovereignty was tentative. During the recent revolution, the provisional government had incurred millions of dollars in debt, debt which the current government lacked the resources to

Even before he became president, Martin Van Buren made it clear that he had no intention of opening the can of worms that annexing Texas would entail. *Courtesy of the Library of Congress.*

repay. If that were not enough, a boundary dispute soured relations with Mexicans, who insisted Tejas—despite the Battle of San Jacinto—remained part of their national domain. For those reasons and more, Morfit counseled the United States should postpone recognition of the breakaway republic.

President Jackson heeded Morfit's counsel. On December 21, 1836, he referenced Morfit's findings, observing that the United States only conferred recognition with the prospect that the new nation could sustain its independence. With Texas, the question was much in doubt. Jackson disliked the odds. He noted Mexicans menaced Texas with "an immense disparity of physical force." Although an expansionist and a friend to Houston, the U.S. president believed recognition was premature. Passing on the matter, he consigned it to Congress—where it died in committee.

Back in Texas, President Houston worked for U.S. recognition and annexation. He posted the old War Party hotspur, William H. Wharton, to Washington with orders to pursue recognition. When, and if, Wharton accomplished his mission, he carried his credentials as foreign minister in his saddle bags. Memucan Hunt also traveled to the capital on the Potomac River to aid Wharton. The diplomatic duo wrote to Houston with heartening news. Powhatan Ellis, the U.S. minister to Mexico, had appeared reporting that insolvency, insurrection, and anarchy was rife throughout Mexico. Any possibility of an offensive against Texas was slight—at least in the short term. Moreover, the United States, Great Britain, and France were hounding Mexican officials for compensation for their citizens' claims. The bad news for Mexico proved good news for Texas.

On March 1, 1837, U.S. congressmen approved a resolution to send "a diplomatic agent" to the Texas Republic. During his last night in office, Jackson signed a decree recognizing Texas independence and naming Alcée Louis La Branche as chargé d'affaires. On July 9, 1838, Congress adjourned without addressing annexation. Martin Van Buren, the new president, viewed it as a political liability and indicated he did not plan to pursue the object.

Crestfallen, Houston supplanted Hunt with Anson Jones. Previously, as a Texas congressman, Jones urged President Houston to withdraw the offer of annexation. He maintained Texas had so flourished that it no longer needed to affiliate with the "old states." But the measure was only a face-saving gesture to prevent further humiliation. Acting on Houston's instructions, Jones notified U.S. officials that Texas was withdrawing its application for annexation.

Like a blushing bride, Texas offered herself to the United States, but the groom jilted her at the altar. Texians declared independence believing they would soon join the federal union. Now, they realized they must go it alone. Their rejection embarrassed them, but they remained defiant.

Unable to accomplish annexation, Houston now turned his attention to problems closer to home. Indian relations lay heavy on his mind. During his first term, Houston sought to forestall conflict between Texians and Indians, but the 1838 Córdova Rebellion undermined his endeavors. The outcome of the Texas Revolution had frustrated Vicente Córdova, an influential Tejano resident of Nacogdoches. Disdainful of the new order, he maintained contacts with Mexican authorities. Incited by Mexican agents, disaffected Tejanos joined ranks with disgruntled Kickapoo Indians who lived along the Angelina River. The Cherokees insisted they wanted no part of Córdova's subversion. Learning that more than a hundred armed insurgents had mustered, former secretary of war Thomas Jefferson Rusk called up the Nacogdoches militia and entreated surrounding towns for more troops. Observing his peace initiatives going up in smoke, President Houston issued a proclamation ordering the militiamen to stand down. The president then established headquarters in Nacogdoches to manage affairs.

As he normally did, Houston took the middle path. But Rusk took a harder line. Ignoring Houston's directions, he forded the Angelina River to intimidate the Cherokees with a demonstration of strength. Rusk also opened a correspondence with Vice President Mirabeau B. Lamar, who also advocated a stronger stance against local tribes. Texian forces encountered and defeated the insurgents near Seguin. Córdova and most of his lieutenants escaped to Mexico, but Texians had not heard the last of him. With calm restored to East Texas, President Houston returned to the capital; Rusk and the militiamen returned to their homes. Houston's diplomacy had kept bloodshed to a minimum, and Córdova's upheaval proved a minor distraction. Nevertheless, Texians continued to mistrust the loyalty of Tejanos and Indians.

By the end of Houston's first term, something extraordinary had occurred: Texians embraced their nationalism. This phenomenon characterized them and their heirs up to the present day, a sense they were different from other Americans. The notion that they had inherited a singular destiny—what many have branded Texas Exceptionalism—took root.

Independence, Cotton, and Texians
of African Heritage

Notwithstanding numerous assertions to the contrary, slave owners did not incite the Texas Revolution to preserve their "peculiar institution." It was one of the many causes, but not the main one. Professor Randolph B. Campbell, who literally wrote the book on Texas slavery, stated the case succinctly: "The immediate cause of the conflict was the political instability of Mexico and the implications of Santa Anna's centralist regime for Texas. Mexico forced the issue in 1835, not over slavery, but over customs duties and the general defiant attitude of Anglo-Americans in Texas."

At the invitation of the Mexican government, thousands of American settlers poured across the Red and Sabine rivers or through Texas ports. Many from Southern states brought their slaves with them, which posed a dilemma for Mexican officials who were in the processes of abolishing the practice.

Throughout the 1820s and 1830s, the large numbers of Southern Americans who immigrated to Texas drastically altered the social climate. *Tejano* politician José Antonio Navarro introduced a legal loophole whereby American planters might still bring their slaves as "indentured servants." Finally, Mexican politicians in both Texas and Coahuila worked to obtain an exemption from the 1829 Guerrero anti-slave decree. In other words, slavery was illegal everywhere in Mexico . . . *except* Texas. By 1836, about 13,000 enslaved people of African descent lived and worked in Texas.

Victory at San Jacinto heralded the birth of a republic that was wholly and unapologetically committed to the interest of slave holders. The Constitution of 1836 declared that blatantly. (See, Provisions of the 1836 Constitution of the Republic of Texas on page 142.) The delegates did not promote human bondage because they were evil men. They were, rather, pragmatic officials who wished to ensure Southern support for their rebellion, the outcome of which was far from certain at that juncture. Slaves were expensive. For many Southern planters, human chattel constituted their greatest investment. Delegates wished to make sure that potential immigrants understood that if they brought their slaves with them, Texas law would protect their "property."

The plan worked. Independence launched a period of unsurpassed expansion for Texas slavery that ended only when Union victory in the Civil War obliterated the practice. In the wake of San Jacinto, hundreds of

continued

Southern planters invested in Texas lands. Cotton and slavery formed the bedrock of the national economy. While Texian planters largely confined their activities to the eastern portions of the republic, that region alone was the size of Mississippi and Alabama combined. The noxious amalgamation of slavery and cotton chained the Texas economy to the Southern states, a tie that was to have calamitous consequences when Texans cast their lot with the Confederacy in 1861.

Even though unwilling participants, African American Texians were essential contributors. Enslaved people not only planted and harvested the "white gold" that was the life's blood of the Republic, but bondsmen with specialized skills also labored as blacksmiths, masons, and carpenters; enslaved women excelled as cooks, housekeepers, and caregivers, frequently forging deep emotional bonds with white families in their keeping. Texians of African heritage found themselves at the bottom of the social ladder, but with diligence, endurance, and grit they may well have provided its sturdiest rung.

Lamar Takes the Reins

The Texas Constitution hamstrung Sam Houston. It stipulated that the first elected president could serve only two years and was ineligible for immediate reelection. It did not, however, prevent him from supporting Peter W. Grayson, who pledged to continue the president's policies. But Grayson's suicide stymied those plans. The 1838 campaign assumed a morbid tinge when Houston's second choice, James Collinsworth, leapt to his death from the deck of a ship into Galveston Bay. Old Sam Jacinto's third pick, the unknown Robert Wilson, stood for office just to fill the ticket. The results were predictable but still embarrassing. When Texians went to the polls in September, Mirabeau B. Lamar, the contentious vice president, won the presidential post with 6,995 votes. Wilson received 252. Houston's term expired on December 10, 1838, and Lamar took the reins.

Many have remarked the Texas Republic had no organized political parties; it had oversized personalities. And one could hardly imagine two personalities more at odds than Houston and Lamar. In many ways, they were polar opposites. Houston was shrewd, crude, and pragmatic; Lamar was forthright, imaginative, and romantic. Dr. Anson Jones left an astute assessment of the "poet president": "Gen. Lamar may mean well . . . but his mind is altogether of a dreamy, poetic order, a sort of political Troubadour and Crusader and wholly unfit for . . . the every day realities of his present situation." But their differences were not merely political and

211

Politician, poet, and philosopher, Mirabeau B. Lamar was among the most learned and accomplished men in the Texas Republic. Succeeding Sam Houston as president, he won the everlasting gratitude of some and the bitter enmity of others when he transferred the seat of government from Houston to Austin. *Courtesy of the Texas State Library and Archives Commission.*

philosophical. They detested each other.

The contention between these two giants shaped a schizophrenic public policy. Houston worked assiduously for U.S. annexation; Lamar remained indifferent to it. He instead envisioned a Texian empire that would first rival, then surpass, the older North American republic. Aware of the government's precarious finances, Houston followed a frugal course; Lamar, on the other hand, viewed public expenditures as an investment in future greatness. Houston tried to protect Texas Indians; Lamar regarded American Indians as a barrier to westward expansion and vowed to move or destroy them.

Lamar set about dismantling Houston's policies—especially those concerning native peoples. Learning that Cherokee leaders had negotiated with Mexican agents, Lamar determined that military force was warranted. Suspecting an imminent attack, Big Mush, Gatunwali, Di'wali, and other tribal chiefs requested Lamar allow them time to harvest their crops, after which they promised to leave without opposition. The new chief executive would not yield; instead, he issued the following directive: "Push a rigorous war against them; pursuing them to their hiding places without mitigation or compassion, until they shall be made to feel that flight from our borders without hope of return, is preferable to the scourges of war."

On July 15 and 16, 1839, some five hundred Texian forces clashed with eight hundred Cherokees and Delawares at the Battle of the Neches. Yet, of the eight hundred natives, between four and five hundred were non-combatants. Texians came well-armed but later discovered that native warriors had less than twenty-five rifles, muskets, and pistols between them. The outcome was predictable. More than a hundred Indians fell on the field, but they did not go down without a fight. The whites suffered eight killed and twenty-nine wounded. Among those bloodied was Lamar's vice president, David G. Burnet. Soldiers found the corpse of Di'wali (also known as Chief Bowl, or "The Bowl") lying among the slain, still sporting the sword that President Houston had presented him. Captain Robert W. Smith, who shot the wounded chief through the head, later mutilated his body. Most Texians understood that Di'wali was Houston's devoted friend. In a vindictive gesture, General Hugh McLeod dispatched the Bowl's top hat to the previous president. Houston never forgave Lamar for Di'wali's death.

He further begrudged his successor moving the capital. It infuriated Lamar that his rival's namesake city was the governmental seat, so he launched plans to relocate it. On April 13, 1839, commissioners submitted their recommendation. The favored site was the village of Waterloo on the eastern bank of the Colorado River. Lamar had previously inspected the spot and declared it his "seat of Empire." To honor the "Father of Texas"—and to exasperate Houston—officials agreed to name the new capital Austin.

Most representatives were ready to move and had become disgusted with Houston City. Resident Millie Gray complained yellow fever killed as much as 12 percent of the municipal population. Even boosters found it embarrassing to laud the city once it became a yawning graveyard. By the end of October, teamsters had shifted the archives and other papers to Austin. Houston City continued to thrive as a mercantile center, but it ceased to function as the political hub.

Lamar appointed Edwin Waller to plan and build the new capital. He engaged two surveyors and tasked them with preparing the site before the Texas Congress assembled in November 1839. Waller placed the one-story frame capitol on a scenic hillside overlooking the Colorado River—a palisade enclosed the structure as a guard against Indian raids. On August 1, officials auctioned off city lots. President Lamar arrived in October and administrators opened government offices; Congress convened on schedule in November. By 1840, Austin boasted 856 inhabitants, among whom were 145 slaves and several diplomats representing the interests of the United States, France, and Great Britain.

The year 1839 also saw Lamar's most permanent achievement. On December 28, Senator William H. Wharton introduced legislation to adopt a design for a national standard. It was the famous Lone Star flag, which remains the state emblem. On January 25, Congress accepted it. President Lamar championed the Lone Star flag, Wharton introduced it to Congress, and Dr. Charles B. Stewart sketched the pattern that the Third Congress consulted while considering its adoption. Yet, the name of the person who actually conceived the banner is lost to history.

The Council House Fight

President Mirabeau B. Lamar may have crushed the Cherokees, but another tribe posed a much greater threat: The Numunuh, better known to whites as Comanches. Republic officials understood that they could not vanquish these horse-borne warriors as easily as they had the sedentary eastern Indians. So, they tried for negotiation first and scheduled a summit in San Antonio.

On March 19, 1840, twelve chiefs, along with several warriors, women, and children arrived for the conclave. As a condition of the conference, Texians insisted the Comanches return all their white captives. Yet, they produced only one Anglo hostage, sixteen-year-old Matilda Lockhart, along with some Mexican children. Texian negotiators cared nothing for the Mexican youngsters and the state of the white girl did nothing to promote harmony.

She admitted to Béxar resident Mary Maverick that the Comanche women had beaten her, while the men "utterly degraded" her—a Victorian euphuism for gang rape. Lockhart explained how the females woke her by sticking torches in her face. As a result, her nose was gone, burned off, just a seared hole remaining. She further reported she saw fifteen additional prisoners that the Comanches had held back. The chiefs planned to negotiate the highest price and sell them one at a time.

Colonel Hugh McLeod, the ranking Texian negotiator, and Muk-wah-ruh, a civil chief, communicated through an interpreter who spoke both Comanche and English. The pow-wow began with a curt question.

215

Wary Texians watch as Comanches ride into San Antonio. In the background, captive Matilda Lockhart covers her mutilated face with a blanket. *Lee Herring, illustrator. Courtesy of the McWhiney History Education Group.*

McLeod demanded to know why Muk-wah-ruh failed to deliver the other white captives. The chief retorted he had produced all of *his* hostages. Yes, there were others, he admitted, but they belonged to other bands. He was likely telling the truth. Even a chief of Muk-wah-ruh's stature could not compel another war band to surrender its captives. After pleading his good faith, he paused for a long moment, then wryly inquired, "How do you like that answer?"

"I do not like your answer," McLeod snapped. Losing all patience, he excoriated Muk-wah-ruh and expressed his intention of holding him and the other chiefs present as hostages until the Indians returned with all the white captives. The *Tejano* interpreter, a onetime Numunuh prisoner himself, could well anticipate Muk-wah-ruh's reaction. He refused to deliver such a message, but McLeod insisted. The prudent interpreter stood at the door, delivered the verdict, then slipped out.

Bedlam ensued. Muk-wah-ruh raised a war cry. A sentry guarding the door died when an Indian sank a dagger into his chest. He did not long enjoy his triumph; Texian soldiers riddled him with lead. Texian regulars moved in and emptied their muskets into the room. Bullets ricocheted off

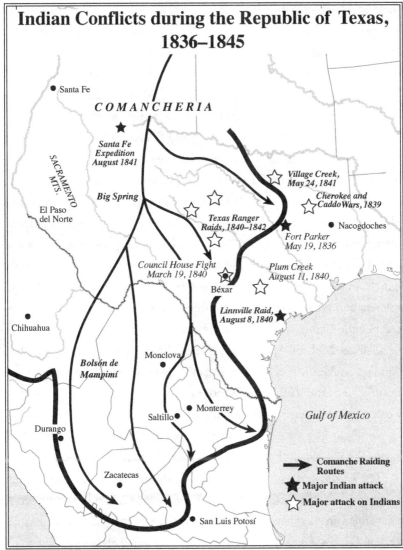

Indian Conflicts during the Republic of Texas, 1836–1845

Santa Fe

COMANCHERIA

★

Santa Fe
Expedition
August 1841

SACRAMENTO MTS.

Big Spring

El Paso
del Norte

Texas Ranger
Raids, 1840–1842

☆ *Village Creek,*
May 24, 1841

☆ *Cherokee and*
Caddo Wars, 1839

● Nacogdoches

★ *Fort Parker*
May 19, 1836

Council House Fight
March 19, 1840

Béxar

Plum Creek
August 11, 1840

●
Chihuahua

Linnville Raid,
August 8, 1840 ★

Bolsón de
Mampimí

Monclova

Gulf of Mexico

Saltillo ● Monterrey

Durango

Zacatecas

San Luis Potosí

➡ **Comanche Raiding**
Routes
★ **Major Indian attack**
☆ **Major attack on Indians**

Map by Donald S. Frazier, Ph.D.

stone walls, striking both friend and foe. Enraged, Muk-wah-ruh lunged at a Texas Ranger captain, stabbing him in the side. Before the chief could strike a deathblow, however, a musket ball slammed his lifeless body to the dirt floor. Matthew "Old Paint" Caldwell, a respected ranger captain, was there only to observe the proceedings, so he was unarmed. Without so much as a penknife, Caldwell found himself in the midst of the lethal affray. A stray round caught him in the leg, engaging his combat instincts. Ignoring the pain, he wrested a musket from a warrior, turned it on the Indian, and blew his head off. As another rushed him, Caldwell brained him with the butt of the empty musket. With little space to maneuver, Comanches and Texians grappled hand-to-hand, each giving full vent to smoldering enmity.

The clash spilled out onto the streets. Suddenly aware of the tumult inside, Comanche women and children fired arrows at Béxar citizens, one of whom fell dead. A small band of warriors broke out of the Council House and tried to fight their way out of town, but Texian regulars pursued them through alleys and into dwellings. Civilians grabbed weapons and joined the fighting. Texians gunned down most escapees in the streets, but those who holed up in buildings offered a greater challenge. At last, soldiers and citizens set the protecting building ablaze. As the fugitives escaped the flames, Texians shot them.

Colonel McLeod reported that sixty-five Comanches rode into San Antonio on March 19. Of those, Texians killed thirty-five: thirty men, three women, and two children. Twenty-nine became captives, twenty-seven women and children and two elderly men. Many have described the Council House Fight as a "massacre," but the Texians did not emerge unscathed. Seven Texians died in the fighting, and ten more suffered serious wounds.

The Council House brawl was a tragedy for both sides. Each group sought peace but immense cultural differences produced misapprehensions that ended in bloodshed. For Plains tribes, the council was sacrosanct. When Texians breached that sacred trust, Comanches reckoned it an inconceivable treachery. It was a Comanche Pearl Harbor—a "day of infamy." But Texians insisted that the natives had acted in bad faith by not bringing in all of their captives, which had been a condition of the meeting. Had events unfolded differently the parties might have reached a lasting peace. Instead, the Council House Fight of 1840 spawned rage that ensured strife for more than three decades.

Rangers Ride

Texians did not invent mounted rangers. During the 1600s, Scots used the term to describe armed men who *ranged* a tract of countryside against raids by hostile clans. The practice migrated to the American colonies where as early as 1739 James Oglethorpe raised a Georgia unit: The Troop of Highland Rangers. Later, settlers hired gunmen to patrol the woods against Indian attacks. In times of immediate crisis, the militiamen mustered, but they looked to the local ranger to organize and lead them. He was the professional.

Along with other trappings of Celtic culture, southern immigrants to Mexican Texas brought their ranging traditions and disdain for regular soldiers. In 1823, Stephen F. Austin paid ten men he termed "rangers" to protect his colony from Indian raids. In the beginning, because these irregular partisans were defending their families, settlers expected each man to arrive for duty well mounted and well armed from his own pocket. They wore no uniform, fought under no flag, and expressed little esprit de corps. Except for paid captains, troopers responded only in case of emergency and took their leave the instant they deemed the threat concluded.

Once they arrived in Texas, Anglo-Celtic Americans encountered another tradition, one which was to influence the way they fought Indians. For generations, the *compañías volantes* or "flying companies" had patrolled the *frontera*. Unlike heavy cavalry units and stationary presidial garrisons, these light cavalry squadrons rapidly responded to hostile raiders.

A typical Texas Ranger of the Republic
period. Note the bandanna, high-horned
saddle, and spike-roweled spurs—all
borrowed from Mexican *vaqueros*. Yet note
also the American rifle, Bowie knife, and
Colt revolvers strapped to his belt. It was the
combination of Tejano experience and U.S.
weaponry that made rangers the most lethal
fighting men on the Southern Plains. *Joseph
Hefter, illustrator. Author's collection.*

These hard-riding *Tejanos* took
the fight to Indian campsites,
conducting extended offensive
patrols, or *cortadas*. Texas Rangers adapted and adopted many
tactics from the compañías volantes. During Spanish colonial
and Mexican republic periods,
Tejano flying companies established routes into *Comanchería*.
Now, rangers serving the Republic of Texas continued to patrol
the trails of previous cortadas.
Anglo rangers further imple-
mented the *caballada*—a string
of horses—to enable prolonged
pursuits. Texians also borrowed
Tejano equipment and horse
gear. Anglos and Tejanos often joined forces and rode and
fought together as allies. Because
of this intensive cultural borrow-
ing, southern rangers adapted
to their new environment and became unique. They morphed into *Texas
Rangers*.

During the Revolution of 1835–1836, officials formalized ranger
organization, but only slightly. On November 24, 1835, the interim
government approved an ordinance providing for a corps of mounted
gunmen. Gone were the casual enlistments. Privates signed on for a
full year and earned $1.25 per day for "pay, rations, clothing, and horse
service." Although rangers saw some action fighting Mexican soldiers,
their primary mission remained to fend off Indian incursions. As Bastrop

resident John Holland Jenkins recalled: "The Indians were growing more and more troublesome, and Captain John Tumlinson raised a minute company of the few boys and men left at home. These held themselves in readiness for protecting . . . homes and families."

President Mirabeau B. Lamar envisioned the infant republic stretching westward toward the Pacific, but harsh realities frustrated his dreams of empire. The government was bankrupt. It possessed a small regular army, which was expensive to uniform, arm, and deploy. Worse, it had little experience fighting horse-borne Indians. Circumstances demanded an inexpensive partisan force that mustered in minutes, provided for itself in the field, and shunned pricey uniforms. In brief, rangers. They supplied their own horses and fodder, sparing the struggling government the cost of supplying mounts and provisioning a cavalry corps.

Ingrained animosity toward regular soldiers remained at the heart of the ranger ethic. Volunteers defending hearth and home considered themselves on higher moral ground than brass-buttoned hirelings. As ranger Nelson Lee explained, "Discipline, in the common acceptation of the term, was not regarded as essential."

Commanding those who rejected conventional authority required a leader who shared his men's egalitarian values. A ranger captain was first among equals, but that was the source of his power. Texians followed a man not because he had attended an academy or perused treatises, but because he had proven his worth in the field. Edward Burleson, roughhewn and barely literate, would never have qualified as an "officer and a gentleman" in the regular army. Yet, Lee and other rangers admired men like Burleson for their "valor, wisdom, and experience."

The Republic's rangers had valor and wisdom aplenty. Yet, at first, they had little experience fighting the mobile Comanche and Kiowa raiders. Riding alongside Tejano, Delaware, and Tonkawa allies, white rangers mastered the skills required to meet mounted Indians on equal terms.

Weapons dictate tactics. In terms of both weapons and tactics, Comanches outclassed Texas Rangers. Although the vaunted long rifle was amazingly accurate, it proved cumbersome for a man on horseback. Texians had to dismount to reload while their adversaries rode rings around them. Even worse, the long rifle was painfully slow to prime and load. A Comanche warrior could gallop a hundred yards and fire a dozen arrows before a grounded man could load and discharge his flintlock. The rangers needed a fast-firing weapon that allowed them to stay in the saddle and take the fight to the enemy. They did not know it, but a Connecticut inventor had conceived a pistol that was about to alter the nature of warfare on the Southern Plains.

The Great Comanche Raid of 1840

Every Comanche burned to avenge the Council House outrage. Vengeful warriors conjured the greatest raid in their history—one that would strike deep into the areas of Texian settlement and show their range and dominance. Yet, such an incursion required time to plan and organize, a venture made more difficult by the loss of prominent chiefs in San Antonio. By August 1840, the Pen-uh-tek-uh had settled on Buffalo Hump to lead the foray. Phallic connotations infused his Numunuh name, Po-cha-na-quar-hip, that most puritanical whites refused to decipher. The most accurate translation is, "erection that will not go down." He summoned other Comanche bands. By August, between four and five hundred warriors had gathered and were preparing to hurl a punitive attack south of Gonzales and eastward along the Guadalupe valley. Because their women and children accompanied them, the band may have totaled one thousand souls. That number included several Kiowa allies and Mexican agents who functioned as guides.

By August 6, the throng approached Victoria on the Guadalupe River's eastern bank. At first, citizens mistook the raiders for Lipan Apaches, a friendly tribe with whom they often traded. The warriors' violent actions soon corrected that impression. Resident John J. Linn recalled, "We of Victoria were startled by the apparitions presented by the sudden appearance of six hundred mounted Comanches in the immediate outskirts of the village." Galloping through town, Comanches killed fifteen citizens and

The Great Comanche Raid

Map by Donald S. Frazier, Ph.D.

captured a herd numbering about fifteen hundred horses. Texians retreated into strongholds and fended off the assault and Buffalo Hump's band flowed like the Guadalupe toward the coast. The windfall of captured horses pleased warriors but limited their mobility. Instead of riding hard and fast, the horde now moved at the sluggish pace of a white man's cattle drive.

Linnville, established by John J. Linnin 1831, was the Texas Republic's second-busiest port. Settler George W. Bonnell described it as an anchorage "where a great many goods have been received. It is finely situated for the commerce of the up country, and will no doubt be a place of considerable importance." In 1840, Linn recorded 130 town lots for taxation. The settlement boasted two hundred residents and eleven slaves. So it was no accident that the Mexican guides led Buffalo Hump's force toward the seaside village. Its destruction would cripple Texian fortunes, offer a rich source of plunder, and gratify both the Comanches' and Mexicans' ambitions.

On August 8, the Comanches struck Linnville like God's own hammer. They cut down three residents to start the terror. Customs official Hugh Oran Watts refused to leave until he retrieved a gold watch from his house. He tarried too long; warriors overtook and killed him. Then they captured his new bride, a slave woman, and her child.

Citizens took refuge on the water. Rowing out in small skiffs, they boarded Captain William G. Marshall's schooner that lay anchored in the bay. Now beyond the range of the Comanches' arrows and lances, Linnville residents remained close enough to witness the wanton destruction of their homes.

One fuming bureaucrat could not bear the sight. Sitting off shore in a row boat, Judge John Hays decided that he would not sit by while barbarians ravaged his town. Shotgun in hand, he waded onto shore, cursing the Comanches to Hell. His behavior mystified the warriors. Believing Hays insane, they rode near but dared not harm him least his bad medicine contaminate them. At length, the crestfallen official returned to his boat and rowed away from the beach. Only then did the magistrate examine his weapon. He had forgotten to load it.

That day, Linnville warehouses bulged with trade goods. Reports placed the value of the merchandise as high as $300,000. Among the ordinary trade items were crates of hats and umbrellas bound for Béxar merchant James Robinson, ornamental objects that delighted the raiders. Linn recalled:

These the Indians made free with, and went dashing about the blazing village, amid their screeching squaws and 'little Injuns,' like demons in a drunken saturnalia, with Robinson's hats on their heads and Robinson's umbrellas bobbing about on every side like tipsy young balloons.

Without opposition, the marauders took their time. They spent the rest of the day plundering and burning. Wanting to leave nothing the Texians could use, the warriors drove cattle into pens and slaughtered them. Adorned with top hats and umbrellas, Numunuh tied calico bolts to their horse's tails and trailed them through the streets. Buffalo Hump left the smoldering town site late that afternoon satisfied. Not a single building or item of value remained. His warriors literally wiped Linnville off the map.

The Comanches were exultant. Each warrior boasted ponies and plunder, which brought status and honors. Yet, their loot slowed them to a crawl, diminishing the mobility that had once made them perilous. Did Buffalo Hump perceive the danger? Probably, but even a chief of his renown would not ask a warrior to part with his booty.

Worse still, the raiders had lost the advantage of surprise. News of their great foray spread across central Texas. Rangers mustered and mounted up. Militiamen, regulars, and Tonkawa allies met and marched. General Felix Huston calculated the Comanches' route back to their Hill Country and Rolling Plains camps and called for Texian fighting men to assemble on the banks of Plum Creek near Lockhart. There, he hoped, he might offer Buffalo Hump a surprise of his own.

On Fighting Comanches

by John Salmon "Rip" Ford, Texas Ranger Captain

In the event of being pursued, immediately after the preparation of depredations, the Comanches move day and night, very often not breaking gallop except to exchange horses (which they do several times) and water the caballada [horse herd], until they deem themselves safe. Under the circumstances they will travel at least 70 miles a day, which is a long distance with the incumbrance of loose animals.

A party of warriors dressed in their trappings—embellished shields, fancy moccasins, long pig tails bedecked with silver, shoulder belts worked with beads and adorned with shells, fine leggings, ornamented cases for bows and arrows—mounted upon spirited horses, singing a war song, and sweeping over a prairie is a beautiful spectacle to a man with plenty of brave fellows to back him.

Their motions are easy and graceful. They sit on a horse admirably, and manage one with a master hand. Charge them and they will retreat from you with double numbers. But beware when pursuing them; keep your men together, well in hand, with at least half their arms loaded, else you will find when it is too late, the flying Comanches will turn on you and charge you to the very teeth.

A Comanche can draw a bow when on horseback, standing or running, with remarkable strength and accuracy. They have been known to kill horses running at full speed over one hundred yards away.

In the commencement of a fight, the yell of defiance is borne to you loud, long, and startling. The war whoop has no romance in it. It thrills even a stout heart with an indescribable sensation. The excitement of battle is quite evident among these people as among others. Let the tide turn against them, send messengers through some of their warriors, and then the mournful wail is heard: its lugubrious notes are borne back to you with uncouth cadences, betokening sorrow, anger, and a determination to revenge.

Never ride upon a bowman's left; if you do, ten to one that he will pop an arrow through you. When mounted, an Indian cannot use his bow against an object behind and to his right.

The dead are usually borne from the field. Nothing but the most imminent danger prevents them from performing the incumbent duty

continued

of not leaving the body of a comrade in the hands of an enemy. Over a fallen chief they will make a desperate stand. Their caution seems merged in the determination to risk everything to bear him from the field. To attain this object, they will fight furiously, bravely, and often. If they abandon him, it is in despair. Flight is no longer methodical and menacing to the pursuer. Retreat degenerates into rout. After this they have seldom if ever been known to resume the offensive. They will hide themselves in the first chaparral affording security against discovery, remain during the day, visit the dead at night, and if not able to remove them will spread blankets or some covering over them.

The bow is placed horizontally in shooting; a number of arrows are held in the left hand; the bow operates as a rest to the arrows. The distance—the curve the missile has to describe in reaching the object—is determined by the eye without taking aim. Arrows are sped after each other in rapid succession. At a distance of 60 yards and over, arrows can be dodged, if but one Indian shoots at you at one time. Under forty yards the six-shooter has little advantage over the bow. At long distances the angle of elevation is considerable. It requires a quick eye to see the arrow and judge the whereabouts of its descent, a good dodger to move out of the way, and a good rider withal to keep in the saddle. A man is required to keep both eyes engaged in an Indian fight.

Plum Creek

he Comanches paraded across the prairie, flushed with the knowledge they had conducted the greatest raid in Numunuh history. Each measured gait brought them closer to Plum Creek, an unremarkable stream like many they had already crossed.

Yet, this one was different; hidden enemies crouched under its banks. Soldiers of the Texas Republic watched their adversaries approach. Even Texians who were there that day could not agree on the exact number of the enemy. They were too many to count. During the morning of August 12, 1840, Texian soldiers viewed the approaching antagonists with both anxiety and admiration. One of them, Texas Ranger Robert Hall, recalled:

> It was one of the prettiest sights I ever saw in my life. The warriors flourished their white shields, and the young chiefs galloped about the field with the long tails streaming from their hats and hundreds of vari-colored ribbons floating in the air, exhibiting great bravado. Some of them dashed courageously very close to us, and two or three of them lost their lives in this foolhardy display of valor.

Regular Army General Felix Huston commanded the disparate Texian force of about two hundred men. He elected to assume a defensive posture, stand his ground, and receive the Comanche attack.

229

"Battle of Plum Creek." In this nineteenth-century woodcut, Comanche warriors brandish items plundered from Linnville. *From J. W. Wilbarger's* Indian Depredations in Texas *(1889). Courtesy of State House Press.*

Comanche warriors obliged, swarming forward to assail the Texian line—but just as quickly to dart away. Most of Huston's troopers remained dismounted, but about thirty mounted rangers pursued the Indians and broke up their attack. One witness testified that they performed "personal heroism worthy of all praise."

Even so, rangers could not provide protection for the grounded regulars and militiamen, several of whom fell wounded. The mounts of the men on the firing line proved easy targets and racing bowmen brought them down like tethered cattle. This one-sided skirmish lasted thirty minutes when Texas Ranger captains Ben McCulloch, Edward Burleson, and Mathew "Old Paint" Caldwell implored Huston to allow the rest of the Texians to mount and countercharge. They explained that while their men remained on foot, the enemy was free to exploit his superior mobility. Still, Huston insisted on maintaining a defensive posture.

The Comanches' arrows found their mark, but so, too, did Texian bullets. When a chief wearing a "tremendous headdress" fell to the accurate rifle fire, his mourning followers "set up a peculiar howl." With their adversaries' sudden demoralization, ranger captains recognized an opportunity. Shaking with anger, Caldwell shouted into Huston's face: "Now, General, is your time to charge them! They are whipped!" The sputtering Huston made no reply; indecisiveness had unmanned him. Without waiting for orders, the captains directed their troops to mount and led them in a spirited rush. Astride their mustangs, they could match the Comanches' mobility and bring deadlier firepower to bear. In a sprawling gunfight the official chain of command became less important than the proven leadership of each troop captain.

Giving full vent to their frenzy, the rangers charged "howling like wolves." The herd of captured horses, as many as two thousand head, stampeded and raised dust "so thick that the parties could see each other but a short distance." Checked by their mass and encumbered with plunder, the Comanches could not maneuver. As Hall told it: "Our boys charged with a yell, and did not fire until they got close to the enemy." Wielding single-shot, flintlock pistols, it was vital that they made each round count. Cramped warriors were unable to break free from the throng; rangers darted along the perimeter. Only then, where they could not miss, did they open fire. They brought down about fifteen amid the press of warriors and ponies.

Captain Caldwell had been right. The Comanches would not stand against a determined charge and close-quarters fire power. General Huston reported: "The Indians scattered, mostly abandoning their horses and taking to the thickets." A running fifteen-mile pursuit ensued as rangers chased fleeing Indians as far as the Balcones Escarpment. Once there, the surviving Indians reached the hilly region of the Edwards Plateau and vanished into the Texas Hill Country.

Toward sundown, ranger detachments returned to the site of the initial engagement near Plum Creek and found the rest of the Texian army sifting loot that the Comanches had discarded. These included items of almost every description: bags of silver, bolts of fabric, kegs of liquor, cases of books, full suits of clothing, pouches of tobacco—even a number of live baby alligators that warriors stashed in saddlebags to convince folks back in the *Comanchería* that they had raided all the way to the coast. Hall recollected: "We hardly knew what to do with all this stuff, and we finally concluded to divide it among ourselves."

As the Comanches broke and fled, they killed many of their captives. Among the hostages was the youthful widow of Linnville customs officer, Major Hugh Oran Watts. Juliet Constance Ewing Watts had been married only twenty-one days before she witnessed her husband's murder and found herself a prisoner. As was their custom, Comanches attempted to rape the young woman but were unable to decipher the intricacies of her whalebone corset. Finally, they gave up and left her virtue intact. When Mrs. Watts had become an encumbrance, a warrior fired an arrow into her torso. But the same corset that had previously preserved her modesty now saved her life. The projectile careened off a bone stay inflicting a painful, but not mortal, flesh wound.

The clash at Plum Creek transformed a Comanche triumph into a bitter defeat. Greed proved their undoing. Texian soldiers could never have intercepted them had warriors not been driving a vast herd of captured livestock. White veterans swore that they had killed at least eighty Indians but produced only twelve enemy bodies. One should recall, however, that the Numunuh carried their dead off the field for ritual burial. The "Lords of the South Plains" continued their attacks against isolated homesteads, but never again did they attack in such large numbers or penetrate so far into areas of Texas settlement.

General Huston dispatched a fulsome postbattle report to President Mirabeau B. Lamar. He claimed victory, but those present on August 12 knew how little he had done to achieve it. Indeed, if the ranger captains had not taken tactical command, Buffalo Hump's warriors would have likely annihilate the entire Texian force a little at a time. The general's military prospects dimmed following the Plum Creek fight. Too many veterans had witnessed his meltdown for it to remain a secret. To some, he became a laughingstock and his pride would not abide it. During the autumn of 1840, he resigned his Texas Army commission and became a partner in a New Orleans law firm. But Texas was never far from his thoughts; four years later, he was a staunch advocate of annexation. He remained a rebel in search of a cause. In 1851, for example, he addressed a New Orleans assembly where he espoused Cuba's independence from Spain. As the states grew further apart, he emerged as a fire-eating secessionist. A civil war might have fulfilled his martial ambitions, but he never found out. In 1857, he passed away in Natchez, Mississippi.

General Felix Huston died as he had lived—a flouncing dilatant out of his depth. Texian officials were about to deal with another flouncing dilatant—this time, of the French variety.

The Pig War

A proud son of Normandy, Jean Pierre Isidore Alphonse Dubois de Saligny entertained a lofty assessment of his prominence, and it exasperated him when people failed to acknowledge it. In 1832 he began his diplomatic duties, serving as secretary of French legations in Hanover, Greece, and the United States. It was during this last assignment, that his superiors directed him to visit Texas and report on its prospects. In 1839, he inspected Galveston, Houston, and Matagorda. Receiving his favorable assessment, French officials recognized Texas and entered into a Treaty of Amity, Navigation, and Commerce.

In January 1840, Dubois returned to Texas, but this time as chargé d'affaires; the new republic did not warrant a full-fledged ambassador. He began to take on the airs he deemed appropriate to the new appointment, signing his name "A. de Saligny," which implied that he descended from French nobility. It was a complete ruse; he was as bourgeois as a wooden shoe. Although the post constituted a promotion, the diplomat resented that his directors had relegated him to such a remote backwater. The primitive conditions in Austin appalled him. In July 1840, he described Austin defenses that were, "limited to surrounding the capitol with a ditch of several feet and with a simple palisade which, to tell the truth, seems to me, with people like Texans to defend it, to be sufficient against enemies like the Comanches and the Mexicans."

235

Among his other duties, Dubois oversaw the construction of a French Legation in Austin. Nations installed legations when the host country was not worthy of an embassy, and in 1841 Texas placed low down in the international pecking order. While builders worked to complete his official residence, he took lodgings in the Bullock House, Austin's first hotel, located at the northwest corner of Pecan Street (current Sixth Street) and Congress Avenue. Dubois and innkeeper Richard Bullock did not get along and the Frenchman soon moved into a modest house on West Pecan Street. In a letter, dated November 6, 1840, he protested having to occupy lodgings so far beneath his station.

> I am thus resigned to entertaining in the humble dwelling where I am encamped rather than installed and to do the honors the best I can. I had all the cabinet and several senators to dinner there, several days ago. I also invited the President, and he did me the honor of accepting.

He purchased twenty-one acres on the town's east side where construction of a proper legation began, one which would reflect the dignity of France—and, of course, his own.

A flare up in the simmering feud between Bullock and Dubois sidetracked diplomatic pursuits. Like most Texians, Bullock kept a sounder of swine to feed his family and customers. Following local custom, he turned them loose to amble along the streets of the capital. In search of fodder, the hogs occupied Dubois's stables and ate corn intended for his horses. That would have been insult enough, but three of the pigs then invaded his bedroom where they devoured his linen and even official state papers. The fuming Frenchman ordered his manservant to dispatch the pigs, which he did with pitchforks and pistols. Bullock later claimed that the diplomat had "most maliciously and wantonly" slaughtered between fifteen and twenty-five of his hogs, the value of which he estimated at one hundred dollars. Then, when the innkeeper learned that it was the butler who had actually killed his pigs, he sought him out and beat him like a

A contemporary sketch of the Bullock House as it appeared during the Pig War.
Courtesy of the Austin Public Library.

dusty rug. Dubois confronted Bullock over the thrashing, but the hot-headed hotelier threatened him with a trouncing of his own.

Bullock and Dubois were in a standoff. One demanded compensation for dead hogs, and the second insisted that under the "Laws of Nations" he fell under diplomatic immunity. Some Texain officials supported Bullock, others Dubois. Following the initial affray, Bullock continued to harangue and bully Dubois and his staff when he met them on the street. Because Austin was still a small town, such occasions were frequent.

The chargé d'affaires exacerbated the situation by embroiling himself in local politics. He was open in his bias for the Sam Houston faction, which alienated Mirabeau B. Lamar supporters. Dubois fired off a number of letters to Lamar's secretary of state, J. S. Mayfield. In these, the diplomat protested Bullock's "scandalous and outrageous" abuse and demanded that Texian officials penalize him for his insolence. Mayfield explained that he had no power to imprison a citizen without due process of law. Besides, who did this Frenchman think he was? Giving orders to national officials, indeed!

In May 1841, Dubois severed diplomatic relations. He explained that he refused to, "remain any longer with a Government which, far from being able to let me enjoy the respect and protection due a Representative of a friendly Power, would not even have the power or the desire to protect my life from the assaults of a scoundrel." He took up residence in culturally comfortable New Orleans and issued proclamations concerning the reprisals his sovereign was about to exact. Actually, his superiors in the Foreign Office were angrier at Dubois than the Texians. Impelled by Gallic pride, he had abandoned his post—and did so without instructions from his government. Even the French grew tired of his tantrums. And all this over wayward swine.

Ultimately, the "Pig War" produced few lasting consequences. The French Foreign Office backed Dubois, at least officially, but had no intention of letting some haughty minion dictate national policy. When Houston won back the president's office in 1841, he made "satisfactory explanations" to the French government and requested Dubois's return. Houston's "explanations" did not entirely appease the sullen chargé d'affaires, but having received severe reprimands from his bosses, he resumed his duties with as much grace as he could muster. He returned to Texas in April 1842, but by then, the new president had returned the capital to Houston City.

Dubois never returned to Austin. Carpenters finished work on the French Legation. The building still stands as Austin's oldest frame structure. But Dubois, the official who secured the land and supervised its construction, never spent a single night in it.

Dreams of Santa Fe

The 1836 Treaties of Velasco denoted the Rio Grande as the southern and western boundary of the Texas Republic and President Mirabeau B. Lamar believed he should assert their claims. A glance at a map revealed that Santa Fe sat on the eastern bank of the Rio Grande, in what was ostensibly Texian territory. *Ostensibly.* Although Texians, in theory, claimed land westward all the way to the Rio Grande, in fact, not one of them lived any further west than Austin—and President Lamar planned to remedy that.

The occupation of Santa Fe was more than a point of pride; it was also a matter of finances. A rich commerce flowed from St. Louis along the Santa Fe Trail. With that track's terminus in Texian hands, that golden stream would roll straight into the republic's near-empty coffers.

Nationalistic considerations also swayed Lamar's judgment. Unlike Sam Houston, he scorned annexation to the United States. In grandiose dreams, the president envisioned the Texas Republic as a continental power, one bounded, not by the Rio Grande, but the Pacific coastline. Taking Santa Fe was but the first step, but like all first steps, a critical one.

Also critical was haste. Lamar needed to pull off his scheme quickly. Lamar's tenure was winding down. His term ended in December and the constitution forbade him another. He must act now or never. Houston, his nemesis, still wielded enormous influence. And "Big Drunk" never

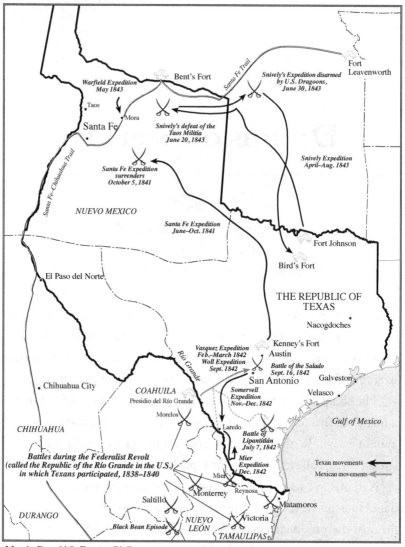

Map by Donald S. Frazier, Ph.D.

tired of singing the praises of the "old flag." By decisive action, President Lamar intended to forestall the growing annexation forces.

The president knew that the arbitrary and ineffective dictates of Mexico City frustrated *Nuevo Mexicanos*. Might they be willing to join forces with an expanding Texian empire? Toward that end, as

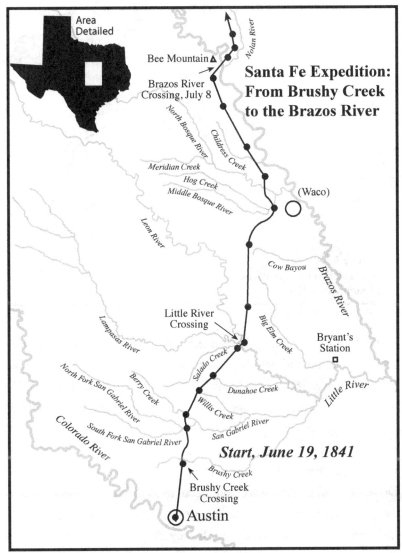

Map by Donald S. Frazier, Ph.D.

early as 1840, he had dispatched commissioners to Santa Fe to woo the locals and assess their pliability. Lamar placed much faith on that ancient proverb, "The enemy of my enemy is my friend." He was about to discover, however, that the enemy of one's enemy can also remain a bitter adversary.

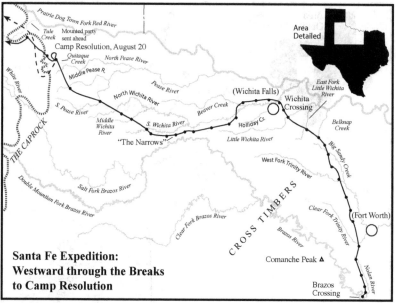

Santa Fe Expedition:
Westward through the Breaks
to Camp Resolution

Map by Donald S. Frazier, Ph.D.

On June 19, 1841, self-styled "pioneers" of the Texian Santa Fe Expedition left Austin brimming with hope and confidence. And with good reason. President Lamar had invested heavily in the success of this enterprise. He wished to dazzle the Santafeans. Oxen hauled twenty-one wagons bursting with trade goods valued at more than $200,000. Some of the republic's most respected citizens served as commissioners. These included William G. Cooke, Richard F. Brenham, George Van Ness, and signer of the Texas Declaration of Independence and Béxar resident, José Antonio Navarro (because they thought it might be handy to have someone along who actually spoke Spanish). Also accompanying the expedition was the thirty-two-year-old correspondent for the New Orleans *Picayune*, George Wilkins Kendall. He captured the pioneers' mood as they set off on their trek: "They were actuated by that love of adventure, which is inherent in thousands of our race; they were anxious to participate in the excitements ever incidental to a prairie tour."

Although a trading expedition, the Texians carried sticks as well as carrots. A veteran of the Battle of the Neches and the Council House

242

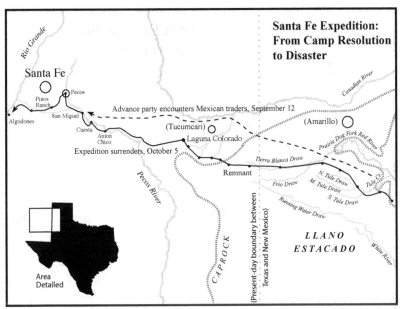

Map by Donald S. Frazier, Ph.D.

Fight, Brigadier General Hugh McCleod rode at the head of 350 men of the regular army organized into five companies of infantry and one of artillery. This force was to provide defense against Indian attacks; the trail to Santa Fe took it through the heart of *Comanchería* . Perhaps naively, the pioneers expected no resistance from the New Mexicans. Indeed, they anticipated a warm welcome. As Kendall noted:

> The universal impression in Texas was, that the inhabitants of Santa Fé were anxious to throw off a yoke, which was not only galling, but did not of right belong to them, and rally under the 'lone star' banner. . . . As for having anything like a regular battle, or forcibly subduing the country should the inhabitants be found hostile, such events were neither intended nor talked of.

The intended "prairie tour" proved disappointing. It was a catastrophe both in its conception and execution. During the 1300-mile march from Austin to Santa Fe, the Texians lost the trail and spent days wandering aimlessly. This roundabout course wasted supplies and undermined

Santa Fe Expedition:
into Mexico as Prisoners

Map by Donald S. Frazier, Ph.D.

morale. Apache warriors killed stragglers. Desertion and death hounded the ill-fated pioneers with every step.

At last, survivors stumbled into Santa Fe—not as liberators—but as starving wretches, begging for food and water. Mexican troops calmly rounded up the pathetic scarecrows and cast them in chains. And what of the array of merchandise meant to astound New Mexicans? The Texians jettisoned some along the trail, and the remainder the Santafeans confiscated. Some $200,000 up in smoke. Lamar's grand vision had been nothing but a pipe dream.

The "poet president" had horribly misjudged the New Mexicans. True, they bore little love for Mexico City bureaucrats, but they had even less for Lamar's government in Austin. Centralist politicos might be arrogant and dismissive, but at least they shared ties of language, religion, and culture. With the Texians they shared, well, nothing.

Now the real suffering began. Texian captives endured an agonizing forced march to Mexico City; many did not survive the journey. Once there, they rotted away in the fetid Perote Prison. The debacle of the Santa Fe Expedition constituted the low point of Lamar's administration and revealed the folly of western conquest.

When news of the disaster arrived in Austin, Texas citizens and their representatives denounced Lamar and his cabinet. A Select Committee proclaimed: "The President, in fitting up and sending out the Santa Fé Expedition [has] acted without the authority of law or the sanction of reason." It further found the chief executive's judgment, "strange, unnatural and unsatisfactory, and that the course pursued by his Excellency meets the disapprobation of Congress." It was probably a blessing that the 1836 Constitution prohibited Lamar from seeking another term.

He would have garnered few votes.

Tejanos in the Texas Republic

Anglo Texians who fought beside Juan Seguín's men during the Béxar and San Jacinto campaigns appreciated how much *Tejanos* had sacrificed to win Texas independence; sadly, most American immigrants flooding into the republic following San Jacinto did not. They were unaware of the region's thorny history, ignorant of the many Tejano contributions, and mistrustful of citizens who spoke a different language, embraced a different religion, and observed different customs. Thus, the differences were all they saw. Many newcomers, believing only what they read in the newspapers, viewed Mexicans as the enemy—all Mexicans.

Had they been more observant, they could have witnessed continuing Tejano allegiance. Seguín won election as a Texas senator. From 1837 to 1840, he and fellow Bexariño, Congressman José Antonio Navarro, labored to represent the interests of their constituents. They sponsored legislation to force officials to print laws of the fledgling nation in both English and Spanish. For Seguín, this issue was intensely personal. He never learned to speak or read English. Despite that disadvantage, he served on the Committee of Claims and Accounts and actually chaired the Committee on Military Affairs—an indication of the high esteem in which fellow congressmen held him. In 1839, Seguín and Captain Henry Karnes led a successful expedition against Comanche raiders. That same year, grateful citizens recognized his patriotism. Residents of a settlement some thirty miles east of Béxar honored him with a parade and formal dinner. They then proclaimed that their community, formerly known as Walnut Springs, would henceforth take the name of his family: Seguin. Despite deep roots in Béxar, he kept an eye on affairs south of the Rio Grande. In 1840, he resigned as senator to fight against the Centralist regime in Mexico City. Returning home in 1841, he won the post of San Antonio mayor.

Yet, not all Tejanos followed Seguín's example. In Nacogdoches, Vicente Córdova grew increasing disenchanted with the new order, plotted with Mexican agents, and in 1838, led an insurgence against the Texas Republic. Texians quickly snuffed out the insurrection, but several of its leaders, including Córdova himself, escaped. Following the uprising, Texas Rangers attacked and killed Mexican agents inside the boundaries of the republic. Rangers discovered documents on the corpses confirming the reality of a conspiracy to provoke disaffected Tejanos and Indians.

In South Texas, another charismatic insurgent earned the wrath of Texian officials. During the Texas Revolution, Carlos de la Garza's company of loyalist rancheros carried out successful guerrilla operations against James W. Fannin's command. Following the Mexican army's retreat after San Jacinto, Garza fortified his ranch and dug in his heels. Throughout the Republic period, he remained a dominant figure in the San Antonio–Guadalupe River region. In troubled times, locals flocked to his ranch seeking protection. During the 1842 Woll incursion, Tejanos and Irish settlers from the nearby towns of Refugio and Goliad took refuge at Carlos Rancho. A tough old bird, Don Carlos earned the grudging admiration (if not the affection) of Anglo Texians, but despite all pressure, he never pledged allegiance to the Republic of Texas.

The actions of Córdova, Garza, and other defiant Tejanos seemed to confirm newly arrived Americans' worst fears. While the Anglo population snowballed, Tejanos found it harder and harder to preserve their rights, their lands, and their lives. In 1836, Texian forces under General Thomas Jefferson Rusk drove the family of Doña Patricia de León out of Victoria— the town that she and husband, *Empresario* Martín de León, had created in 1824. The family went into exile in Louisiana. Doña Patricia was finally able to return to Victoria a decade later, but found that her home and most of the family goods had vanished. Nevertheless, she was able to reclaim most of her land and salvage a measure of her former life. To this day, many of her descendants remain in and around Victoria.

Even in San Antonio, one as highly regarded as Juan Seguín was unable to withstand the onslaught. In 1842, Mexican General Ráfael Vásquez led a foray that briefly captured San Antonio. Although Mayor Seguín pursued the retreating enemy force, many American rowdies alleged that he had collaborated with Vásquez. Ultimately, the drumbeat of opposition became so deafening that Seguín, fearing for his life, fled Béxar.

Seguin had no alternative but to "seek refuge among my enemies." Mexican authorities immediately placed him under arrest. They released him only on condition the that he serve in the Mexican army. Subsequently, he returned to Béxar as a staff officer during the 1842 Woll Raid. In the Mexican War (1846–1848), he fought against many of his former comrades, many of whom condemned him as a defector. In 1848, Seguín returned to his beloved San Antonio, but many old Texians never forgave him. He lived out the rest of his life in peace but never regained the hero's status he once enjoyed.

Seguin's friend and neighbor, José Antonio Navarro was a faithful citizen of the Texas Republic. In 1841, at President Lamar's request, he was

continued

a member of the ill-fated Santa Fe Expedition. Mexican officials captured him, placed him on trial, and delivered a death sentence. Yet, he avoided execution and, along with other Texian prisoners, endured the torturous trek to the infamous Perote prison. While there, he rebuffed repeated offers to collaborate with the Mexicans. He eventually escaped and made his way back to Texas.

Trapped amid a swirl of shifting loyalties, Tejanos had no choice but to adapt to life in the Republic of Texas. Their reactions varied. Some saw their destiny linked to the Texian separatist movement; some remained loyal to Mexico; and others, attempting to protect their families and communities, sat astride the fence. To determine their way, Tejanos weighed political, economic, and cultural concerns. Yet, whichever road they took, far too many of them came to be, in Juan Seguin's mournful phrase, "foreigners in their native land."

Big Drunk's Big Comeback

When Texians went to the polls on September 6, 1841, they had not yet learned of the Santa Fe fiasco. Yet, even without that sorrowful intelligence, most had already lost patience with Mirabeau B. Lamar's extravagant schemes. A blind hog could discern that the nation was bankrupt. Texas paper money, styled "red backs," became more and more depressed. A Roman Catholic priest trying to start a church in Texas described the national mood. Writing from Houston City in July 1841, he commented:

> I arrived last night at this place and found the people in pretty low spirits. Everything looks dull. No money in the country, people move back to the United States much faster than they came in. . . . I am really out of heart. In the States a log church may be at least put up, but here in Texas there is nothing to be done without money, and money can be had nowhere.

The slate of candidates surprised no one. Lamar's vice president and former interim president, David G. Burnet, represented the anti-Houston faction. Sam Houston's supporters urged their man to run, claiming that only he had the experience and ability to untangle the jumble Lamar had left. In the end, he did not require that much prompting.

Nowadays, Texans recall Lamar with disdain. Truthfully, there was much to censure. Still, his administration was not without its successes.

President Lamar pushed through a bill that ensured the future of public education. He famously declared: "The cultivated mind is the guardian genius of democracy and, while guided by and controlled by virtue, the noblest attribute of man. It is the only dictator that freemen acknowledge and the only security that freemen desire." To this day, Texans honor Lamar—not Houston—as the "Father of Texas Education." The "poet president" also fostered the Homestead Act, which prevented citizens from losing their homes to debt. In 1839, he established the city of Austin and moved the capital there. That same year he approved the "Lone Star" flag as the national standard, the one that, even now, flies as the state flag. Lamar was in the tradition of Texas wildcatters, men possessed with, and by, grand dreams, those who either won or lost in spectacular fashion. One may decry their failures but admire their vision.

Indeed, vision and personality were the central issues of the 1841 presidential campaign. Where would the next president take the country; how would he address the republic's multiple difficulties? As Lamar's vice president, Burnet found it impossible to separate himself from that administration's failed policies. His only argument was that Houston would be worse. Diligent and well meaning, Burnet, a New Jersey Yankee, was also cold and contentious. A devout Presbyterian, Burnet neither drank nor swore. In addition, he carried the Holy Bible with him everywhere he went. Dr. Ashbel Smith described him as "a character that Old John Knox would have hugged with grim delight." He was uncomfortable on the stump, where he came across as distant and spiteful. Houston, of course, was in his natural element. Standing six feet, three inches, and weighing in at 240 pounds, Houston looked like every schoolboy's idea of a hero. Some charitably minded individuals might have described Burnet as portly, but most would have called him fat. On the stump, Houston was quick with a joke or an anecdote and— although never shying away from invective—he always delivered it with a gleam in his eye. Unlike his opponent, Houston was notorious for both his drinking and swearing.

Early on, the campaign turned ugly—worse than Texians had ever witnessed. The pious Burnet made Houston's intemperance his central theme. That Ol' Sam Jacinto was an alcoholic was an open secret. His benders were the stuff of legend. One of Houston's friends warned him that his "health and reputation would soon sink under the influence of liquor" and prayed, "May an alwise Providence chain you down to Sobriety and prudence."

Burnet supporters contrasted the two candidates:

> The private character of the individual elected, should be free from blemish or any degrading vice. . . . Burnet has been tried in adversity and prosperity, and ever found capable and faithful to the best interests of the people. Why then should we hesitate? By electing a drunkard, we cast the high destines of our beloved republic upon a die, and leave it to blind chance.

The *Texas Sentinel*, a pro-Burnet newspaper, warned that Houston would "blaspheme his God, by the most horrible oaths, that ever fell from the lip of man." Writing under the pen name, "Truth," Houston fired back in the pages of the *Houstonian*. Addressing Burnet directly, he blasted: "You prate about the faults of other men, while the blot of foul unmitigated treason rest upon you. You political brawler and canting hypocrite, who the water of Jordan could never cleanse from your political and moral leprosy." Discovering Houston's old Cherokee epithet, Burnet began to call his rival, "Big Drunk." He even accused Houston of being part Indian. It was untrue, but Houston—proud of his adopted Cherokee family—turned the tables and wryly thanked Burnet for the compliment. Indeed, emphasizing his native background, Houston rebuked Burnet as a *wetumpka*. The word translated as "hog thief." The towering Houston further dubbed his diminutive challenger "Little Davey." And so it went, each day generating another outlandish defamation. As a younger man, Houston had mastered the bare-knuckled maneuvers of Jacksonian politics, but even he grew disgusted with all the mudslinging. "I am constrained to believe," he commented, "that the people of Texas are thoroughly disgusted with both of us."

Political operatives projected a Houston landslide. Even on the western frontier, where support for Burnet should have been strongest, forecasts were grim. Writing from Austin, San Jacinto veteran Henry Millard recorded, "Burnet is completely done, he could not now in the western counties be elected fiddler Genl. to the old chief."

Predictions proved accurate. Houston carried the election with 7,915 votes. Burnet lagged far behind with 3,616. In the race for vice president, Edward Burleson, a Houston man, received 6,141 votes. Memucan Hunt, representing the Burnet camp, collected 4,336. Yes, the "Sword of San Jacinto" was a functioning alcoholic, but the operative word was *functioning*. The priggish Burnet tried to make Houston's drinking an issue, but it never seemed to register with voters. On Election Day, Texians excused his vices with a wink and a nod. Ultimately, who among his opponents had accomplished half as much sober as Houston had drunk? Explaining the outcome of the election of 1841 to a friend, Texas merchant James Morgan captured the public's disposition: "Old Sam H. with all of his faults appears to be the only man for Texas—He is still unsteady, intemperate, but drunk in a ditch is worth a thousand of Lamar and Burnet."

A Republic in Crisis

When Sam Houston took his oath of office on December 13, 1841, the Texas Republic hovered on the edge of collapse. Conditions were so bad that the government could not afford to buy firewood for the presidential residence. Texians had elected him to clean up Mirabeau B. Lamar's mess, but that proved a herculean task. From its inception, the nation had struggled under the weight of massive debt. In Houston's first term, it rose from $1.25 million to $3.25 million. Lamar viewed expenditures as investments in future greatness and spent like a drunken sailor, adding $4,855,000 to the balance. Houston now implemented a policy of belt tightening, announcing that he intended to reduce expenses from $3 million to a judicious total of $300,000. He cut the number of government "loafers," merged agencies, and slashed salaries—including his own. The debt plunged from $10,000 to $5,000 a year. Chastened by the president's example, congressmen reduced their daily wage from $5 to $3. They also voted to rescind a $5 million loan that they had previously approved. Until the republic could sustain its operating expenses, Congress also deferred payments on the national debt.

Houston was a budget hawk, but the desperate state of affairs forced even him to seek additional loans. An 1839 act permitted the president to borrow up to a million dollars in an emergency. With Antonio López de Santa Anna back in power and promising to plant Mexico's "eagle standard

253

on the banks of the Sabine," Houston figured that qualified. In June 1842, he secured the prescribed amount from New Orleans entrepreneur Alexandre Bourgeois d'Orvanne. The president regretted adding to the debt pile but believed events required it. Nonetheless, Houston boasted a far better fiscal record than Lamar; during the whole of his second term, he spent only $511,000. Houston was never able to balance the budget, but by the time his second term ended, revenues had at least begun to match expenses.

In addition to economic issues, the president had several other problems on his plate. He hated Austin—and not just because it did not bear his name. As he carped to anyone would listen:

> This is the most unfortunate site upon earth for the Seat of Government between water, cold region, indifferent and sparse timber. It is removed outside of the settlement, and not a house between this and Santa Fe. Our eating is very plain, and no society to enjoy in this place.

It was also vulnerable to Indian attack. During Lamar's term, the Comanches were so bold as to raid inside the city limits. One resident admitted, "Indians are as thick as hops about the mountains in this vicinity and occasionally they knock over a poor fellow and take his hair." For all those reasons, the president urged Congress to transfer the capital back to Houston City. Yet, the proposal received considerable resistance, even from members of his own faction. "Ol' Sam Jacinto" cursed his luck and bided his time.

On March 5, 1842, General Rafael Vásquez presented the president with a belated birthday present—he had turned forty-nine on March 2. That Mexican officer had led a foray across the Rio Grande, captured San Antonio, and occupied the place for two days. Then, Vásquez packed up and left, taking his soldiers with him and leaving the town little worse for his visit. What had been the point? Santa Anna evidently wanted to put Texians on notice that Mexicans still considered Texas part of their national domain and had the power to enforce their claims. Houston understood that they did not but exploited the raid to urge Congress to move the capital. If Mexicans had seized San Antonio, he argued, they might have easily taken Austin. Exercising the leverage provided by the Vasquez Raid, Houston ordered the government out of Austin. When the Congress next assembled on June 27, it did so in Houston City. Even so, livid Austin residents retained possession of the national archives.

But Houston's tenure in his namesake city extended less than four months. The squalid conditions that had prompted officials to leave the town in 1839 had not improved. Legislators abhorred the place and made their discontent known. On September 28, to achieve a compromise, Houston moved the capital to the Town of Washington (present-day Washington-on-the Brazos). The president arrived there on October 2—the anniversary of the "Come-and-Take-It" fight—and took up his duties.

In the wake of the Vásquez Raid, Texians, combative as ever, demanded military action. It constituted a stain on national honor, they asserted—an affront they must answer in blood. But the foray had been more of a demonstration than a real menace. In the face of citizen demands, Houston stood fast and clung to his peace policy. With the horrors of the Santa Fe Expedition heavy on his mind, he insisted that the expense of a military excursion would outweigh any possible benefits.

Then, on September 11, General Adrian Woll, a Frenchman in Mexican service, riding at the head of a thousand soldiers, recaptured San Antonio. This time, the Mexicans held it for nine days. Militiamen under Mathew "Old Paint" Caldwell and Texas Rangers under John Coffee "Jack" Hays challenged the enemy incursion. On September 18, the two forces fought at Salado Creek, just outside Béxar. Standing on the defensive, the Texians repelled the Mexican assault but not without cost. On September 17, Captain Nicholas Dawson led a force of fifty-three Fayette County volunteers to reinforce Caldwell. Yet, before he could rendezvous with Caldwell's division, several hundred Mexican cavalrymen surrounded the company. Dawson had his men seek cover in the heavy brush, but when the Mexicans brought up their artillery, he realized his position was hopeless. Dawson walked forward under a flag of truce; the Mexicans gunned him down. Thirty-six of the fifty-three Texians died fighting or while trying to surrender, two escaped, and fifteen others became captives. Texians would recall the episode as "Dawson's Massacre."

On September 20, Woll began a retreat. Caldwell pursued and overtook the Mexican force on the Hondo River. There they fought another battle. Hays and his rangers captured an enemy cannon, but Woll was able to disengage and escape toward the Rio Grande.

Although the raids of 1842 proved bothersome, they also revealed a comforting reality. The Mexican government was too weak to take and hold ground north of the Rio Grande for more than a few days. These swoops were the best they could muster. Even, so Houston came under enormous pressure to respond to them. In November 1842, he yielded to citizen's demands and approved a punitive expedition.

His decision was to produce one of the most darkly dramatic incidents in Texas history.

Black Powder, Lead Bullets, and Black Beans

S am Houston ordered Maryland native and San Jacinto veteran Alexander Somervell to lead the retaliatory expedition to the Rio Grande. He was a Houston man, and the president explained to him that the mission was more a gesture to appease angry citizens of South Texas than a real campaign. His orders were march to Laredo, raise the Lone Star flag, and come home—and to do so with as little bloodshed and expense as possible. Houston hoped that this show of force would be sufficient to appease congressional War Hawks.

At first, all went according to plan. Volunteers and militiamen mustered in San Antonio. All were keen to meet the enemy and strike a blow for Texas pride. Still, visions of fame and spoils also stirred many of them. On November 25, 1842, Somervell steered about 700 men out of San Antonio. Some dropped out during the grueling march, but the excursion numbered 683 effectives when it arrived in Laredo on December 8. Mexican soldiers had evacuated the town and the Texians occupied it without firing a shot. With no one to fight and little plunder to seize, 185 volunteers returned home on December 10. With about 500 men, Somervell rowed down the Rio Grande and captured the Mexican town of Guerrero. Once more, the Texians met little or no resistance, and again, they acquired little or no booty. Increasingly, they were becoming exasperated by the dearth of action and profit. Somervell determined that he had carried out his instructions. The president could now claim to have

257

"Shooting the Decimated Texians." This illustration originally appeared in Thomas Jefferson Green's 1845 edition of *Journal of the Texian Expedition against Mier; Subsequent Imprisonment of the Author, His Sufferings, and Final Escape from the Castle of Perote, with Reflections upon the Present Political and Probable Future Relations of Texas, Mexico, and the United States.*

repelled the Mexican marauders. It was time to call off this charade before someone got hurt.

On December 19, Somervell instructed his men to break camp and return to their homes. Volunteer Joseph McCutchan reported that, upon receiving the order, the men "became perfectly wild." At that juncture, the rowdiness, pigheadedness, and pride that had so often undermined Texian military efforts once again wrought their wicked influence. Disgusted that they had accomplished so little, some 308 diehards refused to obey Somervell's order. Thus, only 189 followed Somervell northward toward San Antonio. The remaining intransigents, including future Texas luminaries Samuel Hamilton Walker, George Bernard Erath, and William "Bigfoot" Wallace, remained in Laredo and formed into five companies. William S. Fisher, a veteran of San Jacinto and the Council House Fight, assumed overall command. Nearly all of them were political opponents of President Houston. They chose to drive across the Rio Grande, drive into Mexico, and capture the border town of Mier. With that decision, the Somervell Expedition ended and the ill-fated Mier Expedition began.

On December 23, Fisher's force entered Mier without opposition. On Christmas Day, a large Mexican unit under General Pedro de Ampudia arrived in town and combat ensued. The firebrands had sought a fight and now had more than they could handle. The Texians held off their attackers throughout the night and into the following day. On the afternoon of December 26, the hopelessness of their situation became apparent. The Mexicans outnumbered Fisher's force ten to one. The invaders had run out of food and water and had exhausted nearly all of their gunpowder. Yet, the lethal Texian long rifles had exacted a fearsome toll. "Bigfoot" Wallace bragged:

> Among us were some of the best marksmen in the world, backwoodsmen from Kentucky, Tennessee, and Arkansas, and every 'greaser' that ventured to peep at us above the parapets of the houses, and round the corners of the streets, was sure to get a bullet through the head.

It was no baseless boast. Ampudia suffered six hundred killed and two hundred wounded. Conversely, Fisher had lost only thirty killed and wounded. Fisher agreed to terms, but recalling the Alamo, Goliad, and Dawson's Massacre, he refused to surrender until Ampudia supplied a written assurance that he would treat the Texians "with consideration."

Antonio López de Santa Anna violated Ampudia's pledge and ordered his soldiers to march the Mier prisoners to Mexico City. On February 11, 1843, the captives overpowered their guards and escaped into the hills outside Salado, Mexico. Without food or water and deep within enemy territory, the effort proved fruitless. Only three escapees made it back to Texas. Mexican troops rounded up the rest, 176 total, and returned them to confinement in Salado.

News of the escape attempt incensed Santa Anna. He ordered the immediate execution of every Mier prisoner. To temper the effects of that barbarous dictate, the governor of Coahuila reduced the sentence to one out of ten. Consequently, 17 of the 176 would die, but how to determine the condemned?

Mexican soldiers placed 159 white beans in an earthenware jar. Then they added seventeen black beans and jumbled the mixture. Blindfolded, each prisoner reach in to pick a bean. A white bean signified survival, a black bean immediate execution. The defiant Texians determined not to cower in the presence of their captors. One of them held aloft a black bean and wryly exclaimed: "Boys, I told you so; I never failed in my life to draw a prize." The seventeen doomed individuals bid farewell to their comrades, and at sunset on March 25, faced the firing squad.

One more, however, fell victim to Santa Anna's malice. Ewen Cameron, a Highland Scot and San Jacinto veteran, had led the breakout at Salado. Although he drew a white bean, "His Excellency" ordered his death. On April 26, he met his fate. Cameron refused a blindfold, declaring, "For the liberty of Texas, Ewen Cameron can look death in the face." Then, he bared his breast for the bullets and shouted the command to fire. Eight musket balls slammed into his chest, killing him instantly.

Many who survived the "Black Bean Episode" succumbed to squalid conditions in Perote Prison. At length, however, Mexican officials exchanged both the Santa Fe and Meir prisoners, bringing a close to this melancholy chapter in Texas history.

The Texas Navy

The antagonism that surged back and forth across the Rio Grande, much like that torrent itself, flowed into the Gulf of Mexico. In November 1835, representatives of the Texian provisional government established an official navy. In January 1836, agents in New Orleans bought four schooners: *Brutus, Independence, Invincible,* and *Liberty.*

During the Texas Revolution, those vessels provided essential service. They protected sea lanes between New Orleans and Texas, along which streamed supplies and volunteers. Those ships and sailors also prevented an amphibious invasion of Texas. Antonio López de Santa Anna marched his *soldados* across miles of bleak prairies to reach Texas, but once there, he relied upon stores conveyed aboard Mexican ships to sustain them. By intercepting those supply vessels, rebel seadogs denied their land-bound enemies vital provisions. Cargoes seized from the holds of captured Mexican transports helped feed Sam Houston's army.

Commodore Charles Edward Hawkins directed the operations of the first Texas Navy. The New York native was an unlikely choice because he had previously served the Mexicans. While an officer in the U.S. Navy, he served aboard a number of storied frigates, including *Constitution, Constellation,* and *Guerriere.* Hawkins served under Commodore David Porter in the West Indies Squadron. Its mission was to quash piracy in Caribbean waters. The commodore was vehement in accomplishing his

Aboard the Texas Navy sloop-of-war *Austin*, Commodore Edwin Ward Moore commanded a fleet consisting of the brig *Wharton*, several schooners, and five Republic of Yucatán gunboats during the epic naval Battle of Campeche. *Courtesy of the San Jacinto Museum of History.*

assignment—perhaps, overly so. In 1826, Porter faced a court-martial for attacking a Puerto Rican town without proper authorization. His superiors found him culpable and demanded his resignation. Hawkins believed his patron had received a raw deal and, in a demonstration of support, also resigned his commission. Subsequently, both officers accepted positions in the Mexican Navy. Hawkins sailed during the Mexican Revolution as commanding officer of *Hermón*, attacking the Spanish fleet in the Gulf of Mexico. In 1828, he resigned his Mexican commission and returned to the United States.

In the opening stages of the Texas Revolution, Hawkins offered his skills to Governor Henry Smith, who proffered him a post in the Texas Navy and dispatched him to New Orleans to obtain the USS *Ingham*. Taking charge of the schooner, Hawkins renamed it *Independence*. By

January 10, 1836, Hawkins was patrolling the Texas coastline, during which time he sank or captured a number of smaller Mexican craft. In March 1836, Hawkins sailed *Independence* back to New Orleans for a well-deserved overhaul. Arriving at his home port at Matagorda, he discovered that Texian officials had raised him to the rank of commodore, which carried with it full command of the Texas Navy.

Following Texian defeats at the Alamo and Coleto Creek, Mexicans took possession of South Texas ports, forcing Hawkins to operate off of Galveston Island. Texian victory at San Jacinto allowed him to reclaim captured harbors and conduct a blockade of Matamoros.

Sailing vessels were costly to sustain, far beyond the means of the insolvent Texian government. An exasperated Hawkins put into New Orleans and there, in February 1837, fell victim to smallpox. It was a blessing that he did not live to witness the fate of the Texas Navy. By October 1837, all its ships had been lost at sea, captured by the Mexican Navy, run aground, or sold off as surplus.

Houston made no effort to maintain the navy during his first term, but after 1839, it became a critical component in Mirabeau B. Lamar's dreams of empire. In response to Mexican saber rattling, the Texas Congress bought six war ships, adding to the republic's mountain of debt.

Texas now had its second navy but required a man to command it. In 1825, Virginia native Edwin Moore entered the U.S. Navy as a midshipman at the age of fifteen. Promotion came slowly; by 1839, Moore had only attained the rank of lieutenant. Adventure and advancement captured the imagination of this ambitious young officer and he resigned his commission to cast his lot with the Lone Star Republic. Lamar immediately named Moore commander of his entire fleet. From lieutenant to commodore in a single bound—a meteoric rise for a fellow who had not yet celebrated his thirtieth birthday.

For the next three years, Moore's fleet harried the Mexican coastline. In May 1843, it fought alongside ships of the breakaway Republic of Yucatán at the naval Battle of Campeche, during which the Texas Navy sloop-of-war *Austin* and the brig *Wharton* engaged several vessels of the Mexican Navy. Among these were English-built ironclad steamships *Moctezuma* and *Guadalupe*. The battle provided protection for the Yucatán insurgents and compelled the Mexican Navy to lift its blockade of Campeche.

Ironically, Moore's greatest achievement was of ambiguous legality. Houston, who had regained the president's chair in 1841, was determined to cut expenses and swung his budget ax at the Texas Navy. On January 16, 1843, the Texas Congress passed legislation to disband the navy and sell its ships. Houston sent Samuel May Williams, William Bryant, and James Morgan to New Orleans to notify Moore of the congressional decision. Yet, Moore was able to persuade the delegation that it was foolish to sell the navy just as it was ready to sail. Ignoring his instructions, Colonel Morgan accompanied Moore so Congress would have to divide the censure between the commodore and the commissioners. When the president learned his agents had flouted his instructions and Moore had already sailed, he became so angry that he issued an edict that Congress had not sanctioned the mission and the fleet did not represent the Republic of Texas. In terms of international law, Houston had reduced Moore and his men to pirates.

It was fortunate for Moore that the Battle of Campeche was an obvious Texian victory. He suffered five sailors killed, but the Mexicans admitted eighty-seven killed with an undetermined number wounded. The non-sailor Colonel Morgan, was in the thick of the fighting and recorded his impressions:

> The way we knocked H-ll into them & out of them was a caution. We thrashed them soundly & the whole [Mexican] fleet ran off. . . . I expect 'Old Sam' will 'hang me' for I have travelled out of the course his instructions dictated. But as we have played h-ll with the enemy's arrangements and calculations in this quarter, he may be afraid & overlook the matter.

Morgan judged the matter correctly. On July 14, when the fleet arrived in Galveston, Texians of every stripe and persuasion hailed Commodore

Moore and his mariners as national heroes. Houston demanded that Moore face a court-martial, but it not only cleared him of any and all malfeasance, but it also commended him for his conduct. Congressmen later approved resolutions honoring the officers and crews of the Texas Navy—which they had to pass over the president's veto.

Later that year, bureaucratic bean counters auctioned off the fleet. But Galveston citizens purchased all the ships by public subscription and returned them to the nation. But Houston, and his successor Anson Jones, made sure Moore never resurrected the navy.

"Ol' Sam Jacinto" sure knew how to nurse a grudge.

Big Drunk Goes
on the Wagon

T he Cherokees did not call Sam Houston "Big Drunk" without reason. Well into middle age, he sustained an intimate relationship with "ardent spirits." His passion for the "creature" was legendary. Remember, though, he was almost always in pain. Wounds received at Horseshoe Bend in 1814 never completely healed. That would have been agony enough, but his shattered ankle, a souvenir of San Jacinto, only added to his anguish. In an age before over-the-counter pain relievers, he used whiskey to self-medicate. It is a testament to his character and strength of will that he was able to conquer his addiction.

Still, he could not have faced his demons without help—lots of it. The support Houston needed and craved came from the most unlikely of sources, a slip of a girl who was twenty-six years his junior. But what a girl she was. Margaret Moffette Lea was a stunningly striking Alabama belle with violet eyes and dark brown hair. Intensely religious, she relished romantic novels and composed poetry; having mastered guitar, harp, and piano, she was eligible and a pearl of great price. Her charm and beauty struck Houston like a cannonball. Houston had never been a shrinking violet around women. He had known many. Yet, once he met Margaret, he never loved another. Despite the disapproval of the Lea family, the couple wed on May 9, 1840, following a yearlong courtship.

Many of his Texas friends, knowing the general's penchants and personality, were understandably skeptical. Colonel Bernard Bee's

This 1840 photograph reveals Margaret Houston shortly after her marriage. Clearly, descriptions of her beauty were not exaggerated. *Author's collection.*

misgivings were typical: "I see with great pain the marriage of Genl. Houston to Miss Lea! In all my acquaintance with life I have never met an Individual more totally disqualified for domestic happiness—he will not live with her 6 months."The couple fooled the naysayers and remained together until Sam's death in 1863. Their union produced eight children.

Margaret's delicate exterior concealed an iron resolve. Sam's first marriage to Eliza Allen had been a disaster. He never legally wed his Cherokee domestic partner, Tiana Rogers, because he had not divorced Eliza. Nevertheless, Tiana was his wife in all but name and loved him mightily. But she could never constrain the darker forces of his nature. It astonished Texians, long familiarized with Big Drunk's excesses, that Margaret actually rehabilitated the general— something akin to altering the course of the Mississippi River. His friends noted that she was exactly the kind of wife that the great man needed.

Her first job was to get her husband off the bottle. To be fair, he was ready. Now a man of mature years, Sam had long since sown his wild oats. He was ready to settle down; he was sick and tired of being sick and tired. That, and he wanted to prove himself to be the kind of husband Margaret deserved. At an 1841 barbecue to celebrate his reelection, one supporter noted that Houston was a changed man: "Strange to say, it was a cold water doins. The old Chief did not touch, taste, or handle the smallest drop of the ardent."

Houston was spiritual in a Cherokee sort of way, but not religious in a Baptist sort of way and Margaret meant to remedy that. Shortly after coming to Mexican Texas, he accepted baptism into the Roman Catholic Church. One who witnessed that sacrament later avowed that all present thought it a joke—including Houston himself. He knew, however, that he could not hold public office without *officially* swearing his allegiance to Rome. It took Margaret, a lifelong Baptist, a full fourteen years to convince her headstrong husband to accept the doctrines of her church. But on Sunday, November 19, 1854, hundreds of the faithful watched as Houston, a practiced pagan, submitted to the full immersion demanded by Baptist doctrine. The day was chilly and Houston shivered as the pastor dunked all six feet, three inches, of him beneath the waters of the "Baptizing Hole" in Rocky Creek. A few days later, a friend observed:

"Well, General, I heard your sins were washed away."

With tongue firmly fixed in cheek, the convert replied:

"I hope so, but if they were all washed away, the Lord help the fish down below."

Even after his conversion, Margaret could not break Houston's habit of swearing. On one sweltering summer day, the general was riding with District Judge John H. Reagan, a devout Baptist. Houston's mount lost its footing, almost tossing its rider onto the road. Instinctively, he blasted, "God damn a stumbling horse!"

Taken aback, Reagan asked: "Oh! Brother Houston, do you still swear?"

Shamefaced, the hero of San Jacinto inquired, "Well, what must I do?"

"Ask God to forgive you."

"I'll do it. Hold my bridle rein." With that, Houston dismounted, knelt in the dust, and sought the pardon of his redeemer.

According to one version of the story, Ol' Sam rose to his feet, turned to Judge Reagan, and proudly declared, "That was a damned good prayer."

Without his wife's loving guidance, Houston would have drunk himself into an early grave. A family friend remarked, "The truth is Houston is a reformed and improved man. Fortunately married to a lady of fine endowments, combining religion with an amiable simplicity of manners, natural goodness of heart with a romantic taste, he realizes . . . the fruits of a happy union."

Houston owed this remarkable woman a lasting debt of gratitude—but so did all citizens of the Texas Republic.

The President and the Lady Cannoneer

President Sam Houston had used the Woll Raid in September 1842 as an excuse to move the capital out of Austin. He would have preferred to conduct business from his namesake city, but congressmen hated the hot, humid, and grimy municipality and took the governmental seat to the Town of Washington. Houston followed with good grace. Any place, he contended, was better than Austin.

Although Houston was much happier in his new digs, a lingering annoyance remained: the intractable Austin citizens still refused to give over the national archives. The president had attempted to move them following the Vásquez Raid in March. On the tenth day of that month, Houston directed Secretary of War George Washington Hockley to move the records to Houston City.

Getting wind of that order, Colonel Henry Jones, the military commander in Austin, summoned a town meeting to debate this new threat. After a lively discussion, residents concluded that, notwithstanding Houston's handwringing, their town was as safe from enemy attack as any other and that his withdrawal had created a dearth of confidence. That, in turn, had triggered a decrease in property values. On March 16, a "committee of vigilance" declared any relocation of government manuscripts illegal. To enforce their decree, they organized a mounted patrol at Bastrop to search every wagon and repossess any documents they might discover. To assert that Austin citizens disapproved of Houston's

A bird's-eye view of Austin as it appeared in Angelina Eberly's day. *Courtesy of the Austin Public Library.*

actions would be an understatement. The president's private secretary, W. D. Miller, informed his boss that they "would much rather take their rifles to prevent a removal [of the state papers] than to fight Mexicans."

Official pronouncements and executive orders had failed to budge the "seditious" Austinites, so Houston employed his cunning. On December 10, Houston called San Jacinto and Salado Creek veteran Colonel Thomas Ingles Smith and Texas Ranger Captain Eli Chandler into his office. He tasked them with a secret mission: to take possession of the archives and transport them to the Town of Washington—and to do so without arousing the notice of Austin citizens. Houston suggested that Smith and Chandler raise a ranger company on the pretext of providing protection against roving Comanches. Once they had lulled Austin residents into complacency, they were to seize the government papers in the dead of night and haul them away before locals could react.

Writing at the time, Houston explained his rational.

> The importance of removing the public archives and government stores from their present dangerous situation at the City of Austin to a place of security, is

272

becoming daily more and more imperative. While they remain where they are, no one knows the hour when they may be utterly destroyed.

As much as Houston wanted the archives, he admonished his agents not to actually harm anyone. He knew without Congress's sanction his clandestine mission was not strictly legal, and he wished to avoid more scandal. Still, if Smith and Chandler were able to pull off his scheme, he was betting that law makers would not make him return the records to Austin.

On the morning of December 30, Colonel Smith led twenty rangers and three wagons into Austin. The residents bought the deception that they had come to offer defense against marauding Indians. And why not? There were still plenty of those in the neighborhood. Smith, having sold his cover story, waited until citizens turned in for the night. Under the cover of darkness, the rangers loaded the state papers aboard their wagons. As dawn approached, they had almost finished the job. All that remained was for them to make a clean getaway.

And they would have done it had it not been for the intervention of Angelina Belle Peyton Eberly. She had deep roots in Texas and had seen more than her share of misfortune. At twenty years of age, she married Jonathan C. Peyton, her first cousin. From 1825 to 1834, the couple operated a tavern and inn in San Felipe. In 1834, she found herself a widow when he died, but she continued to run the family business on her own. When Houston's retreating Texian forces burned San Felipe in 1836, she lost everything. Later that year, she wed widower Jacob Eberly.

In 1839, they moved to the newly established town of Austin and built an inn called Eberly House, a respectable and high-toned establishment—at least, by frontier standards. On several occasions, President Mirabeau B. Lamar and his cabinet dined there. In 1841, when Houston won back the presidency, he refused to inhabit his predecessor's executive mansion. Instead, he booked a room at the Eberly House. Ol' Sam Jacinto may have been a regular customer, but he seemed to have never endeared himself to Mrs. Eberly. Jacob died in 1841 and Angelina found herself a widow again—and again, by herself, managed the inn.

An early riser, Mrs. Eberly was up and about her business while her neighbors still snoozed comfortably in their beds. As she made her way down Congress Avenue, she observed Smith's rangers loading their wagons and immediately surmised they were trying to pull a fast one. Ever since Lamar's Cherokee War, a six-pound howitzer had sat on government grounds near the capitol. Citizens kept it loaded in case of Indian raids. But this time, the raiders were not Comanches, but Houston's toadies. She pointed the gun toward the General Land Office Building and touched it off. A shower of canister shot shook the structure, but did not strike any of the rangers. It was not from want of trying.

The discharge woke everyone in town. Smith's rangers did not wait for Mrs. Eberly to reload. They whipped their horses and galloped off in a trail of dust—with the state papers. To avoid the Bastrop patrols, the company took the northern route. Rainy weather, muddy roads, and the oxen hauling the wagons, reduced their progress to a crawl. The rangers covered only eighteen miles before they pitched camp at Kinney's Fort along Brushy Creek.

Back in Austin, Captain Mark Lewis assembled a posse to pursue the thieves. During the night of December 30, the Austin vigilantes overtook the rangers, surrounded their camp, and—at gunpoint—forced their surrender. The next morning Lewis brought the archives back into town and sent the empty-handed rangers packing.

This time, the archives would be harder to steal. The state papers, including William B. Travis's famous letter from the Alamo, remained buried in metal boxes and concealed for nearly three years. The House of Representatives later admonished Houston for ordering the removal of the records without congressional approval. On July 4, 1845, a convention convened in Austin to consider an annexation proposal. Officials then sent the files from the Town of Washington on the Brazos River to the former capital. For the first time since 1842, Texians could inspect all their government documents at a single location. The so-called "Archives War" had reached a peaceful resolution.

Its heroine, Angelina Eberly, never remarried. She subsequently operated hotels in Port Lavaca and Indianola where she passed away on August 15, 1860. She left an estate worth fifty thousand dollars. Not bad for a back-country widow woman. In 2004, to commemorate her role in the Archives War, Austinites erected a statue of Mrs. Eberly at the corner of Sixth Street and Congress Avenue.

And appropriately so. Although much of the Archives War reads like a slapstick comedy sketch, it had serious consequences. Had Mrs. Eberly not foiled Houston's conspiracy, it is probable that Austin would not be the state capitol.

Fun and Frolic

espite an "Archives War," Indian raids, Mexican forays, and an insolvent government, Texians still indulged in a vast array of amusements. The type of pastimes they chose depended in large measure on their gender and class, but when it came to having a good time, many of the conventional social barriers fell like the walls of Jericho. In a population so small and democratic, it was possible to rub shoulders with, and talk to, the republic's great men. Gustav Dresel described one cold night in Houston City during the time it served as the nation's capital: "When fall came with its northers and there were only three stoves in the whole of Houston, we used to light fires in front of the saloon in the evening, stand around them, and enjoy—not excepting the President—hot drinks with merry speeches." He would have been aware that Ol' Sam Jacinto was a keen enthusiast of both hot drinks and merry speeches.

Whatever their rank or station, rare was the Texian who did not enjoy dancing. Old settler Noah Smithwick described a country dance in the early days of Austin's first colony:

> The floor was cleared for dancing. It mattered not that the floor was made of puncheons. When young folks danced those days, they danced; they didn't glide around; they 'shuffled' and 'double shuffled,' 'wired' and 'cut the pigeon's wing,' making the splinters fly. There were some of the boys, however, who were not provided with

shoes, and moccasins were not adapted to that kind of
dancing floor, and moreover they couldn't make noise
enough, but their more fortunate brethren were not at
all selfish or disposed to put on airs, so when they had
danced a turn, they generously exchanged footgear with
the moccasined contingent and gave him the ring, and
we just literally kicked every splinter off that floor before
morning. The fiddle, manipulated by Jesse Thompson's
man Mose, being rather too weak to make itself heard
above the din of clattering feet, we had in another fellow
with a clevis and pin to strengthen the orchestra, and we
had a most enjoyable time.

The parties of the gentry were a tad more refined. Kentucky native John
Hunter Herndon recalled an 1838 ball in Houston City. It displayed the
cream of Texas society. Forty gentlemen "and as many ladies" appeared in
full frippery. Stylish was each man, and stunning each woman. Herndon,
a college-educated attorney, was in his element: "Had a fine set, supper,
good wines and interesting ladies." He declared the festivities equal "to
a Kentucky Ball." High praise, indeed! A gaffe occurred when a lady
lost her balance and "fell flat on the floor." She should not have been
self-conscious, for later a "gentleman also came to his marrow bones."
Herndon was too cultivated to mention it aloud, but he noticed something
odd about Houston women: "The ladies have rather large feet, owing
perhaps to their having gone barefooted a little too long." Having relished
a delightful evening, Herndon stumbled back to his hotel around 4 AM.

Quilting bees customarily preceded the dances. They provided
newlyweds quilts for their marriage bed, a gift that was both functional
and symbolic. But such occasions also gave women a chance to visit,
discuss their children, and share the latest gossip. Yet, as one early settler
described them, these events were not the exclusive domain of the ladies.

The quilt was stretched between 4 slats and the
corners each suspended by a rope to the ceiling in the
best room. Now all the ladies are expected to come
early as the quilt has to be finished before the real fun
begins. The Quilters soon take their places—and the

work begins on all sides. The gents on the ground are expected to roll up the sides as fast as needed, to pass the thread and scissors and with anecdotes and small talk to entertain the workers. At last the wonderful quilt is finished—the frames are removed, the Table spread, the Company all called in, and joy unconfined rules the hour. The sound of the violin expedites further preparations—we all danced a reel.

Most Texas men enjoyed games of chance. Rare was the tavern that did not provide a gaming table. Attempting to curb vice, Houston City officials passed an anti-gambling ordinance in 1837. Residents mocked such decrees. District court records revealed several indictments for "dealing faro," for "permitting gambling," and "playing cards." The same registers, however, indicate few convictions. Gambling was just too ingrained in the Southern character and few were willing to forgo this popular diversion. It thrived in large towns and small hamlets. In 1840, Washington on the Brazos River could boast only 350 inhabitants. Of those, one visitor pronounced fifty to a hundred as "gamblers, horse racers, etc. In almost every other house on the public street you could see games of all sorts being played, both day and night." Laying bets may have been popular, but it was also perilous. Many games erupted into violence when despairing men lost all they owned. At other times pistols flared and blades flashed amid charges of cheating.

Racing combined the thrill of gambling with the passion for blooded horseflesh. Houstonians constructed a course at Post Oak that hosted mile and repeat races. By 1837, the Houston Jockey Club was open and flourishing. The "spirit of the people for racing" impressed one visitor from Natchez, Mississippi, where folks knew more than a little about the sport. In an article in the *American Turf Register and Sporting Magazine*, he insisted that in 1837 he had witnessed Texians making side bets of $2500—and that on one race! He was confident concerning the future of the activity in the new republic. "Texas is going to be one of the greatest racing countries in the world, to be racing and betting the way they do now."

WASHINGTON, June 7th, 1845.

WE, the undersigned, do agree to run a Race; one mile and repeat, over the Washington Course, on the last Thursday in November next.

This public agreement to run a horse race first appeared in the *Texas National Register*, Town of Washington, July 3, 1845.

Alcohol consumption accompanied most public holidays. Of these there were many. During the 1830s and 1840s, Christmas was not merely a day, but an entire season that ranged from early December and extended into early January. Texians also observed New Year's Eve, the anniversary of Andrew Jackson's victory at New Orleans, George Washington's birthday, Texas Independence Day, the Fourth of July, and of course, San Jacinto Day.

Some visitors simply could not stomach the drinking. Englishman Nicholas Doran P. Maillard spent only a few months in the republic, but he apparently detested and denounced everything and everyone he encountered. As he recounted in 1842—once he was safely back home:

> Texas [is] a country filled with habitual liars, drunkards, blasphemers, and slanderers; sanguinary gamesters and cold-blooded assassins; with idleness and sluggish (two vices for which the Texans are already proverbial); with pride, engendered by ignorance and supported by fraud, the art of which, though of modern construction, is so well defined, and generally practiced, that it retards even the development of the spontaneous resources of the country.

Texians took no notice of Maillard's slurs, and in truth, they did little to inhibit English interest in Texas. Diplomat and promoter, Dr. Ashbel Smith, declared that it "failed to produce the slightest effect." Certainly, it did little to alter their behavior. Citizens of the republic never allowed such blue-nosed reproaches to hamper their pursuit of fun and frolic.

Texian Tech

O n February 25, 1836—while Mexican cannonballs pounded the walls of the Alamo—Connecticut inventor Samuel Colt patented a new kind of pistol, one the defenders of that crumbling fort would have found valuable on March 6. It featured a revolving cylinder with five chambers aligned with a single stationary barrel. Colt produced a .28-caliber model but followed up with an improved .36-caliber variant the next year. The original design contained no loading leaver. As a result, the owner had to break it into three parts every time he need to reload, a cumbersome disadvantage in a firefight. The weapon also featured a folding trigger that dropped down when one cocked the hammer. Because he had his factory in Paterson, New Jersey, Colt christened his invention the "Paterson" revolver. Although it attracted little notice at the time of its introduction, in the hands of the Texas Rangers, this tiny pistol was destined to revolutioize warfare on the Southern Plains.

The Paterson's journey to Texas was slow and circuitous. In 1839, Svante M. Swenson, a Swedish trader, brought a dozen he had acquired from Colt's agent in New York. Later that year John Fuller, a mutual friend of Colt's and the newly elected Mirabeau B. Lamar, visited the republic. He demonstrated the five-shooter for the "poet president," who became enamored of it. He sent two of Fuller's Patersons to Captain John Coffee "Jack" Hays, commander of the San Antonio ranger company. "Captain

281

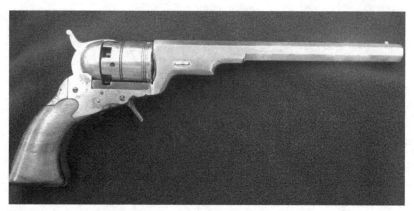

Texas Rangers wielded the five-shot, .36-caliber "Paterson Colt," designated as the Number 5 Holster Model or, more commonly, as the "Texas Paterson." *Author's photograph.*

Jack," as his men called him, immediately recognized the value—and potential—of the weapon. With such a firearm, his rangers could stay in the saddle and take the fight to the Comanches. The revolving cylinder boosted the Texians' rate of fire. For the first time, they could unleash lead bullets as rapidly as the Numunuh fired their arrows.

Captivated by Fuller's pitch, Lamar placed an order for 180 of the .36-caliber "Number 5 Holster" model, which acquired the tag, "Texas Paterson." But then, in one of his biggest blunders, he assigned the entire allotment to the Texas Navy. No doubt Commodore Edwin Moore was pleased to receive them, but during their shipboard service, records do not indicate that the pistols ever left their holsters. Meanwhile, the only revolvers available to Hays and his rangers were those obtained through private purchase. Officials also equipped a few units of the regular army with Patersons, but most of them were destroyed by their owners or captured by the Mexicans during the Santa Fe Expedition.

In December 1841, Sam Houston regained the presidency and deactivated the navy. Finally, he could transfer the Colt pistols from sailors who did not need them to rangers who did—desperately. On New Year's Day, the president convened with Captain Hays and allocated 227 of the

"Texas Patersons" to his rangers. At last, Captain Jack had the weapon he needed to succeed in the ongoing frontier campaigns.

But it was not enough to merely acquire the pistols; Hays made sure his rangers knew how to use them. One of them, James Wilson Nichols, left a vivid description of the captain's training regimen:

> We kept out scouts all the time, when one would come in another would go out, and those not on a scout ware every day practicing horsemanship and marksmanship. We put up a post about the size of a common man, then put up another about 40 yards farther on. We would run our horses full speed and discharge our rifles at the first post, draw our pistles and fire at the second. At first thare was some wild shooting but we had not practiced two months until thare was not many men that would not put his balls in the center of the posts.

All that grueling training was about to pay dividends. On June 8, 1844, Captain Hays, Lieutenant Ben McCulloch, and thirteen rangers were on a scout searching for a Comanche raiding party led by the famed war chief Yellow Wolf who had only recently terrorized the region around San Antonio. Hays yearned to engage the marauders. Each of his rangers now carried a brace of Texas Patersons and he was eager to test his tactics in combat.

They rode the Pinta Trail until it crossed the Guadalupe River in present-day Kendall County. There, along the banks of Walker's Creek, Hays called a halt. While the men rested, the captain posted Ranger Noah Cherry in the top of a tall tree to scan the surrounding countryside. They were deep in enemy territory and Captain Jack wished to make sure Yellow Wolf did not take him unawares.

Suddenly, Cherry bellowed: "Jerusalem, captain, yonder comes a thousand Indians!"

The startled Cherry exaggerated just a tad. Yellow Wolf had nowhere near a thousand warriors. Best estimates place the number at around seventy. But in a time like that, no one took time to stop and count the number of enemies bearing down on them. What the rangers knew for a dead certainty was that they had located the raiding party—and it greatly outnumbered them.

In such circumstances, most commanders would have ordered a hasty retreat, but Captain Hays instructed his men to saddle up and follow him *toward* the approaching tribesmen. Yellow Wolf, a wily tactician, tried to lure the rangers into a trap, but Hays refused to fall for it. Finally, the chief led his entire war party forward in a ragged battle line. Ever since Plum Creek, the Comanches had avoided pitched battle with Texians, relying instead on their time-honored strike-and-run tactics. But observing how few rangers he faced, Yellow Wolf was eager to mix it up.

This was the moment Hays had prayed for. Drawing one of his revolvers, he led his rangers in a countercharge right into the mass of the onrushing Indians. As they closed with the enemy, the captain roared, "Crowd them! Powder-burn them!" This was not hyperbole; he knew that the .36-caliber Paterson possessed precious little punching power. To kill, a man had to close to point-blank range.

That was not a problem. Enemies were everywhere and too close for comfort. The rangers remembered their training. They marked their man, fired, and brought him down. But then, to the amazement of their Indian adversaries, they fired again. And again—and again—and again. Then they drew their second Paterson and kept shooting. The braves scattered, but the rangers remained in the saddle and pursued them for almost an hour. The Comanches suffered between twenty and fifty killed. Hays lost one man killed and four more seriously wounded.

The firefight on Walker's Creek marked a strategic pivot point in the history of Indian warfare. Before it, Texians had been unable to equal Comanches on horseback. Afterward, it was the Numunuh who fought at disadvantage. The combination of Texas guts and U.S. technology proved unbeatable. Samuel Colt gave Hays and his rangers the weapon that they carried into legend. And, although Comanches raided the Texas frontier for another three decades, the introduction of the Paterson five-shooter marked the beginning of their inevitable demise. One Comanche warrior who survived the Battle of Walker's Creek knew that he had witnessed a game changer. He swore that he would never fight Hays again because, he declared, Devil Jack "had a shot for every finger on the hand."

"Chew, Chew, Chew &
Spit, Spit, Spit"

T exians of all ages and social classes indulged in the vice of tobacco. No other iniquity provoked more disgust from foreign visitors or prompted more censure. Citizens of the Texas Republic enjoyed the "noxious weed" in all its forms. They smoked it, sniffed it, dipped it, and chewed it. Visitors found this last form especially odious. Arriving at a Houston City hotel in 1846, German traveler Ferdinand Roemer remarked that its patrons were "continually expectorating tobacco juice." The practice also repelled Irish diplomat Francis C. Sheridan, who recounted, "High & low, rich & poor, young & old chew, chew, chew & spit, spit, spit all the blessed day & most of the night."

The unsavory habit was by no means unique to Texas. Along with their long rifles and hoe cakes, Southern immigrants brought their tobacco with them. Back in Tennessee, Congressman David Crockett considered the brown leaf an essential ingredient of his political campaigns. As he explained:

> I [had] me a large buckskin hunting-shirt made, with a couple of pockets holding about a peck each; and in one I would carry a great big twist of tobacco, and in the other my bottle of liquor; for I knowed when I met a man and offered him a dram, he would throw out his quid of tobacco to take one, and after he had taken his horn I would out with my twist and give him another chaw. And in this way he would not be worse off than when I found him; I would be sure to leave him in a first-rate good humor.

In 1836, Friedrich W. von Wrede traveled from Germany to settle in Texas. During the journey he had the opportunity to travel on a U.S. steamboat. The technology impressed him, but the behavior of his fellow passengers left him horrified. As he told it:

The floor [of the vessel] is covered with carpets which at one time must have had colorful patterns, but now only a hard brown crust can be seen which was formed by the disgusting habit of spitting by passengers. Spittoons are placed in every corner of the cabin, but seldom does a gentleman make the effort to direct the squirt of brown juice from his mouth toward these. The Americans are so used to this bad habit that they do not realize that this may seem very loathsome to a foreigner, confirming the old saying that all which is called disgusting has become so by mutual consent.

During the San Jacinto Campaign, General Sam Houston relaxes with a pinch of powered snuff. He also smoked and chewed the "noxious weed." *Courtesy of Gary Zaboly, illustrator, from Phil Collins,* The Alamo and Beyond: A Collector's Journey.

English novelist and travel writer, Matilda Houstoun visited the Texas Republic and not only observed the filthy cycle of chewing and spitting, but offered a remedy to it. She counseled Texian ladies to,

Rise up one and all and say to their husbands, their brothers, and their lovers, "Cast away that lump of tobacco, which disfigures your appearance, and renders your voice and manner of speaking ridiculous; I will have no chewing. I will have no spitting. If you must smoke, do it in moderation, and with propriety, but let our floors, our hearths, be secure from pollution."

Houstoun would have been shocked to learn that many Texian women also indulged. Chappell Hill resident, John Washington Lockhart described an assembly of local women after church services: "The elderly ones would draw their pipes from the long calico bag and have a good smoke, while the younger set would draw from their dress pocket the box and brush and have a social dip." English chronicler N. Doran Maillard confirmed that Texas women favored either "the pipe or the swab," and provided instruction regarding the use of the latter.

> The "swab" is a piece of soft wood about three inches long, which they chew at one end until it forms a brush, then dipping it into a small bottle of brown rappee snuff, which they carry about them for the purpose of cleaning their teeth; this operation being performed, the "swab" is placed on one side of the mouth, while the pipe sometimes takes the other.

Sheridan recalled that Texian parents even initiated their children to the toxic ritual. On Galveston island, he saw a father training his two-year-old son in the "art of spitting," while "loudly applauding every successful effort of the precious prodigy." The beaming sire seemed to believe hocking a brown stream one of the worthiest attainments of manhood. Most of his fellow Texians would have concurred.

Demonstrating enormous resolve President Sam Houston conquered his addiction to "ardent spirits" and even renounced profanity—at least, for the most part. Yet, even his wife Margaret could not curb his passion for the weed. His friend John Lockhart recalled how angry the president made his mother during one of his visits to their home. "Ol' Sam Jacinto" spit tobacco juice all over the freshly swept floor of the front porch. As the indignant matron explained to her son, the distinguished guest could have just as easily spit over the porch rail and into the yard as on her clean floor.

Many of the republic's plantation owners raised tobacco alongside their cotton. Although the soil produced a pleasing product, it never took off as a profitable export crop. Most growers seemed to have tended a patch for their own use and that of their neighbors. During the 1840s, English travel writer William Bollaert visited one estate where he observed "segars of home manufacture being lighted" after dinner.

The "segar's" stench may have affronted dainty noses, but in none of its forms, did the wicked leaf create as much exasperation as the chewing quid. Observing a session of the Texas Congress, one guest commented: "The way the members were chewing the Tobacco & squirting was a sin to see." Even church houses fell victim to the spew of brown juice. It became so unpleasant, that one Austin minister posted the following on his sanctuary door:

Tobacco in Church
Ye chewers of that noxious weed
Which grows in earth's most cursed sod,
Be pleased to clean your filthy mouths
Outside the sacred House of God.
Throw out your "plug and Cavendish,"
Your "pig Tail," "Twist," and "Honey-dew,"
And not presume to spit upon
The pulpit, aisles, or in the pew.

Did the notice persuade his obstinate flock?
God only knows.

Blood on the Pines

A s if President Sam Houston did not have enough troubles, it seemed as if one-half of East Texas citizens were trying to kill the other. Raging from 1839 to 1844, the violence culminated in what locals called the "Regulator-Moderator War." Rather, it was a grand feud that began in Shelby County but grew to engulf surrounding vicinities. Even so, as dustups go, it was the biggest in Texas history. The ruckus had its roots in a quarrel over land titles, but it eventually mutated into a brawl over domination of the regional economy. Character assassination, cattle rustling, and finally bushwhacking became the favored tactics of the two factions. Before the hostility ran its course, more than forty men lost their lives, including Robert Potter, a lawyer, signatory of the Texas Declaration of Independence, and former Secretary of the Texas Navy.

Even before the "war" began in 1839, East Texas fostered a tradition of lawlessness. In the wake of the 1803 Louisiana Purchase, New Spain's administrators became weary of U.S. encroachments of their territory. In 1805, skirmishing broke out along both banks of the Sabine River. By the following year, a Spanish army under Lieutenant Colonel Simón de Herrera stood on the western bank of that stream, while a U.S. army under General James Wilkinson inhabited the eastern. Across this contested torrent, the two forces bristled and glared at each another; most observers believed war inevitable.

TEXAS

LOUISIANA

Tenaha   • Logansport

Red River

SHELBY COUNTY

Shelbyville
•

• Terrapin Neck

Natchitoches •

• Nacogdoches

• San Augustine

NEUTRAL GROUND

Battleground
of the
Regulator–Moderator War

Sabine River

Map by Donald S. Frazier, Ph.D.

But cooler heads prevailed. Wilkinson and Herrera realized that it served the interest of neither country to squander blood and treasure on a trivial backwater. They signed an "agreement" declaring the disputed territory neutral ground until bureaucrats of their respective governments could sort out a final arrangement. But the understanding never became a formal treaty and neither government's officials ever ratified it. Still, they mostly observed its provisions.

The Neutral Ground Agreement solved one problem only to create another. Neither country controlled the nonaligned patch between the Sabine River and the Arroyo Hondo, and the wilderness of the Calcasieu bottoms. Consequently, that no-man's land became a haven for criminals on the lam from both countries' laws. Even while New Spain retained jurisdiction, the pandemonium surging across the Sabine infected the Piney Woods of East Texas. The 1819 Adams-Onís Treaty settled the boundary question and Mexicans gained their independence in 1821, but those momentous events did nothing to address the region's chaos. Even after Texians declared their independence in 1836, East Texas continued its culture of anarchy.

For years, a feud had been brewing. Charles W. Jackson and Charles W. Moorman emerged as leaders of a faction that they branded the "Regulators," ostensibly to thwart "cattle rustling." They brutalized and bullied local settlers by contesting land titles, thieving cattle, and burning barns. In the years before 1839, many had already fallen victim to the dissension. But in 1840, tensions came to a boiling point. That year, Jackson, already a fugitive from Louisiana sheriffs, shot and killed Joseph Goodbread at Shelbyville.

As a counter, Edward Merchant, John M. Bradley, and James J. Cravens headed a group aiming to "moderate" the excesses of the Regulators. On July 12, 1841, Merchant and his "Moderators" were hopeful as Jackson stood trial for the murder of Goodbread. The judge was John M. Hansford, a friend of Goodbread's and a defender of the Moderators. But Regulators terrorized the court to such a degree that Judge Hansford had to declare a mistrial. It was also about that time that Jackson's Regulators torched the homes of Moderator stalwarts, the McFadden family and "Tiger Jim" Strickland. Receiving reports of the escalating violence in East Texas, a disgusted President Houston reportedly declared:

> I think it advisable to declare Shelby County, Tenaha, and Terrapin Neck free and independent governments, and let them fight it out.

Following the travesty of Jackson's trial and the house burnings, both sides abandoned any pretense of due process; rifle and firebrand dislodged judge and jury. The McFadden brothers subsequently bushwhacked and killed Jackson and another man named Lauer. By all accounts, Lauer was innocent of any wrongdoing. Moorman, vowing to avenge his predecessor's murder, assumed leadership of Shelby County Regulators. Moorman and his men tracked Jackson's killers to a point twenty-five miles north of Crockett in Houston County. In October 1841, the McFadden brothers stood trial for the murder of Jackson and Lauer in Shelbyville. The verdict was predictable. Sparing only the youngest, Moorman and his Regulators strung up the McFadden brothers.

Moderators swore vengeance for the McFaddens. Over summer 1844, they assembled at Bell Springs and changed their name to the "Reformers." The newly labeled faction elected to attack and occupy Shelbyville, a hotbed of Regulator activity and focus of the strife. Despite his previous glib comments, Houston could no longer ignore the dispute roiling an entire region of the republic. News of the conflict had reached the United States, where it endangered annexation negotiations. The president dispatched his associate, George W. Terrell, to assess conditions and he reported: "It really appears to me as if society were about to dissolve itself into its original elements."

On August 14, 1844, Houston—appalled by the East Texas unruliness—dispatched five hundred militiamen to the region. The president himself soon arrived and established his headquarters at San Augustine to oversee operations. Even then, the carnage continued. Eventually, however, Houston's diplomacy—and his show of force— brought the ringleaders to the negotiating table.

Although the Regulator–Moderator War officially ended in 1844, the bad blood continued. During the Mexican War, some feuders put aside their differences to serve in Captain L. H. Mobitt's company and the bonds of wartime service diminished their acrimony. John J. Kennedy, Harrison County Sheriff, and Joseph U. Fields, a county judge, were instrumental in finally curbing the fighting, affiliating with the emerging law-and-order party. Even then, peace proved elusive. Lingering resentment forced many families to move out of East Texas altogether. But no matter how far they traveled, the hatred provoked by the Regulator–Moderator War pursued them. On February 14, 1850, Dr. Robert Burns unearthed Moorman in Logansport, Louisiana, and shot him to death.

With judicious application of coercion, diplomacy, and cunning, President Houston managed to, if not completely freeze the feuding, at least reduce it to a simmer. Indeed, it lists among his greatest presidential achievements—but also one of his last. On December 9, 1844, his second term ended. It remained for his successor, the prosaic Anson Jones, to fulfill Ol' Sam Jacinto's fondest dream.

Anson and Annexation

nson Jones was, and remains, a hard man to fathom. A native of Great Barrington, Massachusetts, he came to Texas in 1833. A physician by profession, he served as Sam Houston's Secretary of State and was the fourth, and final, president of the Texas Republic. No one worked harder, or more deftly, to achieve union with the United States and scholars justly remember him as the "Architect of Annexation."

But when he completed his presidential term, the people of Texas discounted him. In the words of his biographer, "for twelve years Jones brooded over his neglect [and] became increasingly moody and introspective." Disregarded and unappreciated, Jones viewed himself as a failure. Following Thomas Jefferson Rusk's 1857 suicide, he had reason to hope that the state legislature might at last designate him U.S. Senator. He received not a single vote. This final indignity was more than he could bear; on January 9, 1858, he passed a bullet through his brain. He had once written, "I trust truth will ultimately prevail & posterity judge me correctly." In his last moments Jones determined it had not and probably never would.

But Jones was no failure. Houston's second administration ended before his machinations could bear fruit. Once again he had to step away from the presidency, but Jones, who assumed the office on December 9, 1844, continued to correspond with annexation advocates in the United

Having declared "The Republic of Texas is no more," Anson Jones—last president of the Texas Republic—solemnly lowers the Lone Star standard. Although Sam Houston had worked for years to attach Texas to the "old states," historians accurately characterize President Jones as the "Architect of Annexation." *Courtesy of the Texas State Library and Archives Commission.*

States. Although he was in Houston's camp, Jones did not always agree with his predecessor's policies and sought to plot an independent path.

In the United States a new mood was sweeping the nation. The allure of "Manifest Destiny" greatly influenced the election of 1844. Three candidates sought the executive office. Henry Clay, a Whig, claimed to support Texas annexation—unless such actions led to war with Mexico. He was totally disingenuous. Mexican diplomats had stated repeatedly that if Texas joined the United States, they *would* declare war. So Clay did not, in reality, support annexation. James G. Birney, an abolitionist and nominee of the Liberty Party, opposed the admission of Texas in any way, shape, or form. Democrat James K. Polk was the only candidate who was forthright in his support of expansion and Texas annexation. When Americans cast their votes, Polk won by a wide margin. His victory rekindled annexation prospects.

With Polk's election, events unfolded quickly. Now that Manifest Destiny had captured the national imagination, John Tyler, the lame-

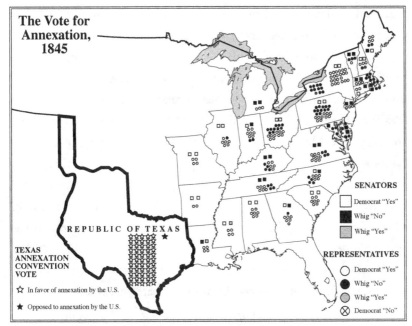

The Vote for Annexation, 1845

REPUBLIC OF TEXAS

SENATORS
☐ Democrat "Yes"
■ Whig "No"
▨ Whig "Yes"

REPRESENTATIVES
○ Democrat "Yes"
● Whig "No"
◐ Whig "Yes"
⊗ Democrat "No"

TEXAS ANNEXATION CONVENTION VOTE
☆ In favor of annexation by the U.S.
★ Opposed to annexation by the U.S.

Map by Donald S. Frazier, Ph.D.

duck president, wished to seize the moment and achieve annexation on his watch. He pitched the notion to Polk, who agreed. The president-elect just wanted Texas in the Union; he did not care who took credit. Having previously failed to annex Texas by treaty—too many abolitionists and Northerners had opposed the measure—Tyler resorted to admission by joint resolution of Congress. This approach required a simple majority in both houses instead of a two-thirds vote in the Senate. On January 25, 1845, the House endorsed the annexation proposal; the Senate followed suit on February 26. After a long and rancorous process, Tyler signed the resolution and dispatched it to Texas. The pro-annexation forces had cleared the path for admission. All that remained was Texian acceptance of the offer, which most considered a foregone conclusion.

When President Jones did not immediately accept the proposal, Washington observers found themselves bewildered. Having been rebuffed on so many occasions, were Texians now playing coy? No, Mexican officials had fundamentally altered the political landscape with an offer of formal recognition of Texas independence and a lucrative trade agreement. The deal was contingent, however, on Texians *not* joining the United States. Mexican politicians finally came to understand that it was preferable to have the weak and ineffectual Texas Republic as their northern neighbor, if the alternative was the brawny and expansionist United States. Many Texians wished to accept the Mexican offer and retain their sovereignty. Jones was a nationalist, but offered to submit both proposals to the Texas Congress.

Meeting in Austin on July 4, 1845 (the date was not coincidental), a convention overwhelmingly approved Tyler's annexation resolution. Given their agonizing history with their southern neighbor, Texians had little confidence in Mexican promises. On December 29, 1845, President Polk signed the bill of formal admission, but republic officials were to remain in office until February. As Jones accurately recorded:

> I had a difficult task to perform to secure success to this great measure by exciting the rivalry and jealousy of the three greatest powers in the world & at the same time so act as to affect my object and to maintain the perfect good faith of Texas towards all these powers.

On February 19, 1846, in a formal ceremony in Austin, President Jones transferred control of the government to the newly elected state governor, James Pinkney Henderson. Hundreds of officials and citizens attended the procedure. In a prepared address, Jones spoke to the assembled throng:

> The lone star of Texas, which ten years since arose amid clouds over fields of carnage, and obscurely shone for a while, has culminated, and, following an inscrutable destiny, has passed on and become fixed forever in that glorious constellation which all freemen and lovers of freedom in the world must reverence and adore—the American Union. . . . Blending its rays with its sister stars long may it continue to shine, and may a gracious Heaven smile upon this consummation of the wishes of the two Republics, now joined together in one.

He ended with a flourish: "The final act in this great drama is now performed. The Republic of Texas is no more."

With that, Jones strode toward two flag poles erected for the occasion. One flew the Lone Star banner; the other was empty. As he hauled down the standard of Texas nationhood, something incredible occurred. The shaft from which it had flown snapped in two. People gasped at the omen. Recovering himself following the uncanny accident, the former president ran up the Stars and Stripes on the remaining staff.

The experiment in nationhood was a heroic failure, but nonetheless a failure. When Texas joined the Union one could almost perceive a collective sigh of relief. San Antonio matron Mary Maverick spoke for the majority of her fellow citizens: "Thank God, we are now annexed to the United States, and can hope for home and quiet." But some diehards—Texas always had its share of those—believed their neighbors had been too eager to surrender their national sovereignty. As he looked back on his life, the old Indian fighter Robert Hall regarded the years of the Texas Republic as his happiest and viewed statehood as a mistake. He spoke for many old warriors of his generation: "I was opposed to annexation, and voted first, last, and all time for the Lone Star."

Legacy

The Republic of Texas was an ephemeral empire. Like spring bluebonnets, it bloomed, blossomed, and blanched with the sands of time. But also like the state flower, its scent lingers in the hearts and imaginations of contemporary Texans. A distinct history produces a distinct culture; a distinctive culture produces a distinctive people. Texans express pride in their ancestors. "The past," as novelist William Faulkner reflected, "is never dead. It's not even past." In Texas, that is especially true. In the Lone Star State, not only is the past never dead, it lives—vibrantly.

But more than any other epoch, the revolutionary and republic periods shaped what some have termed "Texas Exceptionalism." In the United States, the Panic of 1819 devastated many frontier families. Reports that Texas had lowered barriers to U.S. settlers seemed a godsend for poor folks seeking a place to start over. The Mexican government was so openhanded that newcomers could hardly believe their good fortune. Indigents who had arrived in Texas with nothing built spreads ten times larger than those back in the "old states."

We've all heard it. "Everything's bigger in Texas." The enormity of Mexican land grants was likely the source of this popular adage. It may be a myth, but the state is still larger than France. Even so, the "bigger-in-Texas" cliché misses the point. It's not the size of their ranches, or Cadillacs, or Stetson hats, or belt buckles that define Texans. It is the size of their dreams. Texas

Much altered from its 1836 appearance and no longer relegated to the outskirts of town, the Alamo church now stands at the heart of a vibrant, modern city. The most iconic building in Texas, it serves as reminder of the state's heroic age. *Keith Durham, photographer. Author's collection.*

provided possibilities for ambitious visionaries: The Richard Kings, the Charlie Goodnights, the Clint Murchisons, the H. Ross Perots, the Mary Kay Ashes, the "Red" McCombs—dreamers and schemers who savored the doing more than the payoff. What proved impossible elsewhere became feasible west of the Sabine River. That spirit remains firmly entrenched.

The Texas Republic was born in the blood of rebellion. From the beginning, cultures clashed at this crossroad of empires; some came to settle, others to slaughter. Mayhem and carnage rendered the region one enormous battlefield. Thus, a warrior myth imbedded itself in the public imagination. But are Texans really more aggressive than others? Perhaps so. Given their history, how could they be otherwise? Yet theirs is rarely the mindless violence of the thug, terrorist, or sociopath. Texans pack the ranks of the national armed forces, and military installations dot the landscape. The Lone Star has always produced—and honored—fighting sons and daughters.

Early Texians fought to live by their own lights, to plot their own course. That trait continues to burn in their descendants. Texans, having witnessed what individuals breathing the fresh air of freedom can attain, bristle under restraint. Their tendency to strike an independent course, to observe their own customs, annoys foreigners. Presidents and politicians

Map by Donald S. Frazier, Ph.D.

living in remote capitals, bureaucrats who knew nothing of conditions in Texas, have always tried to foist one-size-fits-all policies suited for places with milder climes, for persons of more yielding dispositions. They never worked; they never will. Texas—and Texans—are simply too different from those other places and those other people.

Texans celebrate their history and the unique culture it forged. There is integrity in tradition, value in the verdict of experience, of lives lived, and principles cherished. It does not venerate the ashes; it feeds the flames. And Texans heat multiple irons in that fire. Explain to the heirs of William Barret Travis, James Bowie, and Juan Seguín that compliance is a virtue, submission but another form of patriotism. Texans have spent enough time in feed lots to recognize this notion for what it is—and their mamas taught them to scrape it off their boots before they came into the house. Ultimately, identity remains the best argument for Texas Exceptionalism.

It's just this simple: If a people *decide* that they're different, they are.

Many vestiges of the revolution and republic remain to remind Texans of that difference. Each year, more than a million people from all over the world visit the Alamo, the state's number-one tourist attraction. The huge number of foreign visitors serves as proof that the 1836 battle is not merely a Texas tale. The love of liberty, veneration of courage, and defiance of tyranny is the birthright of all free men and women. The church's battered façade is among the world's most iconic images. It is, far and away, the state's most famous building.

While vacationing in northern England, my wife and I toured Flodden battlefield, the site of the decisive 1513 victory of the Earl of Surrey over an invading Scots army under King James IV. It was a breezy, rainy day and we had the place virtually to ourselves. I say virtually because an elderly English couple were the only other people silly enough to be out in such nasty weather. They represented a previous generation of Englishmen, all tweed and teatime; they might have been characters from an Agatha Christie mystery. We introduced ourselves and, recognizing our accents, they asked us which of the states we were from.

"Texas," I said.

The wife beamed. "Ah, yes, that's the Alamo isn't it?"

"Yes," I assured her, "that's us."

There's no escaping it. Even if we sometimes wish to forget it, the rest of the world will always remember the Alamo.

The Old Three Hundred, Come and Take It, the Alamo, San Jacinto, the Horse Marines, and Plum Creek, all have become global metaphors that transcend mere history. John Steinbeck insisted:

> The word Texas becomes a symbol to everyone in the world. There's no question that this Texas-of-the-mind fable is often synthetic, sometimes untruthful, and frequently romantic, but that in no way diminishes its strength as a symbol.

Who can deny that this emblematic Texas is firmly rooted in the quarter-century between 1821 and 1846? It was the Lone Star State's heroic age.

Steinbeck said it best. "Texas is a state of mind. Texas is an obsession. Above all, Texas is a nation in every sense of the word." Even today it is common to hear natives of the state claim that they are, "Texans first, Americans second." The degree of Texas nationalism is a question for debate. Yet, it is perhaps significant that the citizens of the Lone Star Republic refused to forsake their cherished flag. To this day, the emblem of a sovereign nation continues to swell over the forests, hills, and prairies of that exceptional state.

Bibliography

Note to Readers: This list is wide-ranging—and for good reason.

If you are a teacher or a parent, you have probably heard your student or child say, "I don't know how to pick a topic. How can I? I don't know anything about Texas history. I hate history!" This bibliography is for you.

Turn the question around. "Okay, I get that. So what do you like?" If a student answers music, you might direct him or her toward Chemerka and Wiener's *Music of the Alamo*. If a student says fashion, suggest Holman and Persons's *Buckskin and Homespun: Frontier Texas Clothing, 1820–1870*, or Marks's, *Hands to the Spindle: Texas Women and Home Textile Production, 1822–1880*. If the young scholar is of a poetic bent, you might recommend Graham's *Early Texas Verse, 1835–1850*. You get the idea. Every discipline or interest has a history, and history is not always about politics and battles.

Better yet, don't recommend a topic at all. Sit down with the student and read through the bibliography together. Discuss various topics. Students—if left to make their own choices—will almost always select topics that engage their interests, which usually makes for a better paper or project.

I have included a number of Spanish-language sources. If you have Latino students who struggle with English, they would probably enjoy researching materials in their native language. Afterward, have them report their findings to their English-only classmates. This approach not only involves Latino students in class assignments, but also allows them to make singular contributions.

Good luck. I hope you find what follows beneficial.

—S.L.H.

PRIMARY MATERIALS

Manuscripts

Archives and Library Division, Texas State Library, Austin, Texas

Army Papers

Audited Military Claims

Audited Republic Claims

Home Papers

Andrew Jackson Houston Collection

Valentine O. King Collection

Mirabeau B. Lamar Papers

Memorials and Petitions

Juan N. Seguín Papers

Catholic Archives of Texas, Chancery of the Austin Diocese, Austin, Texas.

Sam Houston Papers

The Daughters of the Republic of Texas (DRT) Collection, Texas A&M University—San Antonio

Dickson Family Papers, Manuscript Collection

Dolph Briscoe Center for American History, University of Texas at Austin

Eugene C. Barker Papers

Valentine Bennett Papers

Béxar Archives

John Sowers Brooks Letters

Nathan Boon Burkett Reminiscences

Andrew Davis Narrative

Kelsey H. Douglass Papers

John C. Duval Papers

Vicente Filisola Papers

Philip Smith Hale Papers

James Hatch Papers

Sylvanus Hatch Narrative

John Hunter Herndon Papers

Hobart Hudson Narratives

Kuykendall Family Papers

Adele Lubbock Briscoe Looscan Papers

Nathan Mitchell Papers

Muster Rolls

Henry Raguet Family Papers

Sherwood Reams Letter

Thomas B. Rees Letter

Samuel C. A. Rogers Reminiscence

Thomas Jefferson Rusk Papers

Julia Sinks Papers

Ashbel Smith Papers

S. F. Sparks Papers

James Harper Starr Papers

Texas Veterans Association Papers

Anne Raney Thomas Papers

William Barret Travis Papers

Amasa Turner Papers

Newspapers

[Houston] *Morning Star*, 1839

[Houston] *Telegraph and Texas Register*, 1837–1839

[New Orleans] *Daily Picayune*, 1837–1838

Books

Almonte, Juan Nepomuceno. *Almonte's Texas: Juan N. Almonte's 1834 Inspection, Secret Report and Role in the 1836 Campaign.* Edited by Jack Jackson. Translated from the Spanish by John Wheat. Austin: Texas State Historical Association, 2003.

Barker, Eugene C., ed. *The Austin Papers.* 2 vols. Washington, DC: Government Printing Office, 1924, 1928; 3rd vol. Austin: University of Texas, 1927.

Barker, Nancy Nichols, comp. and ed. *The French Legation in Texas.* Two volumes. Austin: Texas State Historical Association, 1971–1973.

Barnard, Joseph H. *Dr. J. H. Barnard's Journal, December 1836–June 1836.* Ed. and annotated by Hobart Huson. N.P.: Goliad Bicentennial Edition, 1949.

Becerra, Francisco. *A Mexican Sergeant's Recollections of the Alamo and San Jacinto . . . as told to John S. Ford in 1875.* Introduction by Dan Kilgore. Austin: Jenkins Publishing Co., 1980.

Berlandier, Jean Louis, and Rafael Choval. *Journey to Mexico during the Years 1826 to 1834.* Translated by Sheila M. Ohlendorf, Josette M. Bigelow, and Mary M. Standifer. Introduction by C. H. Muller. Botanical notes by C. H. Muller and Katherine K. Muller. Two volumes. 1850; reprint, Austin: The Texas State Historical Association, 1980.

Binkley, William C., ed. *Official Correspondence of the Texas Revolution, 1835–1836.* 2 vols. New York: D. Appleton-Century Co., 1936.

Bollaert, William. *William Bollaert's Texas.* Edited by W. Eugene Hollon and Ruth Lapham Butler. Norman: Published in Cooperation with the Newberry Library, Chicago, by the University of Oklahoma Press, 1956.

Breeden, James O., ed. *A Long Ride in Texas: The Explorations of John Leonard Riddell.* College Station: Texas A&M University Press, 1994.

Bryan, Moses Austin. *Reminiscences of Moses Austin Bryan.* Edited by Wilson W. Crook. Report No. 27. Houston: Houston Archeological Society, 2016.

Burnet, D[avid] G. *Review of the Life of Gen. Sam Houston, as Recently Published in Washington City, by J. T. Towers.* Galveston: News Power Press Print, 1852.

[Coleman, Robert M.] *Houston Displayed; or, Who Won the Battle of San Jacinto? By a Farmer in the Army. Velasco Herald,* 1837. Reprint, Austin: Brick Row Book Shop, 1964.

Crockett, David. *A Narrative of the Life of David Crockett of the State of Tennessee.* Introduction by Paul Andrew Hutton. 1834; reprint, Lincoln: University of Nebraska Press, 1987.

Daughters of the Republic of Texas. *Muster Rolls of the Texas Revolution.* Lubbock: Printed by Craftsman Printers, Inc., 1986.

Day, James M., comp. *The Texas Almanac, 1857–1873: A Compendium of Texas History.* Waco: Texian Press, 1967.

De Cordova, Jacob. *Texas: Her Resources and Her Public Men: A Companion for J. De Cordova's New and Correct Map of the State of Texas.* Philadelphia: Printed by E. Crozet, Cor. Thirteenth & Market, 1858. Reprint, Waco: Texian Press, 1969.

Delgado, Pedro. *Mexican Account of the Battle of San Jacinto.* Deepwater, TX: W. C. Day, 1919.

DeShields, James T., comp. *Tall Men with Long Rifles: Set Down and Written out by James T. DeShields as Told to Him by Creed Taylor, Captain during the Texas Revolution.* San Antonio: Naylor Co., 1935.

Dresel, Gustav. *Houston Journal: Adventures in North America and Texas, 1837–1841.* Translated by Max Freund. Austin: University of Texas Press, 1954.

Dubois de Saligny, Jean Pierre Isidore Alphonse. *Alphonse in Austin: Being Excerpts from the Official Letters Written to the French Foreign*

Ministry by Alphonse Dubois de Saligny, Chargé D'affairs of the Kingdom of France to the Republic of Texas, With Divers Notes Concerning the Pig War. Austin: A Waterloo Book published by the Encino Press for the Friends of the Austin Public Library, 1967.

Dunt, Detlef. *Journey to Texas, 1833.* Translated from the German by Anders Saustrup. Edited and with an Introduction by James C. Kearney and Geir Bentzen. 1834; reprint, Austin: University of Texas Press, 2015.

Duval, John C. *Early Times in Texas, or the Adventures of Jack Dobell.* Austin: H. P. N. Gammell & Co., Publishers, 1892.

Edward, David Barnett. *The History of Texas; or, The Emigrant's, Farmer's, and Politician's Guide to the Character, Climate, Soil, and Production of That Country; Geographically Arranged from Personal Observation and Experience.* Cincinnati: J. A. James & Co., 1836.

Ehrenberg, Hermann. *With Milam and Fannin: Adventures of a German Boy in Texas's Revolution.* Dallas: Tardy Publishing Company, Inc., 1935.

Erath, George B. *The Memoirs of Major George B. Erath, 1813–1891: As Dictated to Lucy A. Erath.* Waco: The Heritage Society of Waco, 1923; reprinted 1956.

Field, Joseph E. *Three Years in Texas, Including a View of the Texas Revolution, and an Account of the Principal Battles, Together with Descriptions of the Soil, Commercial and Agricultural Advantages, etc. 1836;* reprint, Austin: Steck Co., 1935.

Filisola, Vicente. *Evacuation of Texas: Translation of the Representation Addressed to the Supreme Government by Gen. Vicente Filisola, in Defence of his Honor, and Explanation of his Operations as Commander-in-Chief of the Army Against Texas.* Columbia, TX: G. & T. H. Borden, Public Printers, 1837.

———. *General Vicente Filisola's Analysis of José Urrea's Military Diary: A Forgotten 1838 Publication by an Eyewitness to the Texas Revolution.* Edited by Gregg J. Dimmick. Translated from the Spanish by John R. Wheat. Austin: Texas State Historical Association, 2007.

———. *Memoirs for the History of the War in Texas.* 2 vols. Translated by Wallace Woolsey. 1849; reprint, Austin: Eakin Press, 1986, 1987.

Forester, John, *Memoirs of John Forester, Soldier, Indian Fighter, and Texas Ranger of the Republic of Texas.* Foreword by John H. Jenkins. Austin: The Pemberton Press, 1969.

Gaddy, Jerry J., comp. and ed. *Texas in Revolt: Contemporary Newspaper Accounts of the Texas Revolution.* Fort Collins, Colorado: Old Army Press, 1973.

Gaillardet, Theodore Frederic. *Sketches of Early Texas and Louisiana.* Translated with an Introduction by James L. Shepherd III. Austin: University of Texas Press, 1966.

Gammel, Hans Peter Nielson. *The Laws of Texas, 1822–1897.* 10 vols. Austin: Gammel Book Co., 1898.

Garrison, George Pierce. *Diplomatic Correspondence of the Republic of Texas.* Three volumes. Washington: Government Printing Office, 1908, 1911.

Gouge, William M. *The Fiscal History of Texas: Embracing an Account of Its Revenues, Debts, and Currency from the Commencement of the Revolution in 1834 to 1851–52, with Remarks on American Debts.* Philadelphia: Lippincott, Grambo, and Co., 1852, Reprint, New York: Burt Franklin, 1969.

[Gray, Millie]. *The Diary of Millie Gray, 1832–1840 (nee Mildred Richards Stone, Wife of Col. Wm. Fairfax Gray) Recording her Family Life Before, During and After Col. Wm. F. Gray's Journey to Texas in 1835, and the Small Journal Giving Particulars of all that Occurred during the Family's Voyage to Texas in 1838.* Houston: The Fletcher Young Publishing Company, 1967.

Gray, William Fairfax. *The Diary of William Fairfax Gray: From Virginia to Texas, 1835–1837.* Edited from the original manuscript, with an Introduction and notes, by Paul Lack. Dallas: De Golyer Library & William P. Clements Center for Southwest Studies, Southern Methodist University, 1997.

Green, Rena Maverick, ed. *Samuel Maverick, Texan: 1803–1870. A Collection of Letters, Journals and Memoirs.* San Antonio: Privately printed, 1952.

Green, Thomas Jefferson. *Journal of the Texian Expedition against Mier; Subsequent Imprisonment of the Author, His Sufferings, and Final Escape from the Castle of Perote, with Reflections upon the Present Political and Probable Relations of Texas, Mexico, and the United States.* New York: Harper & Brother, Publisher, 82 Cliff Street, 1845.

Gulick, Charles Adams, Jr., ed. *The Papers of Mirabeau Buonaparte Lamar.* 6 vols. Austin: Texas State Library, 1922.

Hale, Edward Everett. *How to Conquer Texas before Texas Conquers Us, with a Speech by Charles J. Jack of Re-Annexation of Texas.* Edited & with an Introduction by James C. Martin. N. P.: Roger Beacham, Publisher, 1978.

Hall, Robert. *Life of Robert Hall: Indian Fighter and Veteran of Three Wars.* Austin: Ben C. Jones & Company, 1898. Reprint, Austin: State House Press, 1992.

Hamilton, Jeff. *My Master: The Inside Story of Sam Houston and His Times by His Former Slave, Jeff Hamilton, as Told to Lenoir Hunt.* Foreword by Franklin Williams. Austin: State House Press, 1992.

Hansen, Todd, ed. *The Alamo Reader: A Study in History.* Mechanicsburg, PA: Stackpole Books, 2003.

Hatcher, Mattie Austin. *Letters of an Early American Traveller: Mary Austin Holley, Her Life and Her Works, 1784–1846.* Dallas: Southwest Press, 1933.

Helm, Mary S. *Scraps of Early Texas History, by Mrs. Mary S. Helm Who, with Her First Husband, Elias R. Wightman, Founded the City of Matagorda in 1828–9.* Austin: Printed for the author at the Office of B. R. Warmer & Co., 1884.

Holley, Mary Austin. *Texas.* 1836, reprint, Austin: Texas State Historical Association, 1985.

———. *The Texas Diary, 1835–1838.* Edited with an introduction by J. P. Bryan. Austin: The Humanities Research Center, University of Texas, 1965.

Honor Roll of the Battle of San Jacinto: The Complete List of Participants and Personnel on Detached Services. La Porte: San Jacinto Museum of History Association, 1993.

Houston, Sam. *The Writings of Sam Houston. 1813–1863.* 8 vols. Edited by Amelia Williams and Eugene C. Barker. Austin University of Texas Press, 1938–1943.

Houstoun, Matilda Charlotte (Jesse) Fraser. *Texas and the Gulf of Mexico; or, Yachting in the New World.* Edited by Marilyn McAdams Sibley. Philadelphia: G. B. Zieber & Co., 1845. Reprint, Austin: W. Thomas Taylor, 1991.

Hunter, Robert Hancock. *Narrative of Robert Hancock Hunter.* Introduction by William D. Wittlif. 1936; reprint, Austin: Encino Press, 1966.

Jenkins, John H., ed. *The Papers of the Texas Revolution, 1835–1836.* 10 vols. Austin: Presidial Press, 1973.

Jenkins, John Holland. *Recollections of Early Texas: The Memoirs of John Holland Jenkins.* Edited by John Holmes Jenkins III. Austin: University of Texas Press, 1958.

Johnson, Frank W. *A History of Texas and Texans.* 5 vols. Chicago: American Historical Society, 1916.

Johnston, William Preston. *The Life of General Albert Sidney Johnston, Embracing His Services in the Armies of the United States, the Republic of Texas, and the Confederate States.* New Introduction by T. Michael Parrish. New York: Da Capo Press, 1997.

Jones, Anson. *Memoranda and Official Correspondence Relating to the Republic of Texas, Its History and Annexation: Including a Brief Autobiography of the Author.* New York: D. Appleton & Company, Inc., 1859.

Kendall, George Wilkins. *Narrative of the Texan Santa Fe Expedition, Comprising a Description of a Tour through Texas, and across the Great Southwestern Prairies, the Camanche and Caygua Hunting-grounds, with an Account of the Sufferings from Want of Food, Losses from Hostile Indians, and Final Capture of the Texans, and Their March, as Prisoners, to the City of Mexico.* New York: Harper & Brothers, 82 Cliff-Street, 1844.

Kennedy, William. *Texas: The Rise, Progress, and Prospects of the Republic of Texas*. London: R. Hastings, 1841; reprint ed., Fort Worth: Molyneaux Craftsmen, 1925.

Lawrence, A. B. *Texas in 1840; or the Emigrant's Guide to the New Republic*. New York: W. W. Allen, 1840.

Lamar, Mirabeau Buonaparte. *The Papers of Mirabeau Buonaparte Lamar*. 6 vols. Edited by Charles A. Guluck, Katherine Elliot, Winnie Allen, and Harriet Smither. Austin: Pemberton Press, 1968.

Lane, Walter P. *The Adventures and Recollections of General Walter P. Lane, a San Jacinto Veteran, Containing Sketches of the Texan, Mexican, and Late Wars with Several Indian Fights Thrown In*. Edited by Jimmy L. Bryan. 1887; reprint, Dallas: DeGolyer Library, William P. Clements Center for Southwest Studies, Southern Methodist University, 2000.

[Lawrence, A. B.]. *Texas in 1840; or the Emigrants Guide to the New Republic; Being the Result of Observation, Enquiry and Travel in That Beautiful Country, by an Emigrant, Late of the United States, with an Introduction by the Rev. A. B. Lawrence, of New Orleans*. New York: Published by William W. Allen, and Sold by Robinson, Pratt & Co., 73 Wall Street, Collins, Keese & Co., 254 Pearl Street, and by Booksellers Generally, 1840.

Laws and Decrees of the State of Coahuila and Texas, in Spanish and English. to which Is Added the Constitution of Said State: Also: The Colonization Law of the State of Tamaulipas and Naturalization Law of the General Congress. By Order of the Secretary of State. Translated by J. P. Kimball, M. D. with a new Introduction by Joseph W. Knight. Clark, NJ: The Lawbook Exchange, Ltd., 2010.

Leclerc, Frederic. *Texas and Its Revolution*. Translated from the French with an Introduction by James L. Shepherd III. Houston: The Anson Jones Press, 1950.

Lee, Nelson. *Three Years Among the Camanches: The Narrative of Nelson Lee, the Texas Ranger, Containing a Detailed Account of His Captivity among the Indians, His Singular Escape through the Instrumentality of His Watch,*

and Full Illustrating Indian Life as It Is on the War Path and in the Camp.
Albany: Baker Taylor, 58 State St., 1859.

Linn, John J. *Reminiscences of Fifty Years in Texas*. New York: D. & J.
Sadlier & Co., 1886.

Lockhart, John Washington. *Sixty Years on the Brazos: The Life and Letters
of Dr. John Washington Lockhart, 1824–1900*. Los Angeles: Press of
Dunn Bros., 1930.

Lubbock, Francis R. *Six Decades in Texas; or, Memoirs of Francis Richard
Lubbock, Governor of Texas in War Time, 1861–63. A Personal Experience
in Business, War, and Politics*. Edited by C. W. Raines. Austin: Ben C.
Jones & Co., 1900.

Ludecus, Eduard. *John Charles Beales's Rio Grande Colony: Letters by
Eduard Ludecus, a German Colonist, to Friends in Germany in 1833–
1834, Recounting His Journey, Trials, and Observations of Early Texas*.
Translated from the German and with an Introduction by Louis E.
Brister. Austin: Texas State Historical Association, 2008.

Maillard, Nicholas Doran P. *The History of the Republic of Texas, from
the Discovery of the Country to the Present Time; and the Cause of Her
Separation from the Republic of Mexico*. London: Smith, Elder, and Co.,
1842.

Manford, Erasmus. *Twenty-five Years in the West*. Chicago: E. Manford
Publisher, 1867.

McCutchan, Joseph D. *Mier Expedition Diary: A Texan Prisoner's Account*.
Edited by Joseph Milton Nance. Austin: University of Texas Press, 1978.

McLean, Malcom D., comp. and ed. *Papers Concerning Robertson's Colony
in Texas*, 19 vols. Fort Worth: Texas Christian University Press (vols.
1–3), and Arlington: UTA Press, University of Arlington (vols. 4–19),
1974–1993.

———, trans. and ed. *Voices from the Goliad Frontier: Municipal Council
Minutes, 1821–1835*. Illustrations by Jack Jackson. Foreword by David
J. Weber. Dallas: William P. Clements Center for Southwest Studies,
Southern Methodist University, 2008.

Menchaca, Antonio. *Memoirs*. San Antonio: Yanaquanna Society Publications, 1937.

Mier y Terán, Manuel de. *Texas by Terán: The Diary Kept by General Manuel de Mier y Terán on His 1828 Inspection of Texas*. Edited by Jack Jackson. Austin: University of Texas Press, 2000.

Moore, Edwin W. *To the People of Texas. An Appeal: In Vindication of His Conduct of the Navy*. Edited by Jonathan W. Jordan. Dallas: The DeGloyer Library and William P. Clements Center for Southwest Studies, Southern Methodist University, 2011.

Morrell, Zachariah Nehemiah. *Flowers and Flowers from the Wilderness; or, Thirty-Six Years in Texas and Two Winters in Honduras*. Dallas: W. G. Scarff & Co., Publishers, 1888.

Muir, Andrew Forest, ed. *Texas in 1837: An Anonymous, Contemporary Narrative*. Austin: University of Texas Press, 1958.

Newell, Chester. *History of the Revolution in Texas, Particularly of the War of 1835 & '36, Together with the Latest Geographical, Topographical and Statistical Accounts of the Country, from the Most Authentic Sources, Also an Appendix*. New York: Wiley & Putnam, 1838.

Nichols, James Wilson. *Now You Hear My Horn: The Journal of James Wilson Nichols, 1820–1887*. Edited by Catherine W. McDowell. Austin: University of Texas Press, 1967.

Parker, Amos Andrew. *Trip to the West and Texas, Comprising a Journey of Eight Thousand Miles, through New York, Michigan, Illinois, Missouri, Louisiana and Texas, in the Autumn and Winter of 1834–5, Interspersed with Anecdotes, Incidents and Observations*. Concord, NH: Printed and Published by White & Fisher, 1835.

Peña, José Enrique de la. *With Santa Anna in Texas: A Personal Narrative of the Revolution*. Translated and edited by Carmen Perry. Introduction by James E. Crisp. College Station: Texas A&M University Press, 1997.

Perry, Cicero Rufus. *Memoir of Capt'n C. R. Perry of Johnson City, Texas: A Texas Veteran*. Edited and with an Introduction by Kenneth Kesselus. Austin: Jenkins Publishing Company, 1990.

Rabb, Mary Crownover. *Travels and Adventures in Texas in the 1820s: Being the Reminiscences of Mary Crownover Rabb.* Introduction by Ramsey Yelvington. Waco: W. M. Morrison Book Dealer, 1962.

Roemer, Ferdinand von. *Texas, with Particular Reference to German Immigration and the Physical Appearance of the Country, Described through Personal Observation.* Translated from the German by Oswald Mueller. Preface by Donald C. Barton. Waco: Texian Press, 1967.

Sánchez-Navarro, Carlos. *La Guerra de Tejas: Memorias de un Soldado.* Mexico, D. F.: Editoral Jus, 1960.

Santa Anna, Antonio López de. *The Eagle: The Autobiography of Santa Anna.* Edited by Ann Fears Crawford. Austin: Pemberton Press, 1967.

[Sedgwick, Theodore]. *Thoughts on the Proposed Annexation of Texas to the United States.* New York: D. Fanshaw, 1844.

Sheridan, Francis C. *Galveston Island, or, a Few Months off the Coast of Texas: The Journal of Francis Sheridan, 1839–1840.* Edited by Willis W. Pratt. Austin: University of Texas Press, 1954.

Smith, Ashbel. *Reminiscences of the Texas Republic: Annual Address Delivered before the Historical Society of Galveston, December 15, 1875.* 1876; reprint, Austin: The Pemberton Press, 1967.

———. *Yellow Fever in Galveston, Republic of Texas, 1839. An Account of the Great Epidemic together with a Biographical Sketch by Chauncey D. Leake, and Stories of the Men Who Conquered Yellow Fever.* Austin: University of Texas Press, 1951.

Smither, Harriet, ed. *Journals of the Fourth Congress of the Republic of Texas, 1839–1840.* 3 vols. Austin: Von Boeckman-Jones Co., 1929.

Smithwick, Noah. *The Evolution of a State; or, Recollections of Old Texas Days.* Compiled by Nanna Smithwick Donaldson. Edited, with an Introduction and Notes by Alwyn Barr. 1900; reprint, Austin: W. Thomas Taylor, 1995.

Solms-Braunfels, Prince Carl of. *Texas, 1844–1845.* Houston: The Anson Jones Press, 1936.

————. *Voyage to North America, 1844–45: Prince Carl of Solms's Texas Diary of People, Places, and Events.* Translated from the German and Notes by Wolfram M. von-Maszewski. Introduction by Theodore Gish. Denton: German-Texas Heritage Society and University of North Texas Press, 2000.

Stapp, William Preston. *The Prisoners of Perote: Containing a Journal Kept by the Author, Who Was Captured by the Mexicans, at Mier, December 25, 1842, and Released from Perote, May 16, 1844.* Foreword by Joe B. Frantz. 1845; reprint, Austin: University of Texas Press, 1977.

Sterne, Adolphus. *Hurrah for Texas! The Diary of Adolphus Sterne, 1838–1851.* Edited by Archie P. McDonald. Austin: Eakin Press, 1986.

Stevens, Kenneth R., comp. and ed. *The Texas Legation Papers, 1836–1845.* Gregg Cantrell and Nancy R. Stevens, associate editors. Fort Worth: TCU Press, 2012.

Stiff, Edward. *The Texan Emigrant: Being a Narration of the Adventures of the Author in Texas, and a Description of the Soil, Climate, Productions, Minerals, Towns, Bays, Harbors, Rivers, Institutions, and Manners and Customs of the Inhabitants of that Country: Together with the Principal Incidents of Fifteen Years Revolution in Mexico: and Embracing a Condensed Statement of Interesting Events in Texas, from the First European Settlement in 1692, Down to the Year 1840.* Cincinnati: G. Conclin, 1840.

Sutherland, John. *The Fall of the Alamo.* San Antonio: Naylor Co., 1936.

Swisher, Col. John M. *The Swisher Memoirs.* Edited by Rena Maverick Green. San Antonio: The Sigmund Press, Inc., 1932.

Teja, Jesús F. de la, ed. *A Revolution Remembered: The Memoirs and Selected Correspondence of Juan N. Sequin.* Austin: State House Press. 1991.

[Texas, General Land Office]. *An Abstract of the Original Titles of Record in the General Land Office.* Preface by Mary Lewis Ulmer. 1838; reprint, Austin: The Pemberton Press, 1964.

Tomerlin, Jacqueline Beretta, comp. *Fugitive Letters, 1829–1836: Stephen F. Austin to David G. Burnet.* Introduction by Catherine McDowell. San Antonio: Trinity University Press, 1981.

Travis, William B. *The Diary of William Barret Travis: August 30, 1833–June 26, 1834*. Edited by Robert E. Davis. Waco: Texian Press, 1966.

Trollope, Francis. *Domestic Manners of the Americans*. Edited by Donald Smalley. New York: Alfred A. Knopf, 1949.

A Visit to Texas, *Being the Journal of a Traveller through Those Parts Most Interesting to American Settlers, with Descriptions of Scenery, Habits, &c. &c.* New York: Van Nostrand and Dwight, 1836.

Webster, Noah. *An American Dictionary of the English Language: Intended to Exhibit, I. The Origin, Affinities and Primary Signification of English Words, as Far as They Have Been Ascertained; II. The Genuine Orthography and Pronunciation of Words, According to General Usage, or to Just Principles of Analogy; III. Accurate and Discriminating Definitions, with Numerous Authorities and Illustrations. To Which Are Prefixed, an Introductory Dissertation on the Origin, History and Connection of the Languages of Western Asia and of Europe, and a Concise Grammar of the English Language.* New York: Published by S. Converse, 1828. Reprint, San Francisco: Foundations for American Christian Education, 1967 and 1995.

White, Cifford E., comp. and ed. *1830 Citizens of Texas: A Genealogy of Anglo-American and Mexican Citizens Taken from Census and Other Records*. Austin: Eakin Press, 1999.

Winfrey, Dorman Hayward, and James Milton Day. *Texas Indian Papers, Edited from the Original Ms. Copies in the Texas State Archives*. Four volumes. Introductions by Joe B. Frantz and H. Bailey Carroll. Austin: Texas State Library, 1958–1961.

Wrede, Friedrich W. von. *Sketches of Life in the United States and Texas*. Compiled by Emil Drescher in accordance with journals and verbal statements. Translated by Chester W. Geue. Waco: Texian Press, 1970.

Zaboly, Gary S., comp. and ed. *An Altar for Their Sons: The Alamo and the Texas Revolution in Contemporary Newspaper Accounts*. With photographs from the Phil Collins Collection. Buffalo Gap, TX: State House Press, 2011.

Zuber, William Physick. *My Eighty Years in Texas.* Edited by Janis Boyle Mayfield. With notes and Introduction by Llerena Friend. Austin: University of Texas Press, 1971.

Periodicals

Almonte, Juan Nepomuceno. "The Private Journal of Juan Nepomuceno Almonte." Introduction by Samuel Asbury. *Southwestern Historical Quarterly* 47 (July 1944): 10–32.

American Turf Register and Sporting Magazine, Vol. 9, No. 12 (December 1838).

Arthur, Dora Fowler, ed. "Jottings from the Old Journal of Littleton Fowler." *Quarterly of the Texas State Historical Association,* 2 (July 1898): 73–84.

Austin, Stephen F. "General Austin's Order Book for the Campaign of 1835." *Quarterly of the Texas State Historical Association* 11 (July 1907): 1–56.

Austin, William T. "Account of the Campaign of 1835 by William T. Austin Aide[e] to Gen. Stephen F. Austin & Gen. Ed Burleson." *Texana* 4 (Winter 1966): 287–322.

Baker, Mosely. "Extracts from Mosely Baker's Letters to Houston." Edited by Eugene C. Barker. *Quarterly of the Texas State Historical Association* 4 (April 1901): 272–287.

[Bannister, Charles B.]. "The Storming of San Antonio de Bexar in 1835." Edited by M. L. Crimmins. *West Texas Historical Association Yearbook* 22 (1946): 95–117.

Bennet, Miles S. "The Battle of Gonzales, the 'Lexington' of the Texas Revolution." *Quarterly of the Texas State Historical Association* 2 (April 1899): 313–317.

Bostick, Sion. "Reminiscences of Sion Bostick." *Quarterly of the Texas State Historical Association* 5 (October 1901) 85–95.

Boyle, Andrew A. "Reminiscences of the Texas Revolution." *Quarterly of the Texas State Historical Association* 13 (April 1910): 285–291.

Cox, C. C. "Reminiscences of C. C. Cox." *Southwestern Historical Quarterly* 6 (October 1902): 113–138.

Calder, R. J. "R. J. Calder's Recollections of the Campaign." Edited by Eugene C. Barker. *Quarterly of the Texas State Historical Association* 4 (April 1901): 334–338.

Darden, Fannie Amelia Dickson. "The Writings of Fannie Amelia Dickson Darden." Compiled by Bill Stein and Jayne Easterling. *Nesbitt Memorial Library Journal. A Journal of Colorado County History* 9, no. 3 (September 1999): 131–194.

Frantz, Joe B., ed. "Moses Lapham: His Life and Some Selected Correspondence." *Southwestern Historical Quarterly* 54 (January 1951): 324–332; (April 1951): 462–475.

Kuykendall, J. H. "Recollections of the Campaign." Edited by Eugene C. Barker. *Quarterly of the Texas State Historical Association* 4 (April 1901): 291–306.

———, ed. "Reminiscences of Early Texas. *Quarterly of the Texas State Historical Association* 6, 7 (January 1903, April 1904, July 1903): 236–253, 311–330, 29–64.

"A Letter from San Antonio de Bexar in 1836." *Southwestern Historical Quarterly* 62 (April 1959): 513–518.

Muir, Andrew Forest, ed. "Diary of a Young Man in Houston, 1838." *Southwestern Historical Quarterly* 53 (January 1950): 276–307.

Nuñez, Félix. "Notes and Documents—The Félix Nuñez Account and the Siege of the Alamo: A Critical Appraisal." Edited by Stephen L. Hardin. *Southwestern Historical Quarterly* 9 (July 1990): 65–84.

Potter, R. M. "Escape of Karnes and Teal from Matamoros." *Quarterly of the Texas State Historical Quarterly* 4 (October 1900): 71–84

"Reminiscences of Mrs. Dilue Harris." *Quarterly of the Texas State Historical Association* 4 (October 1900): 85–125; (January 1903): 204–235; 7 (January 1904): 214–222.

Smith, Henry. "Reminiscences of Henry Smith." *Quarterly of the Texas State Historical Association* 14 (July 1910): 24–73.

Turner, Amasa. "Amasa Turner's Account of the Battle." Edited by Eugene C. Barker. *Quarterly of the Texas State Historical Association* 4 (April 1901): 340–343.

Winters, James Washington. "An Account of the Battle of San Jacinto." *Quarterly of the Texas State Historical Association* 6 (October 1902): 139–144.

Zuber, W. P. "Zuber's Account of the Camp at Harrisburg." Edited by Eugene C. Barker. *Quarterly of the Texas State Historical Association* 4 (April 1901): 338–339.

SECONDARY MATERIALS

Books

Adair, A Garland, and M. H. Crockett, eds. *Heroes of the Alamo: Accounts and Documents of William B. Travis, James Bowie, James B. Bonham, and David Crockett, and Their Memorials.* New York: Exposition Press, 1957.

Allen, Dr. O. F. *The City of Houston: From Wilderness to Wonder.* N.P.: N.P., 1–2.

Alesssio Robles, *Vito. Coahuila y Texas desde la consumación de la independencia hasta Tratado de Paz de Guadalupe Hidalgo,* 2nd ed. Mexico, D. F.: Editorial Porrua, 1979.

Amberson, Mary Margaret McAllen. *A Brave Boy and a Good Soldier: John C. Hill & the Texas Expedition to Mier.* Austin: Texas State Historical Association, 2006.

Baker, DeWitt Clinton. *A Texas Scrap-Book, Made Up of the History, Biography, and Miscellany of Texas and Its People.* New York: A. S. Barnes & Co., 1875.

Bancroft, Hubert Howe. *History of the North Mexican States and Texas.* 2 vols. San Francisco: The History Company Publishers, 1889.

Barker, Eugene Campbell. *The Life of Stephen F. Austin, Founder of Texas, 1793–1836: A Chapter in the Westward Movement of the Anglo-American*

People. Dallas: Cokesbury Press, Importers, 1925. Reprint, Austin: Texas State Historical Association, 1949.

———. *Mexico and Texas, 1821–1835: University of Texas Research Lectures on the Causes of the Texas Revolution*. Dallas: P. L. Turner Co. Publishers, 1928.

Barr, Alwyn. *Black Texans: A History of African Americans in Texas, 1528–1995*. Austin: Jenkins Book Publishing Company, Inc., 1973; 2nd ed., Norman: University of Oklahoma Press, 1996.

———. *Texans in Revolt: The Battle for San Antonio, 1835*. Austin: University of Texas Press, 1990.

Baugh, Virgil E. *Rendezvous at the Alamo: Highlights of the Lives of Bowie, Crockett, and Travis*. New York: Pageant Press, 1960.

Beers, Henry Putney, *The Western Military Frontier, 1815–1846*. 1935; reprint, Philadelphia: Porcupine Press, 1975.

Beeth, Howard, and Cary D. Wintz, eds. *Black Dixie: Afro-Texan History and Culture in Houston*. College Station: Texas A&M University Press, 1992.

Benavides, Adán, ed. *The Bexar Archives (1717–1836): A Name Guide*. Austin: University of Texas Press, 1989.

Bennett, Lenora. *Historical Sketch and Guide to the Alamo*. San Antonio: Privately printed, 1902.

Biesele, Randolph Leopold. *The History of the German Settlements in Texas, 1831–1861*. Austin: Press of Von Boeckmann-Jones Co., 1930.

Billington, Ray Allen. *America's Frontier Heritage*. New York: Holt, Rinehart and Winston, 1966.

Binkley, William Campbell. *The Expansionist Movement in Texas, 1836–1850*. Berkeley: University of California Press, 1925.

———. *The Texas Revolution*. Baton Rouge: Louisiana State University, 1952.

Biographical Dictionary of the Texas Conventions and Congresses, 1832–1845. Austin: Book Exchange, 1941.

Boylston, James R., and Allen J. Wiener. *David Crockett in Congress: The Rise and Fall of the Poor Man's Friend. With Collected Correspondence, Selected Speeches and Circulars*. Houston: Bright Sky Press, 2009.

Brack, Gene M. *Mexico Views Manifest Destiny, 1821-1846: An Essay on the Origins of the Mexican War.* Albuquerque: University of New Mexico Press, 1975.

Brands, H. W. *Lone Star Nation: How a Ragged Army of Volunteers Won the Battle for Texas Independence—and Changed America.* New York: Doubleday, 2004.

Brice, Donaly E. *The Great Comanche Raid: Boldest Indian Attack of the Texas Republic.* Austin: Eakin Press, 1987.

Broussard, Ray F. *San Antonio during the Texas Republic: A City in Transition.* Monograph No. 18. El Paso: Texas Western Press, the University of Texas at El Paso, 1967.

Brown, John Henry. *History of Texas from 1685 to 1892.* Two vols. St. Louis: L. E. Daniell, Publisher, 1892–1893.

———. *Indian Wars and Pioneers of Texas.* Austin: L. E. Daniell, Publisher, 1896.

Bruce, Jr., Dickson D. *Violence and Culture in the Antebellum South.* Austin: University of Texas Press, 1979.

Buchanan, James E., comp. and ed. *Houston: A Chronological & Documentary History.* Dobbs Ferry, NY: Oceana Publications, Inc., 1975.

Butterfield, Jack C. *Men of the Alamo, Goliad, and San Jacinto: An Analysis of the Motives and Actions of the Heroes of the Texas Revolution.* San Antonio: Naylor Company, 1936.

Callcott, Wilfred. *Santa Anna: The Story of an Enigma Who Was Mexico.* Norman: University of Oklahoma Press, 1936.

Campbell, Randolph B. *An Empire for Slavery: The Peculiar Institution in Texas, 1821–1865.* Baton Rouge: Louisiana State University Press, 1989.

———. *Sam Houston and the American Southwest.* New York: HarperCollins College Publishers, 1993.

Canales, José Thomas, ed. *Bits of Texas History in the Melting Pot of America: Native Latin American Contributions to Colonization and Independence of Texas.* San Antonio: Artes Graficas, 1957.

Cantrell, Gregg. *Stephen F. Austin: Empresario of Texas.* New Haven: Yale University Press, 1999.

Cash, W. J. *The Mind of the South.* New York: Alfred A. Knopf, 1941.

Castañeda, Carlos E. *Our Catholic Heritage in Texas, 1519–1936.* Six volumes. Austin: Von Boeckmann-Jones Company, 1936–1958.

Cawthorne, Nigel. *Public Executions.* London: Arcturus Publishing Limited, 2006. Reprint, Edison, NJ: Chartwell Books, Inc., a Division of Book Sales, Inc., 2006.

Chabot, Frederick C. *The Alamo, Altar of Texas Liberty.* San Antonio: Privately printed, 1931.

———. *With the Makers of Old San Antonio, Genealogies of Early Latin, Anglo-American, and German Families with Occasional Biographies, Each Group Being Prefaced with a Brief Historical Sketch and Illustrations.* San Antonio: Privately printed, 1937.

Chance, Joseph E. *José María de Jesús Carvajal: The Life and Times of a Mexican Revolutionary.* San Antonio: Trinity University, 2006.

Chariton, Wallace O. *Exploring the Alamo Legends.* Plano, TX: Wordware Publishing, 1990.

———. *One Hundred Days in Texas: The Alamo Letters.* Plano, TX: Wordware, 1990.

Chartrand, René. *Santa Anna's Mexican Army, 1821–48.* Oxford: Osprey Publishing Ltd., 2004.

Chemerka, William R., ed. *Alamo Anthology: From the Pages of* The Alamo Journal. Austin: Eakin Press, 2005.

Chemerka, William R. and Allen J. Wiener. *Music of the Alamo.* Introduction by Phil Collins. Foreword by Fess Parker. Houston: Bright Sky Press, 2008.

Clark, Carol Lea. *Imagining Texas: Pre-Revolutionary Texas Newspapers, 1829–1836.* Southwestern Studies No. 109. El Paso: Texas Western Press, the University of Texas at El Paso, 2002.

Clark, Sara. *The Capitols of Texas: A Visual History.* Austin: The Encino Press, 1975.

Coalson, George, "Texas Mexicans in the Texas Revolution." In Ronald Lora, ed., *The American West: Essays in Honor of W. Eugene Hollon.* Toledo: University of Toledo, 1980.

Cobia, Jr., Manley F. *Journey into the Land of Trials: The Story of Davy Crockett's Expedition to the Alamo.* Franklin, TN: Hillsboro Press, 2003.

Collins, Phil. *The Alamo and Beyond: A Collector's Journey.* With Illustrations by Gary S. Zaboly. Essays by Richard Bruce Winders, Stephen L. Hardin, and Donald S. Frazier. Buffalo Gap, TX: State House Press, 2012.

Connor, Seymour V. *Adventure in Glory.* Austin: Steck-Vaughn Company, 1965.

————. *The Peters Colony of Texas: A History and Biographical Sketches of the Early Settlers.* Austin: Texas State Historical Association, 1959.

Corner, William. *San Antonio de Bexar: A Guide and History.* San Antonio: Bainbridge and Corner, 1890.

Cox, Mamie Wynne. *The Romantic Flags of Texas.* Dallas: Banks Upshaw and Co., 1936.

Crisp, James E. *Sleuthing the Alamo: Davy Crockett's Last Stand and Other Mysteries of the Texas Revolution.* New York: Oxford University Press, 2005.

Cutrer, Thomas W. *Ben McCulloch and the Frontier Military Tradition.* Chapel Hill: University of North Carolina Press, 1993.

Daniels, A. P. *Texas Avenue at Main Street: The Chronological Story of a City Block in Houston, the Most Significant Block in the History of Texas. An informal but factual history of the block now occupied by the Rice Hotel, site of the Capitol Building of the Republic of Texas when Sam Houston was president.* Houston: Allen Press, 2003, Fannin, A Division of Allen Printing and Letter Service, Publishers, 1964.

Davis, John L. *Houston: A Historical Portrait.* Austin: Encino Press, 1983.

Davis, William C. *Lone Star Rising: The Revolutionary Birth of the Texas Republic.* New York: Free Press, 2004.

———. *Three Roads to the Alamo: The Lives and Fortunes of David Crockett, James Bowie, and William Barret Travis*. New York: HarperCollins Publishers, 1998.

Day, James M., comp. and ed. *The Texas Almanac, 1857–1873: A Compendium of Texas History*. Waco: Texian Press, 1967.

De Bruhl, Marshall. *Sword of San Jacinto: A Life of Sam Houston*. New York: Random House, 1993.

De Leon, Arnoldo. *The Tejano Community, 1836–1900*. Albuquerque: University of New Mexico Press, 1982.

Diccionario Porrua de historia, biografia, y geografia de Mexico, 5th ed. Three volumes. Mexico, D. F.: Editorial Porrua, 1986.

Dienst, Alex. *The Navy of the Republic of Texas, 1835–1845*. 1909; reprint, Fort Collins: The Old Army Press, [1987].

Dimmick, Gregg J. *Sea of Mud: The Retreat of the Mexican Army after San Jacinto, an Archeological Investigation*. Austin: Texas State Historical Association, 2004.

Dixon, Sam Houston, and Louis Wiltz Kemp. *The Heroes of San Jacinto*. Houston: The Anson Jones Press, 1932.

Dobie, J. Frank, Mody C. Boatright, and Harry H. Ransom, eds. *In the Shadow of History*. Dallas: Southern Methodist University Press, 1980.

Donovan, James. *The Blood of Heroes: The 13-Day Struggle for the Alamo—and the Sacrifice That Forged a Nation*. New York: Little, Brown and Company, 2012.

Douglas, Claude L. *Jim Bowie: The Life of a Bravo*. Dallas: Bank Upshaw and Co., 1944.

Drossaerts, Arthur J. *The Truth about the Burial of the Remains of the Alamo Heroes*. San Antonio: Privately printed, 1938.

Eaton, Clement. *The Mind of the Old South*. Baton Rouge: Louisiana State University Press, 1967.

Farrar, R. M. *The Story of Buffalo Bayou and the Houston Ship Channel*. Houston: Chamber of Commerce, [1926].

Fehrenbach, T. R. *Lone Star: A History of Texas and the Texans.* New York: Macmillan Co., 1968.

Foote, Henry Stuart. *Texas and the Texans; or, Advance of the Anglo-Americans to the Southwest including a History of Leading Events in Mexico, from the Conquest of Fernando Cortes to the Termination of the Texas Revolution.* Two vols. Philadelphia: Thomas, Cowperthwait & Co., 1841.

Foreman, Gary L. *Crockett, the Gentleman from the Cane: A Comprehensive View of the Folkhero Americans Thought They Knew.* Dallas: Taylor Publishing Co., n.d.

Frantz, Joe B. *Gail Borden: Dairyman to a Nation.* Norman: University of Oklahoma Press, 1951.

Frantz, Joe B., and Mike Cox. *Lure of the Land: Texas County Maps and the History of Settlement.* College Station: Texas A&M University Press, 1988.

Frantz, Joe B., and David G. McComb. *Houston: A Student's Guide to Localized History.* New York: Teachers College Press, Columbia University, 1971.

Frantz, Joe B., Dorman H. Winfrey, James M. Day, Peck Westmoreland, and Seymour V. Connor. *Battles of Texas.* Waco: Texian Press, 1967.

Friend, Llerena B. *Sam Houston: The Great Designer.* Austin: University of Texas Press, 1954.

Fuentes, Mares José. *Santa Anna: Aurora y Ocaso de un Comediande.* Mexico, D. F.: Editorial Jus, 1956.

Gains, Richard M. *The Federalist War in Coahuila and Texas: 1832–1835.* Gonzales, TX: Clements Creek Press, 1999.

Gambrell Herbert Pickens. *Anson Jones: The Last President of Texas.* 1948; reprint, Austin: University of Texas Press, [1964].

————. *Mirabeau Buonaparte Lamar: Troubadour and Crusader.* Dallas: Southwest Press, 1934.

Geiser, Samuel Wood. *Naturalists of the Frontier.* Dallas: Southern Methodist University, 1937; revised edition, 1948.

Gould, Stephen. *The Alamo City Guide, San Antonio, Texas. Being a Historical Sketch of the Ancient City of the Alamo, and Business Review; With Notes of Present Advantages, together with a Complete Guide to All the Prominent Points of Interest about the City, and a Compilation of Facts of Value to Visitors and Residents.* New York: MacGowan & Slipper, Printers, 1882.

Graham, Philip. *Early Texas Verse (1835–1850) Collected from the Original Newspapers and Edited.* Austin: The Steck Co., 1936.

———. *Life and Poems of Mirabeau B. Lamar.* Chapel Hill: University of North Carolina Press, 1938.

Greenberg, Kenneth S. *Honor & Slavery: Lies, Duels, Noses, Masks, Dressing as Women, Gifts, Strangers, Humanitarianism, Death, Slave Rebellions, the Proslavery Argument, Baseball, Hunting and Gambling in the Old South.* Princeton: Princeton University Press, 1996.

Groneman, Bill. *Eyewitness to the Alamo.* Plano, TX: Republic of Texas Press, 1996.

Hafertepe, Kenneth. *A History of the French Legation in Texas: Alponse Dubois de Saligny and His House.* Austin: Texas State Historical Association, 1989.

Haley, James L. *Passionate Nation: The Epic History of Texas.* New York: Free Press, 2006.

———. *Sam Houston.* Norman: University of Oklahoma Press, 2002.

Hanigen, Frank C. *Santa Anna: The Napoleon of the West.* New York: Coward-McCann, 1934.

Hardin, Stephen L. *The Alamo 1836: Santa Anna's Texas Campaign.* Oxford: Osprey Publishing Ltd., 2001.

———, comp. and ed. *Lone Star: The Republic of Texas, 1836–1846.* Carlisle, MA: Discovery Enterprises, Ltd., 1998.

———. *The Texas Rangers.* Oxford, UK: Osprey Publishing, 1991.

———. *Texian Iliad: A Military History of the Texas Revolution, 1835–1836.* Austin: University of Texas Press, 1994.

———. *Texian Macabre: The Melancholy Tale of a Hanging in Early Houston.* Buffalo Gap, TX: State House Press, 2007.

Harris County Historical Society. *Houston: A Nation's Capital, 1837–1839*. Houston: D. Armstrong Co., Inc., 1985.

Hauck, Richard B. *Crockett: A Bio-Bibliography*. Westport, CT: Greenwood Press, 1982.

Hayes, Charles W. *Galveston: History of the Island and the City*. Two vols. Austin: Jenkins Garrett Press, 1974.

Haynes, Sam, and Gerald D. Saxon, eds. *Contested Empire: Rethinking the Texas Revolution*. Introduction by Gregg Cantrell. College Station: Texas A&M University Press, 2015.

Haynes, Sam W. *Soldiers of Misfortune: The Somervell and Mier Expeditions*. Austin: University of Texas Press, 1990.

Haythornthwaite, Philip. *The Alamo and the War for Texas Independence*. London: Osprey Publishing, 1986.

Hefter, J. *The Army of the Republic of Texas: A Portfolio*. Fort Collins: The Old Army Press, n.d.

———. *The Navy of the Republic of Texas: A Portfolio*. Fort Collins: The Old Army Press, n.d.

Henson, Margaret Swett. *Juan Davis Bradburn: A Reappraisal of the Mexican Commander of Anahuac*. College Station: Texas A&M University Press, 1982.

———. *Lorenzo de Zavala: The Pragmatic Idealist*. Fort Worth: Texas Christian University Press, 1996.

Herring, Patricia Roche. *General José Cosme Urrea: His Life and Times, 1797–1849*. Spokane, WA: The Arthur H. Clark Company, 1995.

Hogan, William Ransom. *The Texas Republic: A Social and Economic History*. Norman: University of Oklahoma Press, 1946.

Hollon, W. Eugene. *Frontier Violence: Another Look*. New York: Oxford University Press, 1974.

Holman, David, and Billie Persons. *Buckskin and Homespun: Texas Frontier Clothing, 1820–1870*. Austin: Wind River Press, 1979.

Houston, Andrew Jackson. *Texas Independence*. Houston: Anson Jones Press, 1938.

Howell, Kenneth W., and Charles Swanland, eds. *Single Star of the West: The Republic of Texas, 1836–1845*. Denton: University of North Texas Press, 2017.

Huffines, Alan C. *Blood of Noble Men: The Alamo Siege & Battle, an Illustrated Chronology*. Austin: Eakin Press, 1999.

———. *The Texas War of Independence 1835–1836: From Outbreak to the Alamo to San Jacinto*. Oxford: Osprey Publishing, 2005.

Humphry, David G. *Peg Leg: The Improbable Life of a Texas Hero, Thomas William Ward, 1807–1872*. Denton: Texas State Historical Association, 2009.

Huson, Hobart. *Captain Phillip Dimmitt's Commandancy of Goliad, 1835–1836: An Episode of the Mexican Federalist War in Texas Usually Referred to as the Texas Revolution*. Austin: Von Boeckmann-Jones Co., 1974.

———. *Refugio: A Comprehensive History of Refugio County from Aboriginal Times to 1953*. Two vols. Woodsboro: Rooke Foundation, 1953–1955.

Huston, Cleburn. *Deaf Smith: Incredible Texas Spy*. Waco: Texian Press, 1973.

Jackson, Donald. *Voyages of the Steamboat Yellow Stone*. New York: Ticknor & Fields, 1985.

Jackson, Jack. *Los Tejanos*. Stamford: Fantagraphics Books, 1982.

———. *Los Mesteños: Spanish Ranching in Texas, 1721–1821*. College Station: Texas A&M University Press, 1986.

———. *The Alamo: An Epic Told from Both Sides*. Austin: Paisano Graphics, 2002.

Jackson, Jr., Ron. *Alamo Legacy: Alamo Descendants Remember the Alamo*. Austin: Eakin Press, 1997.

Jackson, Jr., Ron, and Lee Spencer White. *Joe, the Slave Who Became an Alamo Legend*. Foreword by Phil Collins. Norman: University of Oklahoma Press, 2015.

James, Marquis. *The Raven: A Biography of Sam Houston*. Indianapolis: Bobbs-Merrill Co., 1929.

Jenkins, John H. *Basic Texas Books: An Annotated Bibliography of Selected Works for a Research Library*. Austin: Jenkins Publishing Company, 1983.

Jenkins, John H., and Kenneth Kesselus. *Edward Burleson: Texas Frontier Leader*. Austin: Jenkins Publishing Company, 1990.

Johnson, Allen, and Dumas Malone, eds. *Dictionary of American Biography*. 20 vols. New York: Charles Scribner's Sons, 1937.

Johnson, Marguerite. *Houston: The Unknown City, 1836–1946*. College Station: Texas A&M University Press, 1991.

Jones, Oakah L., Jr., *Santa Anna*. New York: Twayne Publishers, 1968.

Jordan, Jonathan W. *Lone Star Navy: Texas, the Fight for the Gulf of Mexico, and the Shaping of the American West*. Washington, DC: Potomac Books, Inc., 2006.

Kane, Harnett T. *Gentlemen, Swords and Pistols*. New York: Bonanza Books, 1951.

Kemp, Louis Wiltz. *The Signers of the Texas Declaration of Independence*. Salado, TX: The Anson Jones Press, 1944.

Kesselus, Kenneth. *History of Bastrop County, Texas, before Statehood*. Austin: Jenkins Publishing Co., 1986.

Kilgore, Dan, and James E. Crisp. *How Did Davy Die? And Why Do We Care So Much?* Commemorative Edition, Enlarged. College Station: Texas A&M University Press, 2010.

King, C. Richard. *The Lady Cannoneer: A Biography of Angelina Belle Peyton Eberly, Heroine of the Texas Archives War*. Burney, TX: Eakin Press, 1981.

———. *Susanna Dickinson: Messenger of the Alamo*. Austin: Shoal Creek Publishers, Inc., 1976.

Kopel, Hal. *Today in the Republic of Texas*. Waco: Texian Press, 1986.

Koury, Michael J. *Arms for Texas: A Study of the Weapons of the Republic of Texas*. Fort Collins: The Old Army Press, 1973.

Lack, Paul D. *The Texas Revolutionary Experience: A Political and Social History, 1835–1836*. College Station: Texas A&M University Press, 1992.

Lamego, Miguel A, Sánchez. *The Siege and Taking of the Alamo.* Translated by Consuelo Velasco. Santa Fe: Blue Feather Press for the Press of the Territorian, 1968.

Lee, Rebecca Smith. *Mary Austin Holley: A Biography.* Austin: University of Texas Press, 1962.

Lemon, Mark. *The Illustrated Alamo 1836: A Photographic Journey.* Foreword by Craig R. Covner. Abilene, TX: State House Press, 2008.

[Lester, Charles Edwards]. *The Life of Sam Houston: The Only Authentic Memoir of Him Ever Published.* New York: J. C. Derby, 1855.

Lindley, E. R., comp. *Biographical Directory of the Texan Conventions and Congresses.* Huntsville, TX: Printed by order of the House of Representatives, 1941.

Lindley, Thomas Ricks. *Alamo Traces: New Evidence and New Conclusions.* Lanham, TX: Republic of Texas Press, 2003.

———. *To Fight the Mexican Eagle: The Ewings of the Texas Revolution.* Austin: Texian Army Investigations, 1993.

Lofaro, Michael A. *Davy Crockett: The Man, the Myth, the Legacy.* Knoxville: University of Tennessee Press, 1985.

Long, Charles J. *1836: The Alamo.* San Antonio: Daughters of the Republic of Texas, 1981.

Lord, Walter, *A Time to Stand.* New York: Harper & Brothers, 1961.

Lowrie, Samuel H. *Culture Conflict in Texas, 1821–1835.* New York: Columbia University Press, 1932.

Lozano, Reuben Rendon. *Viva Tejas: The Story of Mexican-born Patriots of the Republic of Texas.* San Antonio: Southern Literary Institute, 1936.

Lukes, Edward A. *DeWitt Colony of Texas.* Austin: Jenkins Publishing Co., 1979.

Matovina, Timothy M. *The Alamo Remembered: Tejano Accounts and Perspectives.* Austin: University of Texas Press, 1995.

Marks, Paula Mitchell. *Hands to the Spindle: Texas Women and Home Textile Production, 1822–1880.* Illustrated by Walle Conoly. College Station: Texas A&M University Press. 1996.

Bibliography

———. *Turn Your Eyes Toward Texas: Pioneers Sam and Mary Maverick.* College Station: Texas A&M University, 1989.

McComb, David G. *Houston: A History.* Austin: University of Texas Press, 1981.

———. *Houston: The Bayou City.* Austin: University of Texas Press, 1969.

McDonald, Archie P. *The Trail to San Jacinto.* Boston: American Press, 1982.

McGrane, Reginald Charles. *Panic of 1837: Some Financial Problems of the Jacksonian Era.* Chicago: University of Chicago Press, 1965.

McLean, Malcolm D. *Fine Texas Horses: Their Pedigrees and Performance, 1836–1845.* Fort Worth: Texas Christian University Press, 1966.

Meinig, D. W. *Imperial Texas: An Interpretive Essay in Cultural Geography.* Austin: University of Texas Press, 1969.

Merk, Frederick. *Slavery and the Annexation of Texas.* New York: Alfred A. Knopf, 1972.

Miller, Edward L. *New Orleans and the Texas Revolution.* College Station: Texas A&M University Press, 2004.

Miller, Thomas Lloyd. *Bounty and Donation Land Grants of Texas, 1835–1888.* Austin: University of Texas Press, 1967.

Montejano, David. *Anglos and Mexicans in the Making of Texas, 1836–1986.* Austin: University of Texas Press, 1987.

Moore, Stephen L. *Eighteen Minutes: The Battle of San Jacinto and the Texas Independence Campaign.* Dallas: Republic of Texas Press, 2004.

Morphis, J. M. *History of Texas from Its Discovery and Settlement, with a Description of Its Principal Cities and Counties, and Agricultural, Mineral, and Material Resources of the State.* New York: Van Nostrand, 1874.

Morton, Ohland. *Terán and Texas: A Chapter in Texas-Mexican Relations.* Austin: Texas State Historical Association, 1948.

Munoz, Rafael F. *Santa Anna.* Mexico, D. F.: Editorial Mexico Nuevo, 1937.

Murry, Ellen N. *Notes on the Republic: An Anthology of Essays from the Star of the Republic Museum's Quarterly Journal,* The Notes. Washington, TX: Star of the Republic Museum, 1991.

Myers, John Myers. *The Alamo.* New York: E. P. Dutton and Co., 1948.

Nackman, Mark E. *A Nation within a Nation: The Rise of Texas Nationalism.* Port Washington, NY: Kennikat Press, 1975.

Nance, Joseph Milton. *After San Jacinto: The Texas-Mexican Frontier, 1836–1841.* Austin: University of Texas Press, 1963.

———. *Attack and Counter-Attack: The Texas-Mexican Frontier, 1842.* Austin: University of Texas Press, 1964.

———. *Dare-Devils All: The Texan Mier Expedition, 1842–1844.* Austin: Eakin Press, 1998.

Neito, Angelina, Joseph Hefter, and Mrs. John Nicholas Brown. *El Soldado Mexicano, 1837–1847: Organización, Vestuario, Equipo.* Mexico, D. F.: Privately printed, 1958.

Nelson, George. *The Alamo: An Illustrated History.* Second revised edition. Edited by Alicia Beigel Pais, Ph.D. Uvalde, TX: Aldine Books, 1998.

Neven, David. *The Texans.* New York: Time Life Books, 1975.

Nixon, Patrick Ireland. *The Medical Story of Early Texas, 1528–1853.* Lancaster, PA: Published by the Mollie Bennett Lupe Memorial Fund, 1946.

Nosworthy, Brent. *With Musket, Cannon and Sword: Battle Tactics of Napoleon and His Enemies.* New York: Sarpedon, 1996.

Oates, Stephen B., ed. *The Republic of Texas.* Palo Alto: American West Publishing Co., and Texas State Historical Association, 1968.

Oberste, William Herman. *Remember Goliad.* Austin: Von Boeckman-Jones Co., 1949.

———. *Texas Irish Empresarios and Their Colonies: Power and Hewetson, McMullen & McGloin, Refugio-San Patricio.* Austin: Von Boeckmann-Jones Co., 1953.

O'Connor, Kathryn Stoner. *The Presidio La Bahía del Espiritu Santo de Zuniga, 1721–1846.* Austin: Von Boeckmann-Jones, 1966.

Pereyra, Carlos. *Tejas, la Primera Desmembración de Mejico.* Madrid, Spain: Editorial-America, 1917.

Peterson, Harold J. *Ramshot and Rammers.* New York: Bonanza Books, 1969.

Phelps, Marie Lee. *A History of Early Houston*. Houston: Harris County Heritage Society, 1959.

Pickrell, Annie Doom. *Pioneer Women in Texas*. Austin: E. L. Steck Co., 1929.

Pierce, Gerald S. *Texas under Arms: The Camps, Posts, Forts, and Military Towns of the Republic of Texas, 1836–1846*. Austin: Encino Press, 1969.

Pohl, James W. *The Battle of San Jacinto*. Austin: Texas State Historical Association, 1989.

Potter, Reuben M. *The Fall of the Alamo*. 1878; reprint, Hillsdale, N. J.: Otterden press, 1977.

Powers, John. *The First Texas Navy*. Austin: Woodmont Books, 2006.

Prather, Patricia Smith, and Jane Clements Monday. *From Slave to Statesman: The Legacy of Joshua Houston, Servant to Sam Houston*. Introduction by Dan Rather. Denton: University of North Texas Press, 1993.

Procter, Ben H. *The Battle of the Alamo*. Austin: Texas State Historical Association, 1986.

Pruett, Jakie L., and Everett B. Cole, Sr. *Goliad Massacre: A Tragedy of the Texas Revolution*. Austin: Eakin Press, 1985.

Ragsdale, Crystal Sasse. *The Women and Children of the Alamo*. Austin: State House Press, 1994.

Ransom, Harry Huntt. *The Other Texas Frontier*. Austin: University of Texas Press, 1984.

Ratcliffe, Sam DeShong. *Painting Texas History to 1900*. Austin: University of Texas Press, 1992.

Reichstein, Andreas V. *Rise of the Lone Star: The Making of Texas*. College Station: Texas A&M University Press, 1989.

Reid, Stuart. *The Secret War for Texas*. College Station: Texas A&M University Press, 2007.

———. *The Texan Army, 1835–46*. Oxford: Osprey Publishing, 2003.

Remington, Frederic. *Men with the Bark on*. New York: Harper & Brothers Publishers, 1900.

Richardson, Rupert Norval. *Texas: The Lone State*. Englewood Cliffs, NJ: Prentice-Hall, 1958.

Rister, Carl Coke. *Comanche Bondage: Dr. John Beales's settlement of La Villa de Dolores on Las Moras Creek in Southern Texas of the 1830s, with an annotated reprint of Sarah Anna Horn's narrative of her captivity among the Comanches, her ransom by traders in New Mexico, and return via the Santa Fé Trail*. Introduction to the Bison Book Edition by Don Worcester. 1955; reprint, Lincoln: Bison Book, University of Nebraska Press, 1989.

Rives, George Lockhart. *The United States and Mexico, 1821–1848: A History of the Relations between the Two Countries from the Independence of Mexico to the Close of the War with the United States*. New York: Charles Scribner's Sons, 1913.

Roberts, Randy, and James S. Olson. *A Line in the Sand: The Alamo in Blood and Memory*. New York: The Free Press, 2001.

Roell, Craig H. *Matamoros and the Texas Revolution*. Denton: Texas State Historical Association, 2013.

———. *Remember Goliad!* Austin: Texas State Historical Association, 1994.

Roland, Charles P. *Albert Sidney Johnston: Soldier of Three Republics*. Austin: University of Texas Press, 1964.

Rosenthal, Phil. *Alamo Soldiers: An Armchair Historian's Guide to the Defenders of the Alamo*. N.P.: Privately printed, 1989.

Rosenthal, Phil, and Bill Groneman. *Roll Call at the Alamo*. Fort Collins: Old Army Press, 1985.

Ross, Steven. *From Flintlock to Rifle: Infantry Tactics, 1740–1866*. London: Associated University Presses, 1979.

Ryan, William M. *Shamrock and Cactus: The Story of the Catholic Heroes of Texas Independence*. San Antonio: Southern Literary Institute, 1936.

Sanchez Lamego, Miguel A. *The Siege and Taking of the Alamo*. Santa Fe: Printed by The Blue Feather Press for The Press of the Territorian, 1968.

Santos, Richard G. *Santa Anna's Campaign Against Texas, 1835–1836: Featuring the Field Commands Issued to Major General Vicente Filisola.* Waco: Texian Press, 1968.

Scheerr, Mary L., ed. *Women and the Texas Revolution.* Denton: University of North Texas Press, 2014.

Schmitz, Joseph William. *Texas Culture, 1836–1846: In the Days of the Republic.* San Antonio: Naylor Company, 1960.

———. *Texas Statecraft, 1836–1845.* San Antonio: The Naylor Company, 1941.

Schoelwer, Susan Prendergast, with Tom W. Gläser. *Alamo Images: Changing Perceptions of a Texas Experience.* Dallas: De Golyer Library and Southern Methodist University Press, 1985.

Shackford, James Atkins. *David Crockett: The Man and the Legend.* Edited by John B. Shackford. Chapel Hill: University of North Carolina Press, 1956.

Sibley, Marilyn McAdams. *Lone Stars and State Gazettes: Texas Newspapers before the Civil War.* College Station: Texas A&M University Press, 1983.

Siegel, Stanley. *A Political History of the Texas Republic, 1836–1845.* Austin: University of Texas Press, 1956.

Silbey, Joel H. *Storm over Texas: The Annexation Controversy and the Road to Civil War.* Oxford: Oxford University Press, 2005.

Silverthorne, Elizabeth. *Ashbel Smith of Texas: Pioneer, Patriot, Statesman, 1805–1886.* College Station: Texas A&M University Press, 1982.

Smith, Justin Harvey. *The Annexation of Texas.* New York: The Baker and Taylor Co., 1911.

Sowell, Andrew Jackson. *Early Settlers and Indian Fighters of Southwest Texas . . . Facts Gathered from Survivors of Frontier Days.* Austin: Ben C. Jones & Co., Printers, 1900.

———. *Rangers and Pioneers of Texas, with a Concise Account of Early Settlements, Hardships, Massacres, Battles, and Wars by Which Texas Was Rescued from the Rule of the Savage and Consecrated to the Empire of Civilization.* San Antonio: Shepard Bros. & Co., Printers and Publishers, 1884.

Spellman, Paul N. *Forgotten Texas Leader: Hugh McLeod and the Texan Santa Fe Expedition.* Foreword by Stanley E. Siegel. College Station: Texas A&M University Press, 1999.

Struve, Walter. *Germans and Texans: Commerce, Migration, and Culture in the Days of the Lone Star Republic.* Austin: University of Texas Press, 1996.

Taylor, I. T. *The Cavalcade of Jackson County.* San Antonio: Naylor Co., 1938.

Thompson, Frank. *The Alamo.* London: Salamander, 2002.

———. *The Alamo: A Cultural History.* Dallas: Taylor Trade Publishing, 2001.

———. *Alamo Movies.* Plano, TX: Republic of Texas Press, 1994.

Thorp, Raymond W. *Bowie Knife.* Albuquerque: University of New Mexico, 1948.

Tijerina, Andrés. *Tejanos & Texas under the Mexican Flag, 1821–1836.* College Station: Texas A&M University Press, 1994.

Tinkle, Lon. *13 Days to Glory: The Siege of the Alamo.* 1958; reprint, College Station: Texas A&M University Press, 1985.

Tolbert, Frank X. *The Day of San Jacinto.* New York: McGraw-Hill Book Co., 1959.

Tomerlin, Jacqueline Beretta, comp. *Fugitive Letters, 1829–1836: Stephen F. Austin to David G. Burnet.* Introduction by Catherine McDowell. San Antonio, Texas: Trinity University Press, 1981.

Torget, Andrew J. *Seeds of Empire: Cotton, Slavery and the Texas Borderlands, 1800–1850.* Chapel Hill: University of North Carolina Press, 2015.

Trujillo, Rafael. *Olvidate de El Alamo.* Mexico, D. F.: Populibros La Prensa, 1965.

Turner, Martha Anne. *William Barret Travis: His Sword and His Pen.* Waco: Texian Press, 1972.

Valades, José C. *Mexico, Santa Anna y la Guerra de Texas.* Mexico, D. F.: Imprenta Mundial, 1936.

Vigness, David M. *The Revolutionary Decades.* Austin: Steck Vaughn, 1965.

Von-Maszewski, Wolfram M, ed. *Austin's Old Three Hundred: The First Anglo Colony in Texas, as Written by Their Descendants.* Revised & expanded edition with maps. Waco: Eakin Press, 2016.

Walraven, Bill, and Marjorie K. Walraven. *The Magnificent Barbarians: Little Told Tales of the Texas Revolution.* Austin: Eakin Press, 1993.

Webb, Walter Prescott. *The Texas Rangers: A Century of Frontier Defense.* Boston: Houghton Mifflin Co., Riverside Press, 1935.

Weber, David J. *The Mexican Frontier, 1821–1846: The American Southwest under Mexico.* Albuquerque: University of New Mexico Press, 1982.

———. *Myth and the History of the Hispanic Southwest.* Albuquerque: University of New Mexico Press, 1988.

Weems, John Edward. *Dream of Empire: A Human History of the Republic of Texas.* New York: Simon and Schuster, 1971.

Wharton, Clarence R. *El Presidente: A Sketch of the Life of General Santa Anna.* Houston: C. C. Young Printing Co., 1924.

Wheeler, Kenneth W. *To Wear a City's Crown: The Beginnings of Urban Growth in Texas, 1836–1865.* Cambridge: Harvard University Press, 1968.

Wilbarger, J. W. *Indian Depredations in Texas, Reliable Accounts of Battles, War, Adventures, Forays, Murders, Massacres, etc., Together with Biographical Sketches of Many of the Most Noted Indian Fighters and Frontiersmen of Texas.* Austin: Hutchings Printing House, 1889.

Wilkins, Frederick. *The Legend Begins: The Texas Rangers, 1823–1845.* Austin: State House Press, 1996.

Williams, Alfred M. *Sam Houston and the War of Independence in Texas.* Boston: Houghton, Mifflin and Co., 1895.

Winders, Richard Bruce. *Sacrificed at the Alamo: Tragedy and Triumph in the Texas Revolution.* Abilene, TX: State House Press, 2004.

Winfrey, Dorman Hayward, comp. *A History of the Philosophical Society of Texas, 1837–1987.* Austin: The Philosophical Society of Texas, 1987.

Woodrick, James. *The Battle of Gonzales and Its Two Cannons.* N. P.: Privately printed, 2014.

———. *Cannons of the Texas Revolution.* N. P.: Privately printed, 2015.

Wooten, Dudley G., ed. *A Comprehensive History of Texas, 1685 to 1897.* 2 vols. Dallas: William G. Scarff, 1898.

Writers' Program, Work Projects Administration. *Houston: A History and Guide.* Houston: Anson Jones Press, 1942.

Wyatt-Brown, Bertram. *Southern Honor: Ethics and Behavior in the Old South.* Oxford: Oxford University Press, 1982.

Yoakum, Henderson King. *History of Texas from Its First Settlement in 1655 to Its Annexation to the United States in 1846.* Two vols. New York: Redfield, 1855.

Young, Dr. S. O. *True Stories of Old Houston and Houstonians: Historical and Personal Sketches.* Galveston: Oscar Springer, Publisher, 1993.

———. *A Thumb-nail History of the City of Houston Texas: From Its Founding in 1836 to the Year 1912.* Houston: Press of Rein & Sons Company, 1912.

Periodicals

Barker, Eugene C. "Declaration of Causes for Taking Up Arms against Mexico." *Quarterly of the Texas State Historical Association* 15 (January 1912): 173–185.

———. "James H. C. Miller and Edward Gritten." *Quarterly of the Texas State Historical Association* 13 (October 1909): 145–152.

———. "Land Speculation as a Cause of the Texas Revolution." *Quarterly of the Texas State Historical Association* 10 (July 1906): 76–95.

———. "Native Latin American Contribution to the Colonization and Independence of Texas." *Southwest Historical Quarterly* 46 (April 1943): 317–335.

———. "Stephen F. Austin and the Independence of Texas." *Quarterly of the Texas State Historical Association* 13 (April 1910): 257–284.

———. "The Tampico Expedition." *Quarterly of the Texas State Historical Association* 6 (January 1903): 169–186.

———. "The Texas Revolutionary Army." *Quarterly of the Texas State Historical Association* 9 (April 1906): 227–261.

Barton, Henry W. "The Anglo-American Colonists under Mexican Militia Laws." *Southwestern Historical Quarterly* 65 (July 1961): 61–71.

Brack, Gene. "Mexican Opinion and the Texas Revolution." *Southwestern Historical Quarterly* 72 (October 1968): 170–182.

Cleaves, W. S. "Lorenzo De Zavala in Texas." *Southwestern Historical Quarterly* 36 (July 1932): 29–40.

Corner, William. "John Crittenden Duval: The Last Survivor of the Goliad Massacre." *Quarterly of the Texas State Historical Association*, vol. 1 (July 1897): 47–67.

Costeloe, Michael P. "The Mexican Press of 1836 and the Battle of the Alamo." *Southwestern Historical Quarterly* 91 (April 1988): 533–543.

Crane, R. C. "Santa Anna and the Aftermath of San Jacinto." *West Texas Historical Association Year Book* 11 (1935): 56–61.

Crimmins, M. L. "American Powder's Part in Winning Texas Independence." *Southwestern Historical Quarterly* 52 (July 1948): 109–111.

———. "John W. Smith, the Last Messenger from the Alamo and the First Mayor of San Antonio." *Southwestern Historical Quarterly* 54 (January 1951): 344–346.

Crisp, James E. "Sam Houston's Speechwriters: The Grad Student, the Teenager, the Editors, and the Historians." *Southwestern Historical Quarterly* 97 (October 1993): 203–237.

Davenport, Harbert. "Captain Jesús Cuellar, Texas Cavalry, Otherwise 'Comanche'." *Southwestern Historical Quarterly* 30 (July 1926): 56–62.

———. "General José María Jesús Carbajal". *Southwestern Historical Quarterly* 55 (April 1952): 475–483.

———. "The Men of Goliad." *Southwestern Historical Quarterly* 43 (January 1939): 1–41.

De Leon, Arnoldo. "Tejanos and the Texas War for Independence: Historiography's Judgement." *New Mexico Historical Review* 61 (April 1986): 137–146.

Dienst, Alex. "Contemporary Poetry of the Texas Revolution." *Southwestern Historical Quarterly* 21 (October 1917): 156–184.

Dobie, J. Frank. "Jim Bowie, Big Dealer." *Southwestern Historical Quarterly* 60 (January 1957): 337–357.

Dunn, Jeff. "One More Piece of the Puzzle: Emily West in Special Collections." *The Compass Rose* vol. 19 (Spring 2005).

Elliot, Claude. "Alabama and the Texas Revolution." *Southwestern Historical Quarterly* 50 (January 1947): 315–328.

Estep, Raymond. "Lorenzo de Zavala and the Texas Revolution." *Southwestern Historical Quarterly* 57 (January 1954): 322–335.

Franz, Joe B., ed. "Moses Lapham: His Life and Some Selected Correspondence." *Southwestern Historical Quarterly*, vol. 54 (January 1951): 324–332; (April 1951): 462–475.

Garver, Lois. "The Life of Benjamin Rush Milam." *Southwestern Historical Quarterly* 38 (October 1934, January 1935): 79–121, 177–202.

Garwood, Ellen. "Early Texas Inns: A Study in Social Relationships." *Southwestern Historical Quarterly*, vol. 60 (October 1956): 219–244.

Geiser, S. W. "Naturalists of the Frontier." *Southwest Review*, vol. 16 (Autumn 1930): 109–135.

———. "Notes on Dr. Francis Moore (1808–1864)." *Southwestern Historical Quarterly*, vol. 47 (April 1944): 419–425.

Gilbert, Randal B. "Arms for the Revolution and Republic." *Military History of Texas and the Southwest* 9 (1971): 191–216.

Graham, Don. "Remembering the Alamo: The Story of the Texas Revolution in Popular Culture." *Southwestern Historical Quarterly* 89 (1985): 35–66.

Green, Michael Robert. "Activo Battallion of Tres Villas, February–April, 1836." *Military History of Texas and the Southwest* 14 (1976): 53–58.

———. "El Soldado Mexicano, 1836–1836." *Military History of Texas and the Southwest* 13 (1975): 5–10.

———. "To the People of Texas and All Americans in the World." *Southwestern Historical Quarterly* 91 (April 1988): 483–508.

Greer, James K. "The Committee on the Texas Declaration of Independence." *Southwestern Historical Quarterly* 30, 31 (April 1927, July 1927): 239–251, 33–49.

Hardin, Stephen L. "Gallery: Ben McCulloch." *Military Illustrated, Past and Present* 49 (July 1992): 46–47, 50.

———. "Gallery: David Crockett." *Military Illustrated, Past and Present* 23 (February–March 1990): 28–35.

———. "A Hard Lot: Texas Women in the Runaway Scrape." *East Texas Historical Journal* 29 (1991): 35–45.

———. "'We Flogged Them Like Hell': The Capitulation of Lipantitlán and the Battle of Nueces Crossing." *Journal of South Texas* 1 (1988): 49–64.

Henderson, H. M. "A Critical Analysis of the San Jacinto Campaign." *Southwestern Historical Quarterly* 59 (January 1956): 344–362.

Henson, Margaret Swett. "Politics and the Treatment of the Mexican Prisoners after the Battle of San Jacinto." *Southwestern Historical Quarterly* vol. 94 (October 1990): 189–230.

Hogan, William Ransom. "Rampant Individualism in the Republic of Texas." *Southwestern Historical Quarterly*, vol. 44 (April 1941): 454–480.

Howren, Alleine. "Causes and Origin of the Decree of April 6, 1830." *Southwestern Historical Quarterly*, vol. 16 (April 1913): 378–422.

Hutton, Paul Andrew. "The Alamo: An American Epic." *American History Illustrated* 20 (March 1986): 12–37.

King, C. Richard. "James Clinton Neill." *Texana* 2 (Winter 1964): 231–252.

Koury, Mike. "Cannon for Texas: Artillery in the Revolution and the Republic." *Military History of Texas and the Southwest* 10 (1972): 127–139.

Lindley, Thomas Ricks. "Alamo Artillery: Number, Type, Caliber, and Concussion." *Alamo Journal* 82 (July 1992): 3–10.

———. "Alamo Sources." *Alamo Journal* 74 (December 1990): 3–13.

———. "James Butler Bonham. October 17, 1835–March 6, 1836." *Alamo Journal* 62 (August 1988): 3–11.

Looscan, Adele. "Harris County, 1822–1845." *Southwestern Historical Quarterly*, vols. 18 (April 1915): 399–409 and 19 (July 1915): 37–64.

———. "Micajah Autry: A Soldier of the Alamo." *Quarterly of the Texas State Historical Association* 14 (April 1911): 315–324.

———. "The Young Men of the Texas Revolution." *Texana* 3 (Winter 1965): 333–346.

Marks, Paula Mitchell. "The Men of Gonzales: They Answered the Call." *American History Illustrated* 20 (March 1986): 46–47.

McDonald, Archie P. "Lone Star Rising: Texas before the Alamo." *American History Illustrated* 20 (March 1986): 48–51.

Miller, Thomas Lloyd. "Fannin's Men: Some Additions to Earlier Rosters." *Southwestern Historical Quarterly* 61 (April 1958): 522–532.

———. "José Antonio Navarro, 1795–1871." *Journal of Mexican American History* 2 (Fall 1972): 71–89.

———. "Mexican-Texans at the Alamo." *Journal of Mexican-American History* 2 (1971): 105–130.

———. "Mexican Texans in the Texas Revolution." *Journal of Mexican American History* 2 (1971): 105–130.

———. "The Roll of the Alamo." *Texana* 2 (Spring 1964): 54–64.

Moorman, Evelyn Buzzo, ed. "A Red Rover's Last Letter." *Texana* 4 (Spring 1966): 14–22.

Muir, Andrew Forest. "Augustus M. Tomkins, Frontier Prosecutor." *Southwestern Historical Quarterly*, vol. 54 (January 1951): 316–323.

———. "The Destiny of Buffalo Bayou." *Southwestern Historical Quarterly*, vol. 47 (October 1943): 91–106.

———. "The Intellectual Climate of Houston During the Period of the Republic." *Southwestern Historical Quarterly*, vol. 62 (January 1959): 312–321.

Nackman, Mark E. "The Making of the Texan Citizen Soldier, 1835–1860." *Southwestern Historical Quarterly* 78 (January 1975): 231–253.

Nance, J. Milton. "Rendezvous at the Alamo: The Place of Bowie, Crockett, and Travis in Texas History." *West Texas Historical Association Year Book* 63 (1987): 5–23.

Pohl, James W., and Stephen L. Hardin. "The Military History of the Texas Revolution: An Overview." *Southwestern Historical Quarterly* 89 (January 1986): 269–308.

Presley, James. "Santa Anna in Texas: A Mexican Viewpoint." *Southwestern Historical Quarterly* 62 (April 1959): 489–512.

Riviere, Wm. T. "Sam Houston's Retreat." *Southwestern Historical Quarterly* 46 (July 1942): 9–14.

Robertson, Jane M. "Captain Amon B. King." *Southwestern Historical Quarterly*, vol. 29 (October 1925): 147–150.

Roller, John E. "Capt. John Sowers Brooks." *Quarterly of the Texas State Historical Association* 9 (January 1906): 157–209.

Scarborough, Jewel Davis. "The Georgia Battalion in the Texas Revolution: A Critical Study." *Southwestern Historical Quarterly* 62 (April 1960): 511–532.

Schoen, Harold. "The Free Negro in the Republic of Texas." *Southwestern Historical Quarterly* 41 (July 1937): 83–108.

Shuffler, R. Henderson. "The Signing of Texas' Declaration of Independence: Myth and Record." *Southwestern Historical Quarterly* 65 (January 1962): 310–332.

Sibley, Marilyn McAdams. "The Burial Place of the Alamo Heroes." *Southwestern Historical Quarterly* 70 (October 1966): 272–280.

Siegal, Stanley. "Santa Anna Goes to Washington." *Texana* 7 (Summer 1969): 126–135.

Smith, Ruby Cumby. "James Walker Fannin, Jr., in the Texas Revolution." *Southwestern Historical Quarterly* 23 (October 1919): 80–90, (January 1920): 171–203, (April 1920): 271–284.

Smith, W. Roy. "The Quarrel between Governor Smith and the Council of the Provisional Government of the Republic." *Quarterly of the Texas State Historical Association* 5 (April 1902): 53–74.

Steen, Ralph W. "Analysis of the Work of the General Council, Provisional Government of Texas, 1835–1836." *Southwestern Historical Quarterly* 41 (April 1938): 324–348.

Vernon, Ida S. "Activities of the Seguins in Early Texas History." *West Texas Historical Association Year Book* 25 (1949): 3–11.

Williams, Robert H. "Travis: A Potential Sam Houston." *Southwestern Historical Quarterly* 40 (October 1936): 154–160.

Winkler, Ernest William. "Membership of the 1833 Convention of Texas." *Southwestern Historical Quarterly* 45 (January 1942): 255–257.

————. "The Seat of Government in Texas." *Quarterly of the Texas State Historical Association*, vol. 10 (October 1906): 164–171.

Winston, James E. "Mississippi and the Independence of Texas." *Southwestern Historical Quarterly* 21 (July 1917): 36–60.

————. "New York and the Independence of Texas." *Southwestern Historical Quarterly* 17 (April 1915): 368–385.

————. "Notes on Commercial Relations between New Orleans and Texas Ports, 1838–1839. *Southwestern Historical Quarterly*, vol. 34 (October 1930): 91–105.

Theses and Dissertations

Adams, Allen F. "The Leader of the Volunteer Grays: The Life of William G. Cooke, 1808–1847." M.A. thesis, Southwest Texas State Teachers College, 1940.

Boyce, Fannie Boyd. "James Bowie." M.A. thesis, Southwest Texas State Teachers College, 1939.

Boyce, Sallie Joy. "James Walker Fannin." M.A. thesis, Southwest Texas State Teachers College, 1939.

Callaway, Carolyn Louise. "'The Runaway Scrape': An Episode of the Texas Revolution." M.A. thesis, University of Texas, 1942.

Curry, Ora Mae. "The Texan Siege of San Antonio, 1835." M.A. thesis, University of Texas, 1927.

Davie, Flora Agatha. "The Early History of Houston, Texas, 1836–1845." M.A. thesis, University of Texas at Austin, 1940.

Downs, Fane. "The History of Mexicans in Texas, 1820–1845." Ph.D. diss., Texas Tech University, 1970.

Garver, Lois Antoinette. "The Life of Benjamin Rush Milam." M.A. thesis, University of Texas, 1931.

George, Catherine. "The Life of Philip Dimmitt." M.A. thesis, University of Texas, 1937.

Hale, Laura Elizabeth. "The Groces and the Whartons in the Early History of Texas." M.A. thesis, University of Texas, 1942.

Hardin, Stephen L. "Long Rifle and Brown Bess: Weapons and Tactics of the Texas Revolution, 1836–1836." M.A. thesis, Southwest Texas State University, 1985.

———. "Texian Iliad: A Narrative Military History of the Texas Revolution, 1835–1836." Ph.D. diss., Texas Christian University, 1989.

Harris, Helen Willits. "The Public Life of Juan Nepomuceno Almonte." Ph.D. diss., University of Texas, 1935.

Jackson, Lillis Tisdale. "Sam Houston in the Texas Revolution." M.A. thesis, University of Texas, 1932.

McDonald, Johnnie Belle. "The Soldiers of San Jacinto." M.A. thesis, University of Texas, 1922.

Mixon, Marie Ruby. "William Barret Travis, His Life and Letters. M.A. thesis, University of Texas, 1930.

Moore, Robert Lee. "History of Refugio County." M.A. thesis, University of Texas, 1937.

Putman, Lucile. "Washington-on-the-Brazos." M.A. thesis, East Texas State Teachers College, 1952.

Smith, Ruby Cumby. "James W. Fannin, Jr., in the Texas Revolution." M.A. thesis, University of Texas.

Tijerina, Andrew Anthony. "Tejanos and Texas: The Native Mexican of Texas, 1820–1850." Ph.D. diss., University of Texas, 1977.

Turkovic, Robert J. "The Antecedents and Evolution of Santa Anna's Ill-fated Texas Campaign." M.A. thesis, Florida Atlantic University, 1973.

Watkins, Willye Ward. "Memoirs of General Antonio López de Santa Anna: Translation with Introduction and Notes." M.A. thesis, University of Texas, 1922.

Webb, Rufus Mac. "Military Campaigns of the Texas Revolution." M.A. thesis, North Texas State College, 1951.

Weiss, August H. "The Texas Revolution." M.A. thesis, Southwest Texas State Teachers College, 1946.

Williams, Amelia. "A Critical Study of the Siege of the Alamo and the Personnel of Its Defenders. Ph.D. diss., University of Texas, 1931.

———. "The Siege and Fall of the Alamo." M.A. thesis, University of Texas, 1926.

Williams, Lawrence Drake. "Deaf Smith: Scout of the Texas Revolution." M.A. thesis, Trinity University, 1964.

Yarbrough, Yancy Parker. "The Life and Career of Edward Burleson." M.A. thesis, University of Texas, 1936.

Websites

Davenport, Harbert. "Notes from an Unfinished Study of Fannin and His Men, with Biographical Sketches." Available at www.tshaonline.org /supsites/fannin/hd_home.html

Dunn, Jeff. "Emily West de Zavala and Emily D. West: Two Women or One?" *The Compass Rose* 20 (Spring 2006). Available at http://www .sonsofdewittcolony.org/images/texforum/drose06.pdf

Texas State Cemetery website. Available at www.cemetery.state.tx.us/

Index

Italic page numbers indicate material may also be found in illustrations, photos, and maps.

Index

Index

About the Author

Michael Daleo, photographer

Stephen L. Hardin is a professor of history at McMurry University in Abilene, Texas. He is the author of *The Texas Rangers* (1991), the award-winning *Texian Iliad: A Military History of the Texas Revolution* (1994), *The Alamo 1836: Santa Anna's Texas Campaign* (2001), and *Texian Macabre: The Melancholy Tale of a Hanging in Early Houston* (2007). Additionally, he is the editor of *Lone Star: The Republic of Texas, 1836–1846* (1998) and is the author of more than a dozen scholarly articles enjoyed by readers on both sides of the Atlantic. *Texian Iliad* achieved distinction as a "Basic Texas Book" when bibliophile Mike Cox included it in *More Basic Texas Books*.

When not engaged in the classroom, he serves as an on-air commentator, appearing on such varied venues as the A&E Network, the History Channel, and NBC's *TODAY* show. Most recently, he appeared on the Fox News series, *Legends & Lies*. Distinguished for his readable style and accessible approach to history, Dr. Hardin is an inductee of the Texas Institute of Letters, an admiral in the Texas Navy, a member of Western Writers of America, and a Life Member and Fellow of the Texas State Historical Association. He also served as historical advisor for the John Lee Hancock film *The Alamo* (2004).

Dr. Hardin lives in Abilene, Texas, with his wife, Deborah. Son, Walker, and Gretchen, their precious daughter-in law, live in Austin, Texas. Daughter, Savannah, resides in Denver, Colorado. Her parents frequently employ emotional blackmail to induce her to return to the sacred soil.